Ontolc

This book gathers together thirteen of Peter van Inwagen's essays on metaphysics, several of which have acquired the status of modern classics in their field. They range widely across such topics as Quine's philosophy of quantification, the ontology of fiction, the part–whole relation, the theory of "temporal parts," and human knowledge of modal truths. In addition, van Inwagen considers the question as to whether the psychological continuity theory of personal identity is compatible with materialism, and defends the thesis that possible states of affairs are abstract objects, in opposition to David Lewis's "extreme modal realism." A specially written introduction completes the collection, which will be an invaluable resource for anyone interested in metaphysics.

PETER VAN INWAGEN is the John Cardinal O'Hara Professor of Philosophy at the University of Notre Dame. His publications include *An essay on free will*, *Material beings*, *Metaphysics*, and *God, knowledge and mystery: essays in philosophical theology*.

CAMBRIDGE STUDIES IN PHILOSOPHY

# Ontology, identity, and modality

# CAMBRIDGE STUDIES IN PHILOSOPHY

General editor ERNEST SOSA

RECENT TITLES

# Ontology, identity, and modality

## Essays in metaphysics

Peter van Inwagen

*University of Notre Dame*

CAMBRIDGE
UNIVERSITY PRESS

PUBLISHED BY THE PRESS SYNDICATE OF THE UNIVERSITY OF CAMBRIDGE
The Pitt Building, Trumpington Street, Cambridge, United Kingdom

CAMBRIDGE UNIVERSITY PRESS
The Edinburgh Building, Cambridge CB2 2RU, UK   www.cup.cam.ac.uk
40 West 20th Street, New York NY 10011–4211, USA   www.cup.org
10 Stamford Road, Oakleigh, Melbourne 3166, Australia
Ruiz de Alarcón 13, 28014 Madrid, Spain

© Peter van Inwagen 2001

First published 2001

*Typeface* Bembo 10/12pt   *System* 3B2   [CE]

*A catalogue record for this book is available from the British Library*

ISBN 0 521 79164 2 hardback
ISBN 0 521 79548 6 paperback

Transferred to digital printing 2003

*To the memory of Roderick M. Chisholm*

# Contents

ix

# Introduction

Almost all my philosophical work falls into four general areas: the problem of free will, ontology, the metaphysics of material objects, and the philosophy of modality.[1] As its title implies, this collection comprises essays on the last three of these subjects. (The essays on the metaphysics of material objects are primarily concerned with their "identity," either their identity across time or their identity "across space" – that is, their unity at a moment. Hence "Identity.") In this Introduction, I will say a few words to tie the essays in each group together.

## ONTOLOGY

Ontology, says tradition, is the science of being as such.[2] Ontology, says the present-day analytic philosopher, is . . . What?

I will try to answer this question.

Many philosophers use "ontology" as a name for the study of the most general structures displayed by objects – "object" meaning "object of (possible) perception that exists independently of the mind." In this sense of the word, if Alicia says that a chair is composed of a bare particular and assorted tropes, and Fritz disputes this characterization, saying

[1] I have often heard myself described as a philosopher of religion. Although I have written a few papers in this area – "Ontological Arguments" and "The Problem of Evil, the Problem of Air, and the Problem of Silence," for example – I don't think I have done enough work in the philosophy of religion to justify this description. The description is probably due to my having written extensively on Christian apologetic. In my view, my apologetic writings are either – depending on how one sees the boundaries of philosophy – not philosophy at all or "applied philosophy." If they are applied philosophy, then the first sentence of this Introduction should read, "Almost all my *pure* philosophical work . . ."

[2] Although the word "ontology" is a seventeenth-century coinage, the tradition can be traced back to Aristotle's statement, in the opening sentence of the fourth book of the *Metaphysics*, that there is an *episteme* that investigates being as being. "Ontology" was invented to be what "metaphysics" could no longer be: an appropriate name for the science of being as such.

1

that a chair is rather a bundle of universals, their disagreement belongs to "ontology." I will use "B-ontology" for this sense of "ontology." ("B" for "Bergmann.") I do not understand much of what B-ontologists write. I do not understand their key terms ("trope," "bare particular," "immanent universal," "bundle"). And I do not understand the sense of "structure" in which they claim to be investigating the structures of objects. For me, structure (< *structus*, pp. of *struere*, to heap together, arrange) is at root a spatial concept, and the questions about the structure of a chair that I can understand are questions to be answered by carpenters, chemists, and physicists. I concede that the concept of structure, spatial in origin, has intelligible non-spatial extensions in many areas, such as logic, linguistics, and mathematics. I do not object to the B-ontologists" use of "structure" on the ground that it is an extension of a spatial concept to a non-spatial domain. I object to it on the ground that it is an extension I do not understand of a spatial concept to a non-spatial domain. I understand (thanks to the explanations of logicians, linguists, and mathematicians) what it is for a proof, a sentence, or an algebra to have a structure, and I can follow their descriptions of the particular structures that are ascribed to these objects, and I can see why "structure" is an appropriate thing to call them. What I cannot see is how a chair could have any sort of structure but a spatial or mereological structure. And, in the matter of mereological structure, I cannot see how a chair could have any parts but smaller spatial things – bits of wood and the more esoteric spatial things we learn about from chemists and physicists. To take one example, I have never been able to think of "tropes" – which most of their proponents say are parts of the things whose tropes they are – as anything but idealized coats of paint. B-ontology, therefore, is no part of this book.

Now a second point about the word "ontology": the word is used not only as a mass term but as a count-noun. A philosopher will say, for example, "My ontology contains only material objects and sets." And ontology, ontology the study, is frequently understood in this sense: it is the study that is productive of ontologies. Ontology in this sense, the study that is productive of ontologies, we may call "A-ontology." ("A" for "all.") The A-ontologist attempts to say what there is, to give a sort of list of *all* that there is, to leave nothing out – and to include nothing that does *not* exist, nothing that there isn't. (The list must, of course, comprise very general, abstract terms like "material object" and "set" – it will not, in its official form, contain "banana" or "football team," although the A-ontologist, when speaking concretely, may say things like, "Yes, unlike van Inwagen, I include bananas in my ontology.")

What is the relation – if any – between A-ontology and "the science of being as such"? Are they perhaps identical? Is the practitioner of the science of being as such engaged simply in an attempt, as one might say, to lay out the *extension* of "being," an attempt to say, in the most complete and general way possible, what there is? (One might also ask what the relation is between B-ontology and the science of being as such. I will leave this question to the B-ontologists.) I think not. Something called "the science of being as such" would obviously be concerned with the intension, as opposed to the extension, of "being." The science of being as such is concerned with the question of the *meaning* of "there is" and "being" (and related terms like "exists"). The practitioner of the science of being as such wants to know what concepts are expressed by these terms and their equivalents in other natural languages and related terms or devices in formal languages (such as quantifiers and bound variables). The question of the meaning of being is of fundamental philosophical importance, whatever the science or study that addresses it may be called. In my own work, I have called this study "meta-ontology." (To be precise: As I use the term, meta-ontology comprehends both questions about the meaning of being and questions about the proper method of A-ontology.) In the essays of Part I, I generally use "ontology" as a count-noun. When I do use "ontology" as a mass term, I use it in the sense of "A-ontology."

The first two of the four essays of Part I are meta-ontological. The third is an exercise in A-ontology. I shall discuss the fourth essay presently. The meta-ontology presented in Essays 1 and 2 is broadly Quinean. (This statement brings into stark relief the distinction between meta-ontology and ontology: I agree entirely with Quine about the nature of being and the method one should use in trying to determine what there is. I disagree with him almost entirely about what there is.) Essays 1 and 2 are essays on the philosophy of quantification. Essay 1 presents an account of "objectual" quantification (and presents, in a sense, an account of "ontological commitment"). Essay 2 is an attack on the intelligibility of substitutional quantification, its main rival. It is of the essence of my philosophy of quantification that objectual quantification *has* no rivals and might just as well be called simply "quantification." (Here is a related thesis which I accept, which is not touched on in the essays, and which I cannot defend here. Quine has said that higher-order

3

logic is "set theory in sheep's clothing"; I agree, although I should prefer to say "attribute theory in sheep's clothing." It is of the essence of my philosophy of quantification that first-order quantification has no rivals and might just as well be called simply "quantification.")

Now Essay 4. I begin with some remarks whose relevance to Essay 4 will not be immediately evident. One of the most important divisions between "continental" and "analytic" philosophy has to do with the nature of being.[3] (This division is discussed in Essay 1.) Quine's meta-ontology – and mine: he has formulated it; it is mine only in that I have read his work and have been convinced by it – is the highest development of what may be called the "thin" conception of being.[4] (The most important earlier stages in the line of development that led to Quine's meta-ontology are represented by the treatment by Kant and earlier critics of Descartes's ontological argument, and by Frege's *Begriffsschrift*.) The thin conception of being is this: the concept of being is closely allied with the concept of number: to say that there are Xs is to say that the number of Xs is 1 or more – and to say nothing more profound, nothing more interesting, nothing more. Continental philosophers of being have not seen matters this way. (The continental philosophy of being is, I believe, rooted in Thomism.) For these philosophers, being is a "thick" concept, and they see the thin conception of being – those of them who take note of it at all – as a travesty, an evisceration of the richness of being. (An allegiance to a thick conception of being is reflected in the titles *L'Etre et le Néant* and *Sein und Zeit*.) I can say little about this issue. Analytic philosophers, at least for the most part, will regard what I have to say as obvious, and continental philosophers will believe that anything I say on the topic is shot through with (perhaps wilful) misunderstanding. I can say only that, in my view, it is possible to distinguish between the being and the nature of a thing – any thing; anything – and that the thick conception of being is founded on the mistake of transferring what belongs properly to the nature of a chair – or of a human being or of a universal or of God – to the being of the chair. To endorse the thick

---

[3] I use these two traditional terms for want of anything better (I am aware that analytic philosophers are common enough on the European continent, and, whatever passports they may hold, do not generally regard the analysis of concepts as the only business of philosophy). *Some* terms are needed to do the work "continental philosophy" and "analytic philosophy" have done since the fifties, for the divide in philosophy they have been used to mark still exists, even if it is not the yawning gulf it once was.

[4] I owe the terms "thin conception of being" and "thick conception of being" to Professor Wilfried VerEecke.

conception of being is, in fact, to make (perhaps for other reasons; perhaps in a more sophisticated way) the very mistake of which Kant accused Descartes: the mistake of treating being as a "real predicate."

Even if it were possible for me to disagree profitably with the continental conception of being, the introduction to a collection of essays would not be the place for it. I mention the thick conception of being only to justify (in a way) placing Essay 4, "Why Is There Anything at All?", under the heading "Ontology." Heidegger has suggested that reflection on the question "Why is there something and not rather nothing?"[5] can, if the question is honestly addressed, expose the inadequacy of the thin conception of being. (These are not, of course, Heidegger's words, but I think that the attribution of the idea expressed by these words to him is fair.) Well – "Why Is There Anything at All?" is a reflection on the question that is its title, carried on by someone who subscribes to the thin conception of being. Heideggerians and other continental philosophers will, no doubt, regard it as simply a clever (if that) exercise in missing the point. In any case, the essay had to go somewhere. (To which the continental philosopher will no doubt reply, "Je n'en vois pas la nécessité.")

I will make one remark about the conclusion of the central argument of "Why Is There Anything at All?" Since I believe that there is a necessary being, I believe it is impossible for there to be nothing (those who believe, on Humean grounds, that it is possible for there to be nothing are directed to Essay 13). The conclusion of the central argument of the essay, that the probability of there being nothing is 0, follows from the impossibility of there being nothing. The central argument of "Why Is There Anything at All?" prescinds from my belief that it is impossible for there to be nothing. It is an argument for the conclusion that even if it is possible for there to be nothing, the probability of there being nothing is nonetheless 0. (The third of the four premises of this argument – "There is at most one possible world in which there are no beings" – is, of course, true if there are beings in every possible world. The arguments I give for the other three premises are independent of the question whether it is possible for there to be nothing.)

---

[5] Heidegger formulates this question ("the fundamental question of metaphysics" – but not in the sense "the most basic question that *belongs to* metaphysics"; rather, "the question that founds or underlies metaphysics") in various ways. The following formulation is the first sentence of *Einführung in die Metaphysik*: "Why are there beings [*Seienden*] rather than nothing?"

## IDENTITY

The essays of Part II are episodes in an attempt, some two decades in length, to think to some philosophical effect about the metaphysics of material objects.[6]

The metaphysics of material objects has come to be recognized as one of the most difficult parts of philosophy. This is a remarkable development. When I was a graduate student (in the 1960s) it seemed to most philosophers that it was *everything but* material objects (the usual examples of which were those things that Austin characterized as "moderate-sized specimens of dry goods") that was puzzling: sense-data, thoughts, universals, God, elementary particles . . . Material objects, it was thought, were what we *did* have a good philosophical grip on. And, it was thought, a major aim of philosophy ought to be to "eliminate" everything but material objects – or, failing that, to provide an understanding of such other things as there might be that was as good as our understanding of material objects. But the puzzles that material objects raise are undeniable. There are puzzles that arise from particular cases or examples – the famous Ship of Theseus, or the more recent but almost equally famous case of the cat Tibbles and his part Tib. And there are puzzles that arise from appealing metaphysical principles, either because these principles are in conflict or because certain of them, appealing as they may be when considered in the abstract, seem to imply that important "common sense" beliefs about material objects are false.

Perhaps it would be of service to the reader of Part II if I were to list the most important of the principles that are (individually or in clumps of two or three; no philosopher accepts them all) the source of the puzzles:[7]

- Any region of space that is wholly filled with solid matter is occupied by a material object that exactly fills it.
- Any material objects whatever have a mereological sum (which is also a material object).
- Every material object has all its parts essentially.
- If an object *x* is the mereological sum of certain objects, the *y*s, then the *y*s have essentially the property of having *x* as their sum.
- Material objects are extended in time in a way very strongly analogous to the

---

[6] The body of this attempt is contained in my book *Material Beings* (Ithaca, 1990). The essays in Part II of the present book concern matters not touched on or touched on only lightly in *Material Beings*.

[7] In order not to subject the reader to a cloud of notes in what follows, I will simply cite, collectively, the essays in the excellent collection *Material Constitution* (1996), ed. Michael Rea. The essays in the present book may also be consulted for references.

way they are extended in space; objects that are extended in time are composed of temporal parts, just as objects that are extended in space are composed of spatial parts.

If certain combinations of these metaphysical principles lead to violations of "common sense," why should that be thought to generate a "puzzle"? Why not accept the appealing principles and say, "So much the worse for common sense"? The answer to this rhetorical question is, of course, that there is a widespread allegiance among analytic philosophers to various epistemological principles that (as our literary colleagues say) "privilege" common sense. The simplest example would be:

- One must not endorse theses that are at variance with common sense (this seems to come down to the thesis that one must not reach the conclusion that material-object count-nouns in common everyday use – "table," "banana," "cat" – do not apply to anything, or ascribe to the things to which they do apply properties substantially different from the properties that are ascribed to them by people engaged in the ordinary business of life).

There are, moreover, widely accepted principles about thought and language that are not straightforwardly epistemological but which work to much the same effect as an epistemological privileging of common sense:

- It is not possible for most of what human beings believe to be false.
- If a philosopher maintains that material-object count-nouns in common everyday use do not apply to anything (or maintains that, e.g., "table" applies to things that have properties substantially different from the properties tables are ordinarily supposed to have), that philosopher must mean something different by these terms from what they mean in ordinary English.
- If someone says, for example, "There are some apples in the bowl on that table," what that person says cannot be true unless the predicates "is an apple," "is a bowl," and "is a table" have non-empty extensions.

Philosophers who have accepted various combinations of the metaphysical principles have been led, because of their allegiance to common sense (or something in that vicinity), to accept certain further principles, principles that belong not to metaphysics, epistemology, or the philosophy of language, but to logic (in a suitably broad sense of the word), principles in conflict with what might be called "the standard view of numerical identity":

- Identity must be relativized to kinds: it makes no sense to ask whether the (object that is the) ship $x$ is identical with the (object that is the) ship $y$ *sans phrase*, for $x$ may be the same ship as $y$ but not the same aggregate of planks.
- Identity must be relativized to times; $x$ and $y$ may be two objects at a certain moment and *later become*, or *once have been*, numerically identical. (For

7

example, if Tibbles is a cat and Tib is "all of Tibbles but his tail," then, if Tibbles loses his tail, Tibbles and Tib were two things before the loss of the tail and one and the same thing after the loss of the tail.)

- Identity is a relation that many things can bear to one thing. (And not as *ancestor of* is a relation that many things can bear to one thing. Identity is a relation that many things can bear to one thing not individually, so to speak, but collectively. For example, certain trees – numbering in the hundreds of thousands – are identical with the Forest of Arden; the legs and the seat of the stool, which are four in number, are identical with one thing, the stool.)

These philosophers have embraced revisions of the standard view of numerical identity because these revisions block the derivation of "anti-common-sense" conclusions from the metaphysical principles they find appealing. It is my conviction, displayed in the essays of Part II, that logic is better left alone. My maxim has been: retain the standard view of identity, and try to achieve theoretical coherency by a suitable choice of metaphysical principles (and by resolutely maintaining a healthy skepticism about "common sense").

It will be noted that in these essays I take a very strong "realist" line about *personal* identity (sc. across time). Only Essay 9 is directly concerned with personal identity, but in all the essays I more or less take it for granted that a theory of material objects can be satisfactory only if it is consistent with the thesis that human beings strictly and literally persist through time.

An apology is required in connection with Essay 8 ("Temporal Parts and Identity across Time"): it contains some of the same material (about 1,200 words" worth) as Essay 11 ("Plantinga on Trans-world Identity"). The buyer of this book may with some justice protest paying for two tokens of the same type. But the duplicate passages are essential to the essays in which they occur, and there seemed to be no serious alternative to printing the same words twice.

## MODALITY

There have been two main influences on my philosophy of modality: the work of Alvin Plantinga and Saul Kripke, on the one hand, and David Lewis on the other. The essays in Part III have mainly to do with "modal ontology" – with questions about the nature of objects like possible worlds and possible individuals, with the nature of the property (if it is a property) *actuality*, with the nature of the relations *exists in* and *is true*

*in*, and with essence and accident and "identity across possible worlds."[8]
(The exception is Essay 13, "Modal Epistemology," whose topic is adequately conveyed by its title. If the question, What is an essay on epistemology doing in a collection of metaphysical essays? is raised, I have an answer: It is an essay in the epistemology of metaphysics.) It is well known that there are two main schools of modal ontology. One is the product of the endlessly rewarding thought of David Lewis, and its membership comprises him and very few other people. According to this school, the universe (the mereological sum of all spatiotemporal things[9]) is "the actual world" and other possible worlds are "things of the same sort," separated from the actual world by the fact that they bear no spatiotemporal relations to it. We "exist in" the actual world in that we are parts of it, and we call it "actual" because it is the one we are parts of; people who are parts of other worlds correctly call the worlds they are parts of "actual" in virtue of just that fact: that they are parts of them. The other school (the school of Plantinga and Kripke and Stalnaker and Robert Adams and myself and – very nearly – everyone but Lewis) holds that the actual world is not the universe, but rather a necessarily existent proposition-like abstract object that is "actual" in virtue of the fact that it (or a proposition closely associated with it) happens to be true; it (or this proposition) is true because of the properties of concrete reality – of the whole system of things with causal powers and accidental intrinsic properties –; it makes certain claims about concrete reality, and these claims get the properties of the one concrete reality right. Other possible worlds, the non-actual ones, are similar proposition-like abstract objects, and are non-actual in virtue of getting the properties of the one concrete reality wrong. (Actuality for Plantinga *et al.* is thus a relational property, like that property, desirable in maps, called *accuracy* – the property that is conferred on a map just in virtue of its getting the territory right.)

Part III is largely a defense of the Plantinga–Kripke modal ontology and a sustained argument against Lewis's modal ontology. Only one

---

[8] David Lewis has convinced me that the phrase "trans-world identity," which figures prominently in both the title and the text of Essay 11, is a solecism.

[9] If there could be causal things that were not spatiotemporal – such as God, according to many theologians and philosophers –, one would have to say "the mereological sum of all causal things." Lewis believes, however, that anything with causal powers must be in space and time. It is a nice question whether this thesis about causality is properly a part of Lewis's modal ontology, or is simply a thesis he happens to hold (for reasons that are largely independent of his views on modality) that yields an important modal-ontological consequence when it is conjoined with the theses that properly belong to his modal ontology.

essay calls for comment. "Indexicality and Actuality" was written when I did not really "get" Lewis's modal ontology. (It was published in 1980; it was written for the most part in 1978.) When I was writing that essay, I charitably made Lewis a present of a Plantinga–Kripke-style modal ontology – I charitably supposed that he could not really have meant literally the scattered remarks suggesting that his metaphysic of possible worlds was quite different from the metaphysic of Plantinga and Kripke, that he was what he later came to call a "genuine modal realist." I will say in my defense that it was not really clear to anyone at the time – except, no doubt, to Lewis – that those scattered remarks were meant to be taken strictly, seriously, and literally. The essay, therefore, does not accomplish what it sets out to accomplish: a refutation of Lewis's "indexical theory of actuality." Nevertheless, it contains – so it seems to me on re-reading it – much interesting material, and it does, I think, stand as an argument for the following conclusion: no one who accepts an "abstractionist" modal ontology can accept any account of actuality that could possibly be described as "indexical."

# PART I

*Ontology*

# 1

# Meta-ontology

Quine has called the question "What is there?" "the ontological question." But if we call this question by that name, what name shall we use for the question, "What are we asking when we ask 'What is there?'"? Established usage, or misusage,[1] suggests the name "the meta-ontological question," and this is the name I shall use. I shall call the attempt to answer the meta-ontological question "meta-ontology" and any proposed answer to it "a meta-ontology." In this essay, I shall engage in some meta-ontology and present a meta-ontology. The meta-ontology I shall present is broadly Quinean. I am, in fact, willing to call it an exposition of Quine's meta-ontology. (We must distinguish Quine's meta-ontology from his ontology – from his various theses about what there is and isn't. Quine's meta-ontology comprises such propositions as his theses on quantification and ontological commitment. His ontology comprises such propositions as the proposition that there are no propositions.)

Quine's meta-ontology may be formulated as a fairly short list of theses: about five, depending on how one divides them up. Let us say five. Some of the theses I shall list have never been explicitly stated by Quine – the first in the list certainly has not – , but I do not doubt that he would accept all of them.

## THESIS I. BEING IS NOT AN ACTIVITY

What J. L. Austin said of "exist" – we shall consider the relation between "exist" and "be" presently – , he might equally well have said of "be": "The word is a verb, but it does not describe something that things do all the time, like breathing, only quieter – ticking over, as it

First published in *Erkenntnis* 48 (1998), pp. 233–250.

[1] Such coinages as "meta-language" and "metaphilosophy" (which I am imitating) are based on a misconception about the origin of the word "metaphysics."

were, in a metaphysical sort of way."[2] In order to understand what we are denying when we deny that being is an activity, let us try to understand those who accept, or talk as if they accepted, what we are denying. Let us try to get into their minds.

Some activities are more general than others. What am I doing now? I am writing. I am writing a philosophical essay. These are both answers to the question I have asked, but the correctness of the latter entails the correctness of the former, and the correctness of the former does not entail the correctness of the latter. Let us say that an activity A is *more general than* an activity B if a thing's engaging in B entails its engaging in A and the converse entailment does not hold.

We may ask with respect to each thing (or, at least, with respect to each thing that engages in any activity) whether there is a most general activity it engages in: an activity it engages in in virtue of engaging in any activity at all. If I understand them correctly, many representatives of the existential-phenomenological tradition would answer Yes; they would call this activity the thing's "being" or "existence."

We may also ask whether there is a most general activity *simpliciter*, an activity that things engage in in virtue of engaging in any activity at all. At least some representatives of the existential-phenomenological tradition would, I believe, answer No. As I interpret Sartre, for example, he would say that your and my most general activity (*être pour-soi*) is not the same as the most general activity of a table (*être en-soi*). Thus Sartre can say that the table and I have different kinds of *être*, since the most general thing the table does (just standing there; undergoing externally induced modifications) is not the most general thing I do (being conscious of and choosing among alternative possibilities; acting for an end I have chosen from a motive I have created.)

Now I do not wish to deny that there is a most general activity that I engage in. I suppose that if I had to put a name to it, I should call it "lasting" or "enduring" or "getting older." But I would differ from Sartre and from most other members of the existential-phenomenological tradition on two points. First, I would say that I share this most general activity with everything – or at least with every concrete inhabitant of the natural world. Secondly, I would say that it is just wrong to call this activity "existing" or "being" or "être" or to use any word for it

---

[2] J. L. Austin, *Sense and Sensibilia* (Oxford, 1962), p. 68n.

that contains a root that is related to "être" or "esse" or "existere" or "to on" or "einai" or "Sein" or "be" or "am" or "is."

I cannot say that "lasting" or "enduring" has nothing to do with being, for being (like truth and identity) is what the medievals called a transcendental, and has a great deal to do with everything. But, in my view, enduring is no *more* intimately connected with being than are color or shape or intelligence or the ability to ride a bicycle, for the plain reason (as Newman said in another connection) that one idea is not another idea.

There is, of course, a vast difference between rational beings and mere inanimate objects. I believe this quite as firmly as Sartre does. But to insist, as I do, that this difference does not consist in the one sort of thing's having a different sort of being from the other's is not to depreciate it. The vast difference between me and a table does not consist in our having vastly different sorts of being (*Dasein, dass sein,* "that it is"); it consists rather in our having vastly different sorts of *nature* (*Wesen, was sein,* "what it is"). If you prefer, what the table and I are *like* is vastly different. This is a perfectly trivial thing to say: that a vast difference between A and B must consist in a vast difference in their natures. But if a distinction can be made between a thing's being and its nature, then this trivial truth is in competition with a certain statable falsehood. And if one denies the trivial at the outset of one's investigations, one is bound to get into trouble down the road.

### THESIS 2. BEING IS THE SAME AS EXISTENCE

Many philosophers distinguish between being and existence.[3] That is, they distinguish between what is expressed by "there is" and "exists." Following Quine, I deny that there is any substance to the distinction: to say that dogs exist is to say that there are dogs, and to say that Homer existed is to say that there was such a person as Homer. This may seem obvious, but on reflection it can seem less obvious. Suppose I am discussing someone's delusions and I say, "There are a lot of things he believes in that do not exist." On the face of it, I appear to be saying that there are things – the poison in his drink, his uncle's malice, and so on – that do not exist. Perhaps someone who reflects on this example will conclude that it is not obvious that to be is the same as to exist. But

---

[3] See, for example, Terence Parsons, *Nonexistent Objects* (New Haven, 1980).

whether or not it is obvious, it is true. There *is* no nonexistent poison in the paranoid's drink. There *is* no such thing as his uncle's malice. In sum, there are no things that do not exist. This thesis seems to me to be so obvious that I have difficulty in seeing how to argue for it. I can say only this: if you think that there are things that do not exist, give me an example of one. The right response to your example will be either, "That does too exist," or "There is no such thing as that."

Since I know of no way of arguing for the identity of being and existence (other than a case-by-case examination and refutation of all known attempts to give examples of non-existent objects), I shall have to try to find some means other than argument of persuading you to see things as I do. I will tell you a funny story. At least I think it's funny. But I expect that if you think that there is an important difference between "there is" and "exists," you will find the story more annoying than funny. (This expectation is grounded on a certain amount of empirical evidence: W. V. Quine thinks the story is funny and Terence Parsons thinks it is annoying.[4])

One day my friend Wyman told me that there was a passage on page 253 of volume IV of Meinong's *Collected Works* in which Meinong admitted that his theory of objects was inconsistent. Four hours later, after considerable fruitless searching, I stamped into Wyman's study and informed him with some heat that there was no such passage. "Ah," said Wyman, "you're wrong. There is such a passage. After all, you were looking for it: there is something you were looking for. I think I can explain your error; although there *is* such a passage, it doesn't *exist*. Your error lay in your failure to appreciate this distinction." I was indignant.

My refusal to recognize a distinction between existence and being is simply my indignation, recollected in tranquility and generalized.

### THESIS 3. BEING IS UNIVOCAL

And, we might add, since existence is the same as being, existence is univocal. Many philosophers have thought that "there is" and "exists" mean one thing when they are applied to material objects, and another when they are applied to, say, minds, and yet another when they are applied to (or withheld from) supernatural beings, and one more thing again when applied to abstractions like numbers or possibilities. This is

[4] Quine's opinion was expressed in personal correspondence, Parsons's in "Are There Nonexistent Objects?", *American Philosophical Quarterly* 19 (1982), p. 365.

evidently an extremely attractive position. Undergraduates fall effortlessly into it, and it is very hard to convince anyone who subscribes to it that it is false, or even that it is not obviously true. But it is false. Perhaps the following consideration will show why it is at least not obviously true. No one would be inclined to suppose that number-words like "six" or "forty-three" mean different things when they are used to count different sorts of object. The very essence of the applicability of arithmetic is that numbers may count anything: if you have written thirteen epics and I own thirteen cats, then the number of your epics *is* the number of my cats. But existence is closely tied to number. To say that unicorns do not exist is to say something very much like saying that the number of unicorns is 0; to say that horses exist is to say that the number of horses is 1 or more. And to say that angels or ideas or prime numbers exist is to say that the number of angels, or of ideas, or of prime numbers, is greater than 0. The univocacy of number and the intimate connection between number and existence should convince us that there is at least very good reason to think that existence is univocal.

The thesis that existence is equivocal has found its most outspoken twentieth-century exponent in Ryle, who says,

It is perfectly proper to say, in one logical tone of voice, that there exist minds and to say, in another logical tone of voice, that there exist bodies. But these expressions do not indicate two different species of existence . . . They indicate two different senses of "exist," somewhat as "rising" has different senses in "the tide is rising," "hopes are rising," and "the average age of death is rising." A man would be thought to be making a poor joke who said that three things are now rising, namely the tide, hopes and the average age of death. It would be just as good or bad a joke to say that there exist prime numbers and Wednesdays and public opinions and navies; or that there exist both minds and bodies.[5]

To my mind, there are at least two reasons why it sounds silly to say, "There exist prime numbers and Wednesdays and public opinions and navies." For one thing, "There exist Wednesdays" and "There exist public opinions" sound pretty silly all by themselves. Secondly, it is hard to think of any excuse for mentioning all these items in one sentence, no matter what one says about them. I invite you to try to devise a sentence about the items in Ryle's list that does *not* sound silly. If we restrict ourselves to just two of the items in the list, we can produce an entirely plausible sentence: "The Prime Minister had a habit of ignoring the existence of things he didn't know how to deal with, such as public

---

[5] Gilbert Ryle, *The Concept of Mind* (London, 1949), p. 23.

opinion and the Navy." But we need not make up examples. Here is a real one.

In the USSR . . . as we know, there is a prohibition on certain words and terms, on certain phrases and on entire . . . parts of reality. It is considered not only impermissible but simply indecent to print certain combinations of graphemes, words, or ideas. And what is not published somehow ceases to exist . . . There is much that is improper and does not exist: religion and homosexuality, bribe-taking and hunger, Jews and nude girls, dissidents and emigrants, earthquakes and volcanic eruptions, diseases and genitalia.[6]

Later in the same essay, the author says,

In the novel of a major Soviet prose writer who died recently the main characters are blinded and start to suffocate when the peat bogs around Moscow begin burning. The peat bog fires actually exist, but then so does Brezhnev's regime.[7]

I conclude that Ryle has made no case for the thesis that existence is equivocal. I know of no argument for this thesis that is even faintly plausible. We must therefore conclude that existence is univocal, for the clear and compelling argument for the univocacy of existence given above (the argument from the univocacy of number and the intimate connection between number and existence) is unopposed.

### THESIS 4. THE SINGLE SENSE OF BEING OR EXISTENCE IS ADEQUATELY CAPTURED BY THE EXISTENTIAL QUANTIFIER OF FORMAL LOGIC

This ought to be uncontroversial. But we find people making statements like this: "Truth-conditions for quantified statements can be given without raising the question whether the objects in the domain of quantification exist. Therefore, quantification has nothing to do with existence. The term 'the existential quantifier' is, in fact, a misnomer. We ought to call it something else – perhaps 'the particular quantifier.'" Now of course I do not think that there are any non-existent objects, and, therefore, I do not think that any domain of quantification could comprise non-existent objects. But that is not what I want to discuss at present. Rather, I want to discuss the nature of quantification. I want to give an account of quantifiers and variables as they appear from the perspective afforded by Quine's meta-ontology. It will be clear that if this

[6] Tomas Venclova, "The Game of the Soviet Censor," *New York Review of Books*, 31 March 1983, pp. 34–37.
[7] Ibid., p. 35.

account is correct, then Thesis 4 should be no more controversial than the thesis that the ordinary sense of the "sum" of two numbers is adequately captured by the arithmetical symbol "+."

I shall present the account of quantification that is endorsed by Quine's meta-ontology by showing how to introduce variables and the quantifiers into our discourse as abbreviations for phrases that we already understand.[8] (This, I believe, is the *only* way – other than ostension – in which one can explain the meaning of any word, phrase, or idiom.) It will be clear that the quantifiers so introduced are simply a regimentation of the "all" and "there are" of ordinary English.

We begin by supplementing the pronominal apparatus of English. We first introduce an indefinitely large stock of third-person-singular pronouns, pronouns whose use carries no implications about sex or personhood. These pronouns are to be orthographically and phonetically diverse, but semantically indistinguishable. Let three of them be: "it$_x$," "it$_y$," "it$_z$"; let the others be of the same sort.

Now let us call the following phrases *universal quantifier phrases*:

It is true of everything that it$_x$ is such that
It is true of everything that it$_y$ is such that
It is true of everything that it$_z$ is such that

.
.
.

Call the following phrases *existential quantifier phrases*:

It is true of at least one thing that it$_x$ is such that
It is true of at least one thing that it$_y$ is such that
It is true of at least one thing that it$_z$ is such that

.
.
.

Any reader of this essay is likely to have a certain skill that will enable him to turn complex general sentences of English into sentences whose generality is carried by quantifier phrases and pronouns. For example:

Everybody loves somebody;

It is true of everything that it$_x$ is such that if it$_x$ is a person, then it is true of at least one thing that it$_y$ is such that it$_y$ is a person and it$_x$ loves it$_y$.

---

[8] The following account of quantification is modeled on, but does not reproduce, the account presented in W. V. Quine, *Mathematical Logic* (Cambridge, Mass., 1940), pp. 65–71.

19

Such sentences, sentences whose generality is carried by quantifier phrases and pronouns, may be hard to read or even ambiguous because of uncertainty about where the "that"-clauses that follow "everything" and "at least one thing" and "such that" end. This difficulty is easily met by the use of brackets:

> It is true of everything that it$_x$ is such that (if it$_x$ is a person, then it is true of at least one thing that it$_y$ is such that (it$_y$ is a person and it$_x$ loves it$_y$)).

A more complex example still:

> Anyone who acts as his own attorney has a fool for a client;

> It is true of everything that it$_x$ is such that (if it$_x$ acts as the attorney of it$_x$, then it is true of at least one thing that it$_y$ is such that (it$_y$ is a client of it$_x$ and it$_y$ is a fool)).

What we have now is a supplemented and regimented version of English. (The only features of the sentences of this new "version" of English that keep them from being sentences of ordinary English are the "new" pronouns and the brackets. If we were to replace each of the subscripted pronouns with "it" and were to delete the brackets from these sentences, the sentences so obtained would be perfectly good sentences of ordinary English – perfectly good from the grammarian's point of view, anyway; no doubt most of them would be stilted, confusing, ambiguous, unusable, and downright silly sentences.) But this supplemented and regimented English is a bit cumbersome, in large part because of the unwieldiness of our "quantifier phrases" and the difficulty of writing or pronouncing all those annoying subscripts. We can to some degree remedy this defect by introducing a few systematic abbreviations:

1. Abbreviate subscripted pronouns by their subscripts, italicized and raised to the line. (Call these abbreviated pronouns "variables.")
2. Abbreviate "it is true of everything that ($x$ is such that" by "$\forall x($" – and similarly for the other variables.
3. Abbreviate "it is true of at least one thing that ($x$ is such that" by "$\exists x($" – and similarly for the other variables.

Our second example, so abbreviated, is:

> $\forall x($if $x$ acts as the attorney of $x$, $\exists y(y$ is a client of $x$ and $y$ is a fool)).

What we have now, of course, are quantifiers and variables. We have, or so I claim, introduced quantifiers and variables using only the resources of ordinary English. And to do this, I would suggest, is to *explain* quantifiers and variables.

We may attribute to Frege the discovery that if the pronominal apparatus of English (or German or any reasonably similar natural language) is supplemented in this way, then it is possible to set out a few simple rules of syntactical manipulation – rules that can today be found in any good logic textbook – such that a truly astounding range of valid inference is captured in the sequences of sentences that can be generated by repeated applications of these rules. It is these rules that give quantifiers and variables their point. The odd-looking, stilted, angular rewriting of our lovely, fluid English tongue that is the quantifier-variable idiom has only one purpose: to force all that lovely fluidity – at least insofar as it is a vehicle of the expression of theses involving universality and existence – into a form on which a manageably small set of rules of syntactical manipulation (rules that constitute the whole of valid reasoning concerning matters of universality and existence) can get a purchase. But while it is these rules that provide the motivation for our having at our disposal such a thing as the quantifier-variable idiom, they are not the source of the meaning of that idiom, the meaning, that is, of sentences containing quantifiers and variables. The meaning of the quantifiers is given by the phrases of English – or of some other natural language – that they abbreviate. The fact that quantifiers are abbreviations entails that we can give them the very best definition possible: we can show how to eliminate them in favor of phrases that we already understand.[9]

Let us now return to Thesis 4: that the single sense of being or existence is adequately captured by the existential quantifier of formal logic. It should be evident that if our explanation of the meaning of the quantifiers – and of the existential quantifier in particular – is correct, then this thesis must be true. If our explanation is correct, then the sentence

$\exists x \; x$ is a dog

is an abbreviation for

It is true of at least one thing that $it_x$ is such that $it_x$ is a dog.

That is,

---

[9] This thesis about meaning and definition has able and articulate enemies. One of these enemies might want to adapt what David Lewis has said about the "semantic marker" method of doing semantics for natural languages; he might want to say that the technique we have presented for eliminating quantifiers from a sentence doesn't tell us "the first thing about the meaning of the . . . sentence: namely, the conditions under which it would be true" ("General Semantics," in *Semantics of Natural Language*, ed. Donald Davidson and Gilbert Harman [Dordrecht, 1972], p. 169).

It is true of at least one thing that it is such that it is a dog.

That is,

It is true of at least one thing that it is a dog.

That is,

At least one thing is a dog.

That is,

There is at least one dog.

The existential quantifier therefore expresses the sense of "there is" in ordinary English. And, if the second thesis is correct, "There is at least one dog" is equivalent to "At least one dog exists," and the existential quantifier expresses the sense of the ordinary "exists" as well. (The name "the existential quantifier" is therefore no misnomer. There is no need to search out some alternative name like "the particular quantifier.") Or this much is true if we have indeed given a correct account of the quantifiers. Many philosophers – proponents of the "substitutional" interpretation of quantification, for example – would dispute the account of the quantifiers that I have presented. A defense of the Quinean account of quantification, however, will not be possible within the scope of this essay.

### THESIS 5

Let us now turn to the last of the five theses that constitute the Quinean meta-ontology. Unlike the first four theses, the fifth cannot be stated in any useful way in a single sentence. It is a thesis about the best way – the only reasonable way – to attempt to answer (and to conduct disputes about alternative answers to) "the ontological question": What is there? Being a thesis about strategy, it involves a large number of pragmatic considerations, and it therefore requires a somewhat lengthy statement.

The fifth thesis pertains to the part of Quine's meta-ontology that is marked out by the words "the criterion of ontological commitment." These words are not always perfectly understood. It would appear that many philosophers think that the words "Quine's Criterion of Ontological Commitment" are a name for a thesis about what the "ontological commitments" of a theory – any theory – are. Many philosophers seem to think that Quine believes that there exists a well-defined class of objects called "theories," and that he believes that he has devised a technique that can be applied to "theories" so as to reveal an objectively present (but often hidden) feature or aspect of their content called their "ontological commitments." This technique could be described as follows: recast the theory in the quantifier-variable idiom, or in "the canonical notation of quantification"; consider the set of all sentences that are formal consequences of the recast theory; consider the members of this set that are closed sentences beginning with an existential quantifier phrase whose scope is the remainder of the sentence; it is these sentences that reveal the ontological commitments of the theory. Each of them will consist of an existential quantifier followed by a variable followed by a sentence in which that variable alone is free.[10] Suppose, for example, that the variable that follows the quantifier is "$x$," and that it has three free occurrences in the open sentence that follows the quantifier phrase. The sentence of our theory that is supposedly partly revelatory of the theory's ontological commitments may therefore be schematically represented like this:

$$\exists x \ldots \ldots x \ldots \ldots x \ldots \ldots x \ldots \ldots$$

An open sentence expresses a condition on objects. The ontological commitment of our theory that this exercise has revealed to us is this: our theory commits us to the existence of at least one object that satisfies the condition we have expressed schematically as

$$\ldots \ldots x \ldots \ldots x \ldots \ldots x \ldots \ldots$$

Here ends the description of what (in my view) many philosophers mistakenly believe is "Quine's criterion of ontological commitment."

The trouble with this representation of "Quine's criterion of ontological commitment" is that it presupposes that there are well-defined objects called theories, and that each of them has a unique translation into the quantifier-variable idiom, or into "canonical notation." If we were to suppose that there were a class of well-defined objects called sentences, we could secure the first of these presuppositions by defining a theory as any class of sentences. This would be a highly artificial account of "theories," since it would normally be supposed that the general theory of relativity, say, or the theory of evolution, was not tied down to any particular class of sentences. But let us simply ignore this problem, and concentrate on the "unique translation" problem. There are two reasons why there is no such thing as the unique translation of a theory

---

[10] Or it may be that no variables are free in that sentence. We ignore this special case.

(or of a set of sentences) into the quantifier-variable idiom. First, the quantifier-variable idiom is not something that a given sentence is "in" or "not in," as a given sentence is in, or not in, Hebrew characters, or italics, or French. Rather, the quantifier-variable idiom is something that is present in varying degrees in various sentences. Secondly, even if we ignore this fact, there will generally be alternative ways of translating a sentence or set of sentences into the quantifier-variable idiom. An example may make these points clear.

Let us consider the following sequence of sentences, a sequence of a type familiar to everyone who has taught logic:

> Every planet is at any time at some distance from every star
>
> $\forall x$ if $x$ is a planet, $x$ is at any time at some distance from every star
>
> $\forall x$ ($x$ is a planet $\rightarrow$ $\forall y$ if $y$ is a star, $x$ is at any time at some distance from $y$)
>
> $\forall x$ ($x$ is a planet $\rightarrow$ $\forall y$ ($y$ is a star $\rightarrow$ $\forall t$ if $t$ is a time, then $x$ is at $t$ at some distance from $y$))
>
> $\forall x$ ($x$ is a planet $\rightarrow$ $\forall y$ ($y$ is a star $\rightarrow$ $\forall t$ ($t$ is a time $\rightarrow$ $\exists z$ ($z$ is a distance & $x$ is at $t$ separated from $y$ by $z$)))).

One should not think of the quantifier-variable idiom (or the canonical notation of quantification) as something that a sentence is "in" or "not in." Rather, this idiom (or this notation) is something that there is *more and more of* in each of the successive sentences in this sequence.[11] In ordinary English, there are various devices and constructions that do the work the quantifiers and variables do in the sentences of the above sequence. We can transform a sentence of English into a sentence that is not, strictly speaking, English by eliminating some of these devices and constructions in favor of quantifiers and variables. And if the English sentence is of any very great degree of complexity, there may be several "sites" within the sentence that afford opportunities to do so. In a given case, one or some or all the opportunities may be taken; how *much* of the original sentence is transformed – how many of the opportunities for the introduction of the canonical notation of quantification are taken – will depend on the purposes of the person who is introducing the notation.

But this description of the opportunities afforded by English sentences for the introduction of quantifiers and variables suggests that within each English sentence there is a fully determinate and objectively present array of "sites" at which quantifiers and variables could be introduced, and

---

[11] Or, rather than "canonical notation," we might say "canonical grammar." See W. V. Quine, *Word and Object* (Cambridge, Mass., 1960), p. 231.

that each of these "sites" has features that dictate the precise way in which these devices are to be introduced. If this were so, of course, then introducing quantifiers and variables into English discourse would always be a mechanical procedure. It may be that the introduction of quantifiers and variables is sometimes very close to being a mechanical procedure, but this is certainly not always the case. For one thing, a choice will sometimes have to be made between alternative ways of introducing these unambiguous devices into a sentence that is ambiguous as to quantificational import. But there is a more interesting way in which the task of introducing canonical notation can be more than mechanical. Sometimes the task requires a certain amount of creativity. For a minor instance of this, consider the four-place open sentence that occurs as a part of the final sentence in the above sequence of sentences. Where did the word "separated" come from? A computer program – any program a human being could actually write, anyway – would probably have produced a sentence that contained, instead of "*x* is at *t* separated from *y* by *z*," the sentence "*x* is at *t* at *z* from *y*." Why didn't I? Well, just because that sounds funny. For one reason or another, although one can say that A is at some distance from B, one can't say of some distance that A is at it from B. Or one can hardly say it. Recognizing that a slavish adherence to the "at" idiom of the original was going to bring me up against this fact of English usage, I cast about for an idiomatic alternative, and came up with the "separated from . . . by . . ." locution. This is creativity if you like; not a very impressive example of creativity if it is measured against many of the daily achievements of human beings, but (I think) greatly in excess of anything a computer could be expected to achieve. It would, of course, be absurd to suppose that the eventual introduction of the "separated from . . . by . . ." locution was in any way dictated by the content of the original English sentence. No doubt there are many other forms of words that would have served as well.

The introduction of quantifiers and variables can, moreover, be accomplished in ways that involve greater creativity than this. Consider again the final sentence in the above sequence. In my opinion, the open sentence "*z* is a distance" does not make much sense, owing to the fact that I cannot give a coherent account of the properties that an object that satisfied it would have.[12] And since I think that the obvious intelligibility of the first sentence in the sequence, the sentence of ordinary English,

---

[12] See Peter van Inwagen, "Searle on Ontological Commitment," in *John Searle and His Critics*, ed. E. LePore and R. Van Gulick (Oxford, 1990), p. 358, n. 11.

does not presuppose that a phrase like "ten miles" denotes a particular "distance," I am inclined to think that the final sentence in the sequence is not a correct paraphrase of the first – although the second, third, and fourth sentences are correct paraphrases of it.

One could say that the fourth sentence is "as far as one can go" as regards the introduction of quantifiers and variables to do the work done by "every," "any," and "some" in the sentence "Every planet is at any time at some distance from every star." One could say that the open sentence "$x$ is at $t$ at some distance from $y$" simply affords no opportunity for the introduction of a quantifier. But if that is so, what about a sentence like "If $x$ is at some distance from $y$, and $y$ is at some distance from $z$, then the distance from $x$ to $y$ is greater than the distance from $y$ to $z$, or the distance from $x$ to $y$ is equal to the distance from $y$ to $z$, or the distance from $x$ to $y$ is less than the distance from $y$ to $z$"? This sentence obviously expresses a truth, or its universal closure does. Are we to say that this sentence is formed from *four unrelated* predicates, the one we have already mentioned, and three others ("the distance from **1** to **2** is greater than the distance from **3** to **4**" etc.)?[13] Surely this is incorrect. The logical structures of the antecedent and consequent of this sentence are more closely related than *that*. We could exhibit an intimate logical relation between the antecedent and the consequent if we were willing to assume that there were things called "distances" that "separated" spatial objects from one another, and that one and the same "distance" might simultaneously "separate" A and B (on the one hand) and B and a third object C (on the other). But we need not be willing to make such an assumption – which, as I have said, I do not find coherent – to exhibit such a relation. There are a lot of alternatives. One of them would be to introduce the predicate "**1** is **2** times farther from **3** than **4** is from **5**." We need no other predicate involving spatial separation to express what is expressed by our sentence (whatever, exactly, "what is expressed by our sentence" may mean; for now, let us take such expressions for granted):

> If $x$ is 1 times farther from $y$ than $x$ is from $y$, and $y$ is 1 times farther from $z$ than $y$ is from $z$, then $\exists n$ $x$ is $n$ times farther from $y$ than $y$ is from $z$, and $n > 1$ or $n = 1$ or $n < 1$.

(Or one might choose to omit the words "and $n > 1$ or $n = 1$ or $n < 1$," regarding them as an "understood" consequence of the properties of the

---

[13] For an account of "predicates," see W. V. Quine, *Elementary Logic*, rev. edn. (Cambridge, Mass., 1966), §40–§42. Where I have used bold-face numerals, Quine uses circled numerals.

real numbers.) If we have this predicate at our disposal, we may replace the last clause in the final sentence in our sequence of sentences with "*x* is 1 times farther from *y* than *x* is from *y*," thus enabling us to avoid the awkward problem of describing the nature of the objects that satisfy the open sentence "*z* is a distance."[14]

To sum up: the transition between "not being in" and "being in" the quantifier-variable idiom is not sharp but gradual – or, better, one's introduction of quantifiers and variables into a piece of English discourse consists in one's seizing some or all of the opportunities afforded by the sentences that discourse comprises for replacing certain constructions within those sentences by constructions involving quantifiers and variables. And this is a procedure that may require a certain amount of creativity. A "mechanical" attempt to introduce the canonical notation of quantification may produce a result that is of dubious grammaticality. More importantly, certain ways of introducing quantifiers and variables that initially suggest themselves may seem to one on reflection to be philosophically objectionable: a way of introducing quantifiers and variables may produce a set of sentences that have as a formal consequence the existential generalization on an open sentence F such that, on reflection, one is unwilling to concede that there is anything that satisfies F. (For "F" read "*z* is a distance," "*x* is a number," "*y* is a set" . . .) And one may be convinced that the "initial" piece of English discourse carried no implication that there were Fs, and that, nevertheless, the discourse contained logical structure that was somehow representable by constructions involving quantifiers and variables. It is at this point – to implement this conviction – that creativity is called for. And there is no unique, preexistent "hidden logical form" for this creativity to uncover. It is certainly not true that any translation of a piece of English discourse into the quantifier-variable idiom is as good as any other, but there will be many interesting cases in which the question whether one proposed translation is as good as another is a philosophical question, with all that *that* implies. (In some cases it may be that the question is an aesthetic or a scientific question. Some "proposed objects" offend the aesthetic sense of certain people, even if these people have no "hard" objections to them. Others

---

[14] To simplify the example, I have omitted the time variable. Strictly speaking, I should have introduced the predicate "at **1**, **2** is **3** times farther from **4** than **5** is from **6**," and I should have replaced the last clause in the final sentence with "at *t*, *x* is 1 times farther from *y* than *x* is from *y*."

may be beautiful and philosophically unobjectionable, but hard to fit in with currently accepted scientific theories.)

It is not true, therefore, that a theory, or a given piece of English discourse, has certain more-or-less hidden but objectively present "ontological commitments." Quine, moreover, is well aware of this fact, and he has not proposed any mechanical technique for uncovering them. (The thesis that a confessed pragmatist has made such a proposal is, surely, little short of incredible.) What, then, *is* "Quine's criterion of ontological commitment"?

I have said that these words are a name for a certain thesis about strategy. More exactly, they are a name for the most profitable strategy to follow in order to get people to make their ontological commitments – or the ontological commitments of their discourse – clear. The strategy is this: one takes sentences that the other party to the conversation accepts, and by whatever dialectical devices one can muster, one gets him to introduce more and more quantifiers and variables into those sentences. (Or, if you will, one gets him to accept new sentences, sentences that come from the sentences he initially endorsed by the progressive replacement of devices and constructions belonging to ordinary English by devices and constructions belonging to the canonical language of quantification. Our sequence of sentences about stars and planets and distances provides an example of what is meant by such "progressive replacement.") If, at a certain point in this procedure, it emerges that the existential generalization on a certain open sentence F can be formally deduced from the sentences he accepts, one has shown that the sentences that he accepts, and the ways of introducing quantifiers and variables into those sentences that he has endorsed, formally commit him to there being things that satisfy F.

"But if someone doesn't believe in, say, numbers, and if he sees that a certain introduction of quantifiers and variables into his sentences would have the result that '$\exists x\ x$ is a number' could be formally deduced from the result, why shouldn't he simply refuse to introduce canonical notation in that way and say, 'Thus far and no farther.' Why can't he stop playing Quine's game at will? In fact, why should he play in the first place?"

Well, any philosopher is perfectly free to resist the application of any dialectical ploy. But the following two points are in order.

- Sometimes, in simple cases involving little or no creativity, a refusal to accept the obvious proposal for the introduction of quantifiers and variables can border on the unintelligible. The symbol "∃" is, after all, essentially an abbreviation for the English "there are," just as "+" is essentially an abbreviation for the English "plus." Suppose, for example, that a certain philosopher maintains that some metaphysical sentences are meaningful – suppose, in fact, that he has actually spoken or written the sentence "Some metaphysical sentences are meaningful." And suppose that he is also a fanatical nominalist who has been known to say that strictly speaking there are no sentences. There is a perfectly obvious proposal for the introduction of the canonical notation of quantification into the English sentence "Some metaphysical sentences are meaningful":

∃x (x is a sentence & x is metaphysical & x is meaningful).

But the philosopher who has written the sentence "Some metaphysical sentences are meaningful" and who denies that (strictly speaking) there are any sentences had better resist this obvious proposal. And yet, given that "∃" just *means* "there are" (as "+" just means "plus") it is very hard to justify such intransigence. (How should we understand someone who was willing to write or speak the sentence "Two plus two equals four" and yet refused – and not because he was unfamiliar with the canonical notation of elementary arithmetic – to write or speak the sentence "2 + 2 = 4"?) As a matter of historical fact, Quine seems to have begun to talk of "the canonical notation of quantification" in ontological contexts because he was confronted with philosophers who accepted English sentences whose obvious "symbolization" was of the form "∃x (Gx & Hx)," and who, nevertheless, rejected the corresponding English sentences of the form "∃x Gx."[15]

- In more complicated cases, a refusal to go beyond a certain point in replacing the idioms of ordinary English with quantifiers and variables could leave English predicates that seem intuitively to be intimately logically related without any apparent logical relation. (We have seen an example of this above.) And this could leave one without any way to account for the validity of inferences that seem intuitively to be valid.

I will end with a little example of how a philosopher might appeal to the latter point in a dispute about what there is. The example is borrowed from David and Stephanie Lewis's classic essay "Holes."[16]

Suppose that a certain materialist refuses to admit that the sentence "There are exactly two holes in this piece of cheese" can be translated into the quantifier-variable idiom in this way:

[15] See, for example, Quine's discussion ("On Carnap's Views on Ontology," *Philosophical Studies* 2 [1951], pp. 65–72) of Carnap's distinction between "internal" and "external" questions, a distinction that allowed Carnap to dismiss as illegitimate the question, "Are there numbers?," but to regard the question "Is there a greatest pair of twin primes?" as legitimate.

[16] David and Stephanie Lewis, "Holes," *Australasian Journal of Philosophy* 48 (1970), pp. 206–212.

$\exists x \, \exists y \, (x$ is a hole & $y$ is a hole & $x$ is in this piece of cheese & $y$ is in this piece of cheese & $\sim x = y$ & $\forall z \, (z$ is a hole & $z$ is in this piece of cheese. $\rightarrow .z = x \lor z = y)).$

(One can well see why a materialist would not want to accept this translation: there would no doubt be occasions on which he accepted what was expressed on that occasion by the sentence of ordinary English; the proposed translation expresses a truth only in the case that there are objects that satisfy the open sentence "$x$ is a hole"; if materialism is true, then there are only material objects; no material object satisfies "$x$ is a hole.") Suppose that one was carrying on an ontological discussion with such a materialist. The exact point of the discussion is not of much importance for present purposes. (One might be an opponent of materialism, or one might simply be trying better to understand what the materialist's position implies.) Here is how one might apply considerations about the validity of inference in such a discussion. One might ask the materialist to consider the ordinary English sentence "If there are three caraway seeds in this piece of cheese, then there are more seeds in this piece of cheese than there are holes in this piece of cheese." This sentence is obviously a logical consequence of "There are exactly two holes in this piece of cheese." Anyone who accepts the above "symbolization" of the latter sentence, and who accepts any symbolization of the second sentence that is constructed along similar lines, can easily account for the fact that the second sentence is a logical consequence of the first: the symbolization of the second is a formal consequence of the symbolization of the first. But our materialist cannot accept this account of that fact, and either must be content to have no account of it or must find some other account of it. The only way that suggests itself to find an alternative account of this fact is this: find alternative symbolizations of the two sentences such that (i) the "new" symbolization of the latter is a formal consequence of the "new" symbolization of the former, and (ii) neither of the new symbolizations is such that its truth requires the existence of objects satisfying some open sentence that – like "$x$ is a hole" – cannot be satisfied by objects acceptable to the materialist.

In the present case, it is easy enough to find such alternative symbolizations – if the materialist is willing to accept the existence of abstract objects of some sort. With some difficulty (as the Lewises have shown) alternative symbolizations can be found that do not presuppose the existence of abstract objects. But these "nominalistic" symbolizations are, not to put too fine a point upon it, bizarre – and they appeal to a very strong principle of mereological summation. Certain untoward consequences of a strict nominalistic materialism thus become evident only when one adopts Quine's strategy for clarifying ontological disputes – and it is unlikely that they would otherwise have been noticed. In my view, a general lesson can be drawn from this: All ontological disputes in which the disputants do not accept Quine's strategy of ontological clarification are suspect. If Quine's "rules" for conducting an ontological dispute are not followed, then – so say those of us who are adherents of Quine's meta-ontology – it is almost certain that many untoward consequences of the disputed positions will be obscured by imprecision and wishful thinking.[17]

[17] This essay is an adaptation of the first chapter of a book, *Being: A Study in Ontology*, which will be published by Oxford University Press.

# 2

# *Why I don't understand substitutional quantification*

I

My difficulty with the notion of substitutional quantification is a very simple – one might almost say simple-minded – one. Yet the friends of substitutional quantification, or those I have talked to, have not been able to resolve this difficulty in conversation. With some trepidation, therefore, I venture to write down my simple problem.

Let us use "Σ" to designate the existential – or "particular" – substitutional quantifier. (I shall assume at the outset that my readers agree with me on one fundamental point: it is not the case that there is something called "the existential – or particular – quantifier" of which philosophers of logic have offered two "interpretations" or "readings," *viz.* the objectual or referential interpretation and the substitutional interpretation. It would be better to say that there are two quantifiers, two distinct variable-binding operators: the objectual or referential and the substitutional.)

If I could understand the sentence

    *S*  Σ*x*  *x* is a dog

then I could understand substitutional quantification. But I cannot understand this sentence. I cannot understand it because I do not know what proposition it expresses. I do not know what proposition it expresses for this reason: those whose business it is to define substitutional quantification have attempted to do this by giving "truth-conditions" for *S* and other sentences containing the substitutional quantifiers. That is, they have attempted to do this by explaining under what conditions whatever proposition it is that is expressed by *S* (to take a particular case) is true. Now I understand these truth-conditions, at least in a rough-and-ready sort of way. My (main) problem with substitutional quantification

First published in *Philosophical Studies* 39 (1981), pp. 281–285.

is not one of interpreting these truth-conditions. It is rather this: I know of a proposition that has just these truth-conditions, and those whose business it is to explain substitutional quantification tell me that the proposition that $S$ expresses is not *that* proposition. And nothing more will they say. Thus, my position with respect to $S$ is what yours would be with respect to the sentence

John cissed Jane

if I told you just these two things and no more:

Whatever proposition is expressed by "John cissed Jane," it is true iff John kissed Jane

"John cissed Jane" does *not* express the proposition expressed by "John kissed Jane."

## II

I do not mean anything mysterious by "proposition." I use this word as a general term for the things people *assent to, reject, find doubtful, accept for the sake of argument, attempt to verify, deduce things from*, and so on. (Some of the phrases on this list take more than one sort of object. One may, for example, reject not only propositions but bribes. I hope no one is going to be difficult about this.) We have plenty of "specialized" words for propositions in the language of everyday life, just as we have plenty of specialized words for human beings. On various occasions, we call propositions "doctrines," "theses," "theories," "premises," "conclusions," "theorems," "views," "positions," "conjectures," "hypotheses," "dogmas," "beliefs," and "heresies," just as, on various occasions, we call human beings "women," "babies," "thieves," "admirals," "Trotskyites," "Australians," and "Catholics."

It is thus uncontroversial that there are propositions. The only question that could arise is: What *are* propositions? Many philosophers apparently think that propositions are sentences, since they think that sentences are what is true or false, and it is evident that those things that are true or false are just the things that are the objects of the activities and states listed above. But I can make no sense of the suggestion that propositions are sentences, and I shall not discuss it further. It is true that I am willing on occasion to speak of sentences being true or false, but this is only shorthand. When I say that a given sentence is *true*, I mean that the proposition – a non-sentence – that that sentence expresses is true. (To say that an English sentence *expresses* a given proposition is to say, roughly, that the result of concatenating "the proposition that" and that sentence *denotes* that proposition.) Similarly, when I say that a name is *honorable*, I mean that the individual or family that bears that name is honorable. I can no more understand the suggestion that a sentence might be true otherwise than in virtue of its expressing a true proposition that I can understand the suggestion that a name might be honorable otherwise than in virtue of its being borne by an honorable individual or family.

III

Let us call a phrase that purports to designate an object a *term*. Thus, "Napoleon," "Pegasus," "the father of King Arthur," "2 + 2," and "the odd prime" are terms. "All men," "something," "just one cat," and "the square of $x$" are not terms.

The friends of substitutional quantification tell us this much and no more about the meaning of *S*:

> TC     "$\Sigma x$ $x$ is a dog" is true [i.e., whatever proposition is expressed by "$\Sigma x$ $x$ is a dog" is true] iff $\exists x$ $x$ is a term and $\ulcorner x$ is a dog$\urcorner$ is true [expresses a true proposition].

Let us stay that a sentence *has the same truth-conditions* as *S* if the result of replacing *S* with that sentence in TC is a truth. Thus – since there *is* a term that, when concatenated with "is a dog," yields a sentence that express a truth – "Grass is green" and "2 + 2 = 4" have the same truth-conditions as *S*. I am *tempted* to say that this fact shows that what the friends of substitutional quantification have told us about *S* has been insufficient to rule out the possibility that *S* expresses the proposition that grass is green; I am *tempted* to accuse the friends of substitutional quantification of having, for this reason alone, told me nothing about what *S* means.

I shall resist these temptations. If I yielded to them, the friends of substitutional quantification would point out that TC is an instance of a *general* statement of truth-conditions for sentences containing "$\Sigma$" and that, in virtue of this general statement, the left-hand constituent of the biconditional TC is *systematically* related to the right-hand constituent of TC by a rule that does not relate any *other* true sentence of the form "$p$ is

34

true" (e.g., " 'Grass is green' is true") to the right-hand constituent of TC.

I am not sure how effective this reply is. In fact I am not quite sure I see why it is a relevant reply to what I am tempted to say. But, since I wish to avoid this issue (for the good reason that I have nothing new to say about it), I shall steadfastly resist temptation.

I therefore do not accuse the friends of substitutional quantification of giving an explanation of "$\Sigma x$ $x$ is a dog" that fails to rule out the possibility that this sentence expresses the proposition that grass is green. But I do want to accuse them of something rather like this. Consider the proposition that $\exists x$ $x$ is a term and $\ulcorner x$ is a dog$\urcorner$ is true. Call this proposition "$\exists$." Suppose $I$ use $S$ to express $\exists$. (*One* way for me to do this would be for me to treat $S$ as an *abbreviation* for the right-hand constituent of TC.) Am I doing anything wrong from the point of view of the friends of substitutional quantification? Should I expect them to accuse me of misusing the symbol "$\Sigma$"? One might suppose not. After all, the proposition $\exists$ is true under just exactly the conditions they specify as the truth-conditions for $S$. Moreover, as is not the case with the proposition that grass is green, the fact that $\exists$ is true under just those conditions is not a contingent, empirical matter.

Nevertheless, the friends of substitutional quantification would deny that $S$ expresses $\exists$. Alex Orenstein, for example, in his recent book *Existence and the Particular Quantifier,*[1] emphatically denies that "substitutional quantification is a metalinguistic species of objectual/referential quantification." This denial, I think, places Orenstein in the standard tradition of interpreting substitutional quantification, a tradition that can be traced to Ajdukiewicz.[2] I take this tradition to be sufficiently "standard" that anyone who departs from it is proposing a *deviant* use for "$\Sigma$." In any case, it is Orenstein's use of the substitutional quantifier, whether it is standard or deviant, that I am unable to understand: I understand objectual quantification over terms and predicates as well as the next philosopher. It is true that some recent writers appear to conflate substitutional quantification and objectual quantification over linguistic objects. Susan Haack in her *Philosophy of Logics*[3] states the "substitutional interpretation" – that this way of talking evidences a mistaken view of the relation between the substitutional and the objec-

---

[1] Alex Orenstein, *Existence and the Particular Quantifier* (Philadelphia, 1978), pp. 34f.

[2] See ibid.

[3] Susan Haack, *Philosophy of Logics* (Cambridge, 1978). See p. 42.

tual quantifier is not to the present point – of the existential quantifier in these words:

> "(∃x) Fx" is interpreted as "At least one substitution instance of 'F . . .' is true."

But I think that the most probable explanation for this statement is that Haack was expressing herself loosely.

"Σx x is a dog," therefore, does not express ∃. But then what proposition does it express? I do not know. No one knows. No one knows because no one has ever *said*. *I* know of only one proposition – ∃ – that one might reasonably suppose (given TC) to be the proposition S expresses, and I am told by those who know what proposition S expresses if *anyone* knows what proposition S expresses that ∃ is *not* the proposition S expresses. Thus my position with respect to S is just what your position is with respect to the sentence "John cissed Jane" that was mentioned in Section I. That is, I do not understand S. And neither, I think, does anyone else. But then neither I nor anyone else understands substitutional quantification.[4,5]

---

[4] I have been asked why, if the arguments of this paper are correct, parallel reasoning does not show that no one understands *objectual* quantification. After all, isn't the meaning of the objectual quantifiers specified by and only by statements like this one: "∃x x is a dog" is true iff at least one object satisfies "x is a dog"? The answer to this question is quite simply No. Our understanding of the (objectual) quantifier-variable idiom resides in our ability to translate sentences couched in it into quantificational idioms of which we have a prior grasp, *viz.* those of ordinary language. Or at least this reply will do as a first approximation. The case is complicated by the fact that the very limited resources for cross-reference in ordinary English probably render it impossible to translate any really complex sentences in the quantifier-variable idiom unambiguously into ordinary English. But, despite this *practical* difficulty, there would seem to be a difference *in principle* between the substitutional quantifier and the objectual quantifier as regards our ability to say, using idioms of which we have a prior grasp, what propositions sentences containing these operators express. At least in the case of relatively uncomplex sentences containing "∃," we *can* say what proposition they express. For example, "∃x x is a dog" expresses the proposition that there is at least one dog. (Someone who knew that "∃x x is a dog" expressed *some* proposition that was true iff at least one thing satisfied "x is a dog," but did not know *which* of the many propositions conforming to this requirement it expressed, would *not* understand objectual quantification.) But *no one* can say what proposition "Σx x is a dog" expresses.

[5] The ideas defended in this paper bear a striking resemblance to some of those presented by William G. Lycan in his fine paper "Semantic competence and funny functors," *The Monist* 64 (1979), which I highly recommend to anyone interested in the general topic of the relationship between knowing what a sentence means and knowing its truth-conditions.

# 3

# Creatures of fiction

I

Some philosophers say there are things that do not exist. In saying this, they mean to assert more than the obvious truth that, on some occasions, sentences like "Mr. Pickwick does not exist" can be used as vehicles of true assertions: They mean to assert that there *are*, there really *are*, certain objects that have, among their other attributes (such as jollity and rotundity), the attribute of non-existence. Let us call such philosophers Meinongians and their doctrine Meinongianism.[1] One argument for Meinongianism proceeds by examples drawn from fiction, or so the Meinongian would say. A typical *anti*-Meinongian, however, would probably want to describe a typical application of this method as follows: "My Meinongian friend uttered 'Mr. Pickwick does not exist' assertively. Then he described what he had done in uttering these words as his having 'given an example of a non-existent object.'" Our typical anti-Meinongian has an obvious reason for so describing the Meinong-

First published in *American Philosophical Quarterly* 14/4 (October 1977), pp. 299–308.
[1] This is merely a convenient label. It is a nice question whether Meinong himself was a "Meinongian" in the present sense. Meinong would certainly say that the English sentence "There are things that do not exist" expressed a truth. But this truth it expressed would be about "ideale Gegenstände," ideal objects, such as Platonic forms and numbers. These subsist (bestehen) but do not exist (existieren), since there *are* such things, but they are not spatio-temporal objects. (On this matter, see fn. 5 to the present essay.) The proposition *I* mean to express by "These are things that do not exist" is, I think, that which Meinong expresses by the words, "There are objects of which it is true that there are no such objects" ("... es gibt Gegenstände, von denen gilt, dass es der gleichen Gegenstände nicht gibt ...") ("Über Gegenstandstheorie," *Alexius Meinong Gesamtausgabe*, ed. Rudolf Haller and Rudolf Kindinger, in collaboration with Roderick M. Chisholm [Graz, 1969–1973], vol. II, p. 490). But it is not clear how seriously he meant these words to be taken, since he prefaced them with "One who was fond of paradoxical modes of expression could ... say." On this topic, see R. M. Chisholm's very enlightening paper (from which most of the points made in this footnote are drawn), "Beyond Being and Nonbeing" in *New Readings in Philosophical Analysis*, ed. Herbert Feigl, Wilfrid Sellars, and Keith Lehrer (New York, 1972), pp. 15–22.

ian's argument. For he is, of course, going to go on to say something like: "But his description of what he did was incorrect; for even if the sentence he uttered was or expressed a truth, its subject-term, 'Mr. Pickwick,' does not denote anything. Therefore, he did not, in uttering this sentence, succeed in giving an example of *anything*, much less of something non-existent."

So the Meinongian thinks that "Mr. Pickwick" is a name for something and that what it names is non-existent.[2] The typical anti-Meinongian thinks that "Mr. Pickwick" is not a name for anything. It will be noticed that their positions are contraries, not contradictories. It would also be at least formally possible to maintain that "Mr. Pickwick" is a name for something and that what it names exists. In this paper, I wish to defend just this thesis. More generally, I shall defend the thesis that there are things I shall call "creatures of fiction," and that every single one of them exists.

I shall show that this thesis has certain advantages over both the Meinongian and what I have called the "typical anti-Meinongian" theories of the ontology of fiction. Its advantage over the Meinongian theory is this: Meinongianism *either* involves a bit of technical terminology that has never been given a satisfactory explanation, *or else* necessitates an abandonment of what are commonly called "the laws of logic." And the theory I shall present does not have this drawback. Consider the Meinongian's claim that there are things that don't exist. If *I* were asked to render this claim into the quantifier-variable idiom, I would write

$$(\exists x) \sim (\exists y) \ (x = y).$$

But the result of prefixing a tilde to this formula is a theorem of logic. Now the Meinongian will probably think my translation wrong-headed. I would expect him to say something like, "Either '$(\exists x)$' means 'there *is* an $x$' or it means 'there *exists* an $x$.' You can't have it both ways. Let's say it means the latter. Then you need to introduce a new piece of notation for the former – say, '$(Ix)$.' *Then* symbolize my general claim as

$$(Ix) \sim (\exists y) \ (x = y)."$$

---

[2] There is, of course, a good deal more to Meinongianism than its treatment of the referents of names like "Mr. Pickwick" and "Hamlet." Even if the theory presented in the present paper, which treats *only* of names drawn from the works of fiction, is true, it might yet be the case that the Meinongian is right in thinking that "the golden mountain," "Pegasus," "the round square," and so on, denote certain objects and that these objects do not exist.

I must confess I do not understand the words I have put into the Meinongian's mouth. I do not see any important difference between "there is" and "there exists," and, therefore, I do not see how it is I am supposed to use "(I$x$)" and "($\exists x$)." Nor is this the end of the Meinongian's difficulties with the usual "laws of logic." For if the Meinongian is asked, "About your Mr. Pickwick – has he an even number of hairs on his head?", he will answer (Dickens having been noncommittal on this matter), "He neither has nor lacks the property of having an even number of hairs on his head; he is therefore what I call an *incomplete object*." And to say this, *I* would say, is to say that some instances of

$$(\forall x)(\mathrm{F}x \ \vee \sim \mathrm{F}x)$$

are false or express falsehoods, though this formula is a theorem of logic. Of course the Meinongian will again find my symbolic formula ambiguous. He will perhaps insist that I choose between two universal quantifiers, one corresponding to " $\sim$ (I$x$) $\sim$ ," and the other to " $\sim$ ($\exists x$) $\sim$ ," and will claim that he assents to the invalidity only of " $\sim$ (I$x$) $\sim$ (F$x$ $\vee$ $\sim$ F$x$)." But this does not make the distinction between "($\exists x$)" and "(I$x$)" any easier to understand. '

These difficulties make the typical anti-Meinongian's position look very attractive by comparison. This philosopher will admit that sentences like "Mr. Pickwick does not exist" and "Mr. Pickwick is jolly" may, in certain contexts (correcting someone who takes *The Pickwick Papers* for history; giving a summary of the plot of that novel), be used by their utterers to express truths. But, he will insist, the utterer of such sentences does not (except in a Pickwickian sense) *refer* to anyone or anything when he utters them. Or, if our anti-Meinongian does not mind talking about such sentences "out of context" (this is how we represented him earlier), he may say that their subject-term does not denote anything, or that they are not subject to existential generalization.

Of course our anti-Meinongian must be able to explain how it is we are able to use declaratively a sentence having "Mr. Pickwick" as its grammatical subject to express a truth when "Mr. Pickwick" is not a name for anything. Usually, when such an explanation is demanded, the anti-Meinongian will produce a *paraphrase* of the "Pickwick"-sentence; that is, he will devise a sentence he claims "really says the same thing as" the "Pickwick"-sentence, in which "Mr. Pickwick" does not even *seem* to function as a name. For example, the anti-Meinongian might offer as a paraphrase of "Mr. Pickwick is jolly" the sentence "If *The Pickwick*

*Papers* were not a novel but a true record of events, then there *would have been* a jolly man called 'Mr. Pickwick'." I do not say this would be a *good* paraphrase. Some philosophers might argue that it fails as a paraphrase because it contains a reference to a novel, which the original does not, and, moreover, contains a reference to the *words* "Mr. Pickwick," which the original does not. (Of course, it would be possible to reply that the original makes a *covert* reference to both these things, which the paraphrase has the virtue of making explicit.) Whether or not this is a good paraphrase, however, it is a good *example* of the sort of thing I mean by "paraphrase."

Well, what is wrong with "typical anti-Meinongianism"? Or perhaps we should ask, What is wrong with adopting it as a *program*?, since, at least as *I* have presented it, it is not an ontological doctrine, but rather a proposal to stick to a certain rather vaguely defined method in dealing with a certain class of ontological problems. I have no particular *a priori* objection to anti-Meinongianism, which has the advantages of leaving the laws of logic unviolated and of requiring no mysterious terminology. And perhaps it appeals to a "robust sense of reality," or, at least, appeals to those philosophers who like to describe themselves as having such a sense. But I am not sure the program it proposes can be carried out. I have no knock-down argument for this, though I shall in the sequel display some sentences that, at the very least, are going to force the typical anti-Meinongian to produce very messy paraphrases. But I am not, in this paper, primarily interested in refuting either "typical anti-Meinongianism" or Meinongianism. I wish only to present, in a very sketchy way, the *prima facie* cases against the way these theories deal with those of our assertions and beliefs that are "about fictional entities," in order to present a *prima facie* case *for* the rival theory I shall presently propose.

II

At this point I am reluctantly going to abandon Mr. Pickwick, despite the fact that, like that old war horse, Pegasus, he has a good claim to tenure in the office of Exemplary Nonentity. I turn instead to Mrs. Gamp. I do this because I have been able to find sentences "about her" that serve my purposes better than any sentences I know of "about Pickwick." Here are three of them:

(1) She was a fat old woman, this Mrs. Gamp, with a husky voice and a moist eye, which she had a remarkable power of turning up, and only showing the white of it. (*Martin Chuzzlewit*, Ch. 19)

(2) Mrs. Sarah Gamp was, four-and-twenty years ago, a fair representation of the hired attendant on the poor in sickness. (From Dickens's preface to an 1867 edition of *Martin Chuzzlewit*)

(3) Mrs. Gamp... is the most fully developed of the masculine anti-women visible in all Dickens's novels. (Sylvia Bank Manning, *Dickens as Satirist* [New Haven, 1971] p. 79)

Now a very naive Meinongian might describe what the authors of these sentences were doing in writing them as follows. "There is a certain non-existent woman, Mrs. Gamp, and both Dickens and Professor Manning wrote about her. In writing (2), Dickens asserted that, in 1843, she was a fair representation of the hired attendant on the poor in sickness; in writing (1), he asserted of her that she was [in 1843?] fat, old, husky-voiced, and so on, while, in writing (3), Professor Manning asserted of her that she was [in 1971?] the most fully developed of the masculine anti-women visible in all Dickens's novels."

Now whatever else may be wrong with the naive Meinongian's description of what the writers of these sentences were doing, surely he is wrong in so assimilating the writing of (1) to the writing of (2) and (3). Sentences (2) and (3) were used by their authors as the vehicles of assertions; (1) was not. It would make sense to say that the authors of (2) and (3), in writing these sentences, wrote something true or wrote something false. If the average "hired attendant on the poor in sickness" in 1843 was rather like the popular picture of Florence Nightingale, then Dickens, in writing (2), wrote something *false* in the same sense as that in which he would have written something false if he had written that he had composed *Martin Chuzzlewit* while living in China. But if someone had been looking over Dickens's shoulder when Dickens was writing (1), and had said to him, "No, no, you've got her all wrong. She is quite thin, about twenty-four, and her voice is melodious," this would simply have made no sense.

Thus, there is a certain sense in which the fact that novelists do things like writing sentence (1) is not directly relevant to questions about the ontology of fictional entities. There is no point in debating what sort of thing Dickens was writing about when he wrote (1) or debating what sort of fact or proposition he was asserting, since he was not writing

41

about anything and was asserting nothing.[3] Sentence (1) does not represent an *attempt* at reference or description.[4]

Sentences (2) and (3), however, do represent assertions: their authors in writing them are expressing propositions of some sort, and these propositions *seem* to be about Mrs. Gamp. A more sophisticated Meinongian will say that *these* sentences, at any rate, are about a non-existent entity, even if (1) is not. Like this Meinongian, I suggest we take Dickens's and Manning's uses of sentences (2) and (3) at face value: as assertions about a certain entity called "Mrs. Gamp." Unlike him, however, I suggest that what Dickens's and Manning's assertions are about exists. In Section III, I shall attempt to answer certain questions that must be answered by anyone who takes these suggestions seriously.

### III

*Question*: Why should we take (2) and (3) as being *about* Mrs. Gamp, in any sense except the uninteresting sense in which "The average American owns 1.02 cars" is "about the average American"? *Answer*: Because, while "the average American" is not a name for anything, "Mrs. Gamp" *is* a name for something – or, if you prefer, there is such a thing as Mrs. Gamp – and if there is such a thing as Mrs. Gamp, then *obviously* (2) and (3) are about her. *Question*: But why do you say there *is* such a thing as Mrs. Gamp? *Answer*: Because there *are* such things as characters in novels. And if there are such things as characters in novels, then Mrs. Gamp is one of them. Anyone who said there were such things as characters in novels, and went on to say that there was no such thing as Mrs. Gamp would simply be factually ignorant. He would be like someone who said that there were such things as irrational numbers, but no such thing as π. *Question*: But why do you say there are such things as characters in novels? *Answer*: Consider sentences like the following:

---

[3] This is a very important point. The reader who does not concede it will get very little out of reading further. The argument in the text of the present paper is not sufficient to establish it. For arguments that are sufficient, see Alvin Plantinga, *The Nature of Necessity* (Oxford, 1974) Ch. 8, pp. 153–163 especially, and J. O. Urmson, "Fiction," *American Philosophical Quarterly* 13 (1976), pp. 153–157.

[4] This is true despite the fact that (1) is what is called a "descriptive" sentence by literary critics. This term is applied to sentences of fiction that would be descriptive sentences in a literal sense if the works of fiction in which they occurred were historical records.

(4) There are characters in some nineteenth-century novels who are presented with a greater wealth of physical detail than is any character in any eighteenth-century novel

(5) Some characters in novels are closely modeled on actual people, while others are wholly products of the literary imagination, and it is usually impossible to tell which characters fall into which of these categories by textual analysis alone

(6) Since nineteenth-century English novelists were, for the most part, conventional Englishmen, we might expect most novels of the period to contain stereotyped comic Frenchmen or Italians; but very few such characters exist.

These sentences, or the propositions expressed by them, certainly *seem* to assert that there are things of a certain sort: if anyone were to utter one of these sentences assertively, it would *seem* that what he would say could be true only if there were such things as characters in novels. Take (4), for instance. If I were asked to render this sentence into the quantifier-variable idiom, I would produce something like:

(4)★ ($\exists x$) ($x$ is a character in a nineteenth-century novel & ($\forall y$) [$y$ is a character in an eighteenth-century novel $\supset$ $x$ is presented with a greater wealth of physical detail than is $y$]).

And, by the rules of formal logic, (4)★ yields:

(7) ($\exists x$) ($x$ is a character in a nineteenth-century novel).

Therefore, since (4) is true, or expresses a true proposition, or is such that if it were uttered in appropriate circumstances its utterer would say something true, *and* since (4)★ is a correct translation of (4) into the regimented idiom of formal logic, *and* since the rules of formal logic are truth-preserving, *and* since "There are such things as characters in nineteenth-century novels" is a correct translation of (7) into ordinary English, it follows that there are such things as characters in nineteenth-century novels, and from this it follows that there are such things as characters in novels.

*Question:* There are several premises in that argument that one might want to look at rather carefully. But let's grant for the sake of argument that there are such things as characters in novels; What do you mean by saying they *exist*? *Answer:* Just what you granted and no more. "There is no cure for cancer," "There is no such thing as a cure for cancer," "A cure for cancer does not exist," and "There exists no cure for cancer" all mean more or less the same thing. Some of them might be slightly more appropriate things to say in certain contexts of utterance than others, but it is not possible that anyone should utter one of these sentences and thereby say something true, and someone else simultaneously utter another of them and thereby say something false. And the same point applies whether we are talking about cures, cabbages, countries, cylindrical algebras, or characters in novels. There is (or exists) a tendency in some quarters to think that "there are" is a harmless and rather empty expression, while "exist" is such an important word that anyone who uses it takes on a great weight of ontological responsibility. But "exist" in (6) above, and "there are" in (4), and, for that matter, "some" in (5), have just exactly the same sort of import. And this is *always* the case, no matter what sort of thing we are talking about.[5]

*Question*: But if Mrs. Gamp really existed, couldn't I, if I had been alive in 1843, have gone and talked with her? *Answer*: Obviously not, since she did exist then (she exists *now*, in fact) and you couldn't have. But now you are touching on matters I will deal with in Section IV. *Question*: But I find her mysterious. What *sort* of thing is she? What ontological categories does she belong to? *Answer*: Well, she is, as I said, a character in a novel. And characters in novels are members of a category of things I shall call *creatures of fiction*. Some things belonging to this category that are not characters in novels are the Wife of Bath, Polyphemus, the Forest of Arden, Dotheboys Hall, and Professor Moriarty's book *The Dynamics of an Asteroid*. And creatures of fiction belong to a broader category of things I shall call *theoretical entities of literary criticism*, a category that also includes plots, sub-plots, novels (as opposed to tangible *copies* of novels), poems, meters, rhyme schemes, borrowings, influences, digressions, episodes, recurrent patterns of imagery, and literary forms ("the novel," "the sonnet"). Or this category includes such things as these if there *are* any such things as these. (Cf. the sequence: the thing that caused this trace in the cloud-chamber, electron, sub-atomic particle, theoretical entity of physics.)

*Question*: And just what are theoretical entities? *Answer*: That's a very good and not very clear question. Of course, it's not *your* fault it's not clear. But let's look at it this way. There are various "theoretical disciplines" like physics and literary criticism. (The former of these is a science, the latter not.) There are various sentences in which the "con-

---

[5] "He [Rush Rhees] thinks we use exists 'chiefly in connexion with physical objects' ... The nearest newspaper shows the contrary; 'conditions for a durable agreement do not exist,' or the like, is the commonest currency of journalism." P. T. Geach, review of Rush Rhees's *Without Answers* in *The Journal of Philosophy* 68 (1971), pp. 531–532.

ceptual machinery" of these disciplines is inextirpably embedded: you couldn't *say* what these sentences say without employing theoretical vocabularies like the ones these disciplines employ. Some of these disciplines may be such that we are comfortable with saying that nothing interesting that can be said only by means of their special vocabularies is ever *true*. (Astrology, for example.) But for many disciplines (physics, say) this would be an absurd thing to say. (Like many absurd things, it has been said.) And I think it would be absurd to think that nothing that can be said only in the language of literary criticism is true, especially if we take "literary criticism" to include all "informed" discourse about the nature, content, and value of literary works. And, sometimes, if what is said in a piece of literary criticism is to be true, then there must be entities of a certain type, entities that are never the subjects of non-literary discourse, and which make up the extensions of the theoretical general terms of literary criticism. It is these that I call "theoretical entities of literary criticism." To say this much, however, is not to answer the question, Which theoretical terms of criticism must be taken as having special sorts of entity as their extension?, or the question, Which, if any, of these terms is in principle eliminable from critical discourse? But I think that "discourse about characters," which is the sort of critical discourse that is our present concern, is not *easily* eliminable from literary criticism. *I see* no way to do it, at any rate. That is, I see no way to paraphrase sentences (4), (5), and (6), and others like them, in such a way as to produce sentences that seem to "say the same thing" and which do not involve "quantification over creatures of fiction." (This is not a very carefully stated claim; taken literally, it is obviously false, since it would be easy enough to paraphrase these sentences in such a way that the paraphrases involve quantification only over, say, unit sets whose members are creatures of fiction. Don't take it *that* literally.)

*Question*: But isn't finding such a paraphrase a fairly easy task? Take sentence (4). It seems obvious that, once all the eighteenth- and nineteenth-century novels have been written, once certain novelists, writing during certain centuries, have finished putting words down on paper in a certain order, then the *facts* relevant to the truth-value of (4) are completely settled, and the truth-value of (4) is determined. Suppose a philosopher is guided by this thought and suppose he is willing to admit novels and classes into his ontology but not willing to admit creatures of fiction. Then he might simply invent an open sentence, e.g., "*x* dwelphs *y*," which is satisfied only by pairs of classes of novels, and

45

which (however its semantics is to be spelled out in general) is satisfied by the pair ⟨the class of nineteenth-century novels, the class of eighteenth-century novels⟩ if and only if what is expressed by (4) is *true*. Couldn't this philosopher then offer "The class of nineteenth-century novels dwelphs the class of eighteeth-century novels" as a paraphrase of (4) that does not involve quantification over creatures of fiction? *Answer*: In a certain trivial sense, this device works. The "dwelphs"-sentence, on the usage of "dwelph" your philosopher has stipulated, expresses the same proposition as (4) – or, at least, expresses a proposition necessarily equivalent to that proposition. But this is not *all* that is required of a good paraphrase. To see this, consider

(8) Every female character in any eighteenth-century novel is such that there is some character in some nineteenth-century novel who is presented with a greater wealth of physical detail than she is.

Now the proposition expressed by this sentence is certainly a logical consequence of the proposition expressed by (4). *I*, who accept the existence of things I call "characters in novels," can account for this fact: (8) is a translation into ordinary English of a sentence in the regimented quantifier-variable idiom that is a *formal* consequence of (4)★, which is a translation of (4) into a quantifier-variable idiom. But if someone were to paraphrase (8) into a sentence consisting of two class-terms flanking a relation-sign (this is what you just now imagined a philosopher doing with (4); let's imagine the paraphrase of (8) looks like this: "The class of eighteenth-century novels praphs the class of nineteenth-century novels"), he would have no way to *account for* the fact that his paraphrase of (8) expresses a proposition that is a logical consequence of the proposition expressed on his usage by "The class of nineteenth-century novels dwelphs the class of eighteenth-century novels."

Because of this consideration, I lay down the following condition of adequacy on any attempt to paraphrase away quantification (or apparent quantification) over "creatures of fiction": an adequate paraphrase must not be such as to leave us without an account of the logical consequences of (the propositions expressed by) the paraphrased sentences. Almost certainly, any paraphrase that satisfies this condition will have a quantificational structure not much simpler than the (apparent) quantificational structure of its "original."

I am not saying it would be *impossible* to devise paraphrases of (4), (5), (6), and similar sentences, that satisfy this condition. Probably the most promising candidates for such paraphrases would involve quantifications mainly over "character-names" (e.g., "Sophia Western," "Rodya Raskolnikov"), the sentences of fiction in which these "names" occur, and the open sentences that can be got by replacing them in these sentences by variables. I do not myself see any way of doing this, but perhaps someone cleverer than I will think of some way to do it.

But (if I may ask *you* a question) why should anyone bother to try to construct such paraphrases? It would probably be very difficult to do this, and the paraphrases would probably be long and messy if they could be got at all; and maybe they *couldn't* be got, in which case one would have been wasting one's no doubt valuable time in trying to get them. So why embark on such an enterprise?

Compare this question with a similar question in the ontology of mathematics: Why should anyone bother to try to construct paraphrases of such sentences as "There is a prime number between 18 and 20" and "There exists a least number that can be expressed in more than one way as the sum of two cubes" that do not involve quantification over numbers? One reason someone might have (there could be others, such as a desire to indulge one's "taste for desert landscapes") is that he finds the idea of there being such things as numbers a very puzzling one. How *could* there be things (he might ask) that *exist* in the same sense as that in which you and I exist, which *have properties* in the same sense as that in which "moderate-sized specimens of dry goods" have properties, and *bear relations* to one another in the same sense as that in which stones and bits of stick bear relations to one another, and which are, nevertheless, intangible and eternal?

And perhaps there are philosophers who find the very idea of creatures of fiction objectionable. We shall investigate just what it is that might be objectionable about them in Section IV. (That is, we shall investigate the question, What is it that is objectionable about creatures of fiction *per se*? We shall not attempt to answer objections that stem from a conviction that theoretical or abstract entities *in general* are objectionable.)

IV

Just what is puzzling or objectionable about Mrs. Gamp? Well, consider the following properties:

47

> being old
> being fat
> being fond of gin
> being named "Sarah Gamp"
> having a friend called "Mrs. Prig."

No one (in 1843) had *all* these properties. (If by chance someone did, we could enlarge the list.) But, someone may argue, Mrs. Gamp has, or had, or is supposed to have had all these properties. Thus, Mrs. Gamp is a very puzzling entity indeed, and, since this point could be generalized so as to apply to all "creatures of fiction," any ontology that includes them is objectionable.

This is a very powerful argument. The Meinongian and I are equally obliged to respond to it. *He* will deny the premise that no one has (or had in 1843) these properties. To the objection that it is simply an empirical fact that no one in 1843 had these properties, he will reply that this is not an empirical fact. What is an empirical fact, he will say, is that no one *existent* in 1843 had these properties. This reply is not available to me, however, who regard "no one existent" as a long-winded way of saying "no one." *I* shall deny the premise that Mrs. Gamp has or had these properties. This thesis will probably strike the reader as odd. But I think it is not so odd as it sounds, and, in fact, something formally very much like it is a familiar philosophical doctrine.

Let us turn for a moment to the Cartesian psychology, that is, to the doctrine that each of us in an immaterial substance. Suppose someone were to say to Descartes, "Your theory is obviously wrong since Jones here has all the following properties:

> being tangible
> being six foot tall
> weighing 190 pounds
> being mainly pinkish-white in color,

and these properties could not be had by an immaterial substance." Descartes, of course, will reply that Jones does *not* have the properties on this list. What he *has*, Descartes tells us, are properties like these:

> thinking about Vienna
> being free from pain
> being in a state of Grace
> animating a body.

Nonetheless, Descartes will concede, Jones bears a certain intimate relation to the properties on the former list that is not the relation of "having" or "exemplifying" but, rather, the relation of "animating a body that has or exemplifies." Descartes will further concede that in ordinary speech we often say "is"; when *strictly speaking* we should say "animates a body that is": what looks like predication in ordinary speech is not always predication.

I want to say something similar with respect to Mrs. Gamp. Here are some of the properties she *has*:

> being a character in a novel
> being a theoretical entity of literary criticism
> having been created by Dickens
> being a satiric villainess.

Moreover, if Dickens and Professor Manning are right, she has the following properties:

> being a fair representation of the hired attendant on the poor in sickness in 1843
> being the most fully developed of the masculine anti-women visible in all Dickens's novels.

Moreover, *if* existence is a property (an hypothesis the correctness of which I take no stand on in this paper), she has that, too. Thus, the properties Mrs. Gamp *has* are just those "literary" properties that are appropriate to what she is: a theoretical entity of criticism. If she shares any properties with you and me, they are "high-category" properties like existence, self-identity, and non-identity with any ordinal number.

Now just as Jones, according to Descartes, does not *have* the property of being tangible, so Mrs. Gamp, according to me, does not *have* the property of being fat. Nevertheless, just as Jones, on the Cartesian view, bears a certain intimate relation to tangibility, Mrs. Gamp bears a certain intimate relation to fatness. And just as, on the Cartesian view, we may *say* "Jones is six foot tall" and be talking *about* an immaterial substance without thereby *predicating* being six foot tall of that immaterial substance, so, on the present view, we may *say* "Mrs. Gamp is fond of gin" and be talking *about* a theoretical entity of criticism without thereby *predicating* fondness for gin of that theoretical entity of criticism.

Such circumlocutions as were employed in the preceding paragraph are cumbersome. Clearly it would be to our advantage to introduce some name or other for this special relation that Mrs. Gamp bears to fatness and fondness for gin. For want of a better name, I shall call it "ascription." Thus, we might write, "Fatness is ascribed to Mrs. Gamp" if we wished to express the proposition expressed in ordinary usage by

"Mrs. Gamp is fat" without using what looks like the "is" of predication. But I think we had better make ascription a three-term relation. For consider the fact that the sentences "Shiela Smith was fat" and "Shiela Smith was not fat" might appear in one and the same novel, owing either to the author's inadvertence or to the passage of narrative time. Suppose there was such a novel. Should we, describing its content in a review, write "Shiela Smith was fat"? This would be misleading. If the two sentences appeared in the novel owing to the author's inadvertence, clearly we ought to write something like "Shiela Smith is described as fat in Chapter Four. But in Chapter Six we are told she is not fat." In order to provide for cases like this, let us use the following open sentence in asserting that the ascription relation holds: "$x$ is ascribed to $y$ in $z$" (Hereinafter abbreviated "$A(x,y,z)$"). For any $x$, $y$, and $z$, if $A(x,y,z)$, then $x$ is a property, $y$ is a creature of fiction, and $z$ is what I shall call a "place." A *place* is either a work of fiction (such as a novel, short story, or narrative poem) or a part or section thereof, even a part or section that is so short as to be conterminous with a single (occurrence of a) sentence or clause. The proposition commonly expressed by "Mrs. Gamp is fat" we may express by "$A$(fatness, Mrs. Gamp, *Martin Chuzzlewit*)" or "$A$(fatness, Mrs. Gamp, Ch. 19 of *Martin Chuzzlewit*)" or "$A$(fatness, Mrs. Gamp, the only occurrence of (1) in *Martin Chuzzlewit*)." Or, if these assertions be thought to be too definite to capture the normal sense of "Mrs. Gamp is fat," we could write

$(\exists x)A$(fatness, Mrs. Gamp, $x$),

or even the conjunction of this last sentence with

$(\sim \exists x)A$(non-fatness, Mrs. Gamp, $x$).

Now the word "ascription" is not a good word for this relation. It is misleading. But I cannot think of a word that would not be misleading. In order to see how this term could mislead, consider the following cases. Suppose Dr. Leavis should write an essay called "Current Nonsense about Dickens," and suppose this essay contained the sentence (used in a straightforward way as the vehicle of an assertion), "Mrs. Gamp is thin." Given the ordinary meaning of "ascription," someone might be led to describe this state of affairs by writing

(9) $A$(thinness, Mrs. Gamp, "Current Nonsense about Dickens").

But this would be a mistake. "Current Nonsense about Dickens" is not a fictional work but a critical essay, and hence is not a "place" and hence sentence (9) does not express a truth.

Or consider the following sentence

(10) A(vanity, Napoleon, *War and Peace*).

Although in the ordinary sense of "ascribe" it is true that Tolstoy ascribed vanity to Napoleon in *War and Peace*, nonetheless (10) is not true since Napoleon is not a creature of fiction.[6]

Finally, it is important to realize that it does not follow from the truth of A(fatness, Mrs. Gamp, *Martin Chuzzlewit*)" that Dickens made a certain sort of silly mistake: viz., that in writing sentence (1), he (mistakenly) ascribed to a certain theoretical entity of criticism the property of being fat. For it is not the case that when Dickens wrote (1) he was ascribing any property to anything, either in our technical sense of "ascribe" or in the ordinary sense; to ascribe a property to something (in either sense of "ascribe"), Dickens would have had to have been expressing some proposition when he wrote (1), and, as I have said, he did not express any proposition by writing (1).

I shall not attempt to give a definition of "A$(x,y,z)$." This three-place predicate must be taken as primitive. But I think its sense is fairly easily grasped. We are saying something *true* about the relations that hold between the novel *Martin Chuzzlewit*, the main satiric villainess of that novel, and the property fatness when we say, "Mrs. Gamp, a character in *Martin Chuzzlewit*, is fat." And I think that we are *not* saying that the relation of *exemplification* holds between Mrs. Gamp and fatness when we say this, since that would *not* be true: if anything *exemplifies* fatness, then it occupies a certain region of spacetime and you and I (if we are appropriately located in spacetime) can touch it; but Mrs. Gamp is a theoretical entity of criticism, and we could no more touch her than we could touch a plot or a sonnet. "A(fatness, Mrs. Gamp, *Martin Chuzzlewit*)" is nothing more than the way I choose to express what we normally express by the above sentence, and that is all the explanation I am able to give of the use of "A$(x,y,z)$." In order to see the difficulties one encoun-

---

[6] That is, *normally* "Napoleon" is used to denote a certain *man*. It *may* be that when critics discuss *War and Peace*, they at least sometimes use "Napoleon" to designate a certain creature of fiction that is (of course) numerically distinct from the man Napoleon. (See fn. 8.) If this is the case, then the triple ⟨vanity, the creature of fiction sometimes called "Napoleon" by critics discussing *War and Peace*, *War and Peace*⟩ satisfies "A$(x,y,z)$." But ⟨vanity, the man Napoleon, *War and Peace*⟩ does not satisfy "A$(x,y,z)$."

ters in attempting to provide an explicit definition of "A($x,y,z$)" let us look at two rather obvious proposals.

First, one might say that "A(fatness, Mrs. Gamp, *Martin Chuzzlewit*)" simply means that if there were a real woman like Mrs. Gamp, that woman would be fat. But this would be either wrong or circular. A "real" woman (I suppose that means, strictly, a woman) could not be "like" Mrs. Gamp, if that means having the properties Mrs. Gamp *has*, since no "real" woman could be a character in a novel, be a theoretical entity of criticism, or have been created by Dickens. Of course, a "real" woman would be "like" Mrs. Gamp in *having* the properties that are *ascribed* to Mrs. Gamp in *Martin Chuzzlewit*. But, obviously, "like" in this sense cannot occur in a *definition* of the ascription relation.

Or one might want to say that "A(fatness, Mrs. Gamp, *Martin Chuzzlewit*)" means that if *Martin Chuzzlewit* were not a novel but a true record of events, then there *would* be a woman *called* "Mrs. Gamp" and she would be fat. But there is a subtle difficulty hidden in this proposal. Consider "A(fatness, the main satiric villainess of *Martin Chuzzlewit*, *Martin Chuzzlewit*)" or "A(fatness, the most important character in *Martin Chuzzlewit* introduced in Ch. 19, *Martin Chuzzlewit*." If we were to try to understand these sentences (which express truths) in the way proposed, we should come up with "If *Martin Chuzzlewit* were not a novel but a true record of events, then there would be a woman denoted by 'the main satiric villainess of *Martin Chuzzlewit*' and she would be fat" in the case of the first of these sentences, and a similar piece of non-sense in the case of the second.

Let us see why this difficulty arises. How is it we are able to use the *proper name* "Mrs. Gamp" to refer to a certain creature of fiction? Normally, an object gets a proper name by being dubbed or baptized. But no one ever dubbed or baptized the main satiric villainess of *Martin Chuzzlewit* "Mrs. Gamp."[7] There is no corresponding problem about how it is this creature of fiction is denoted by "the main satiric villainess of

---

[7] Of course, Dickens might have said to himself, "I'll call the character I'm about to introduce, 'Sarah Gamp.'" He might even have said this out loud, to an audience. And he might *not* have done (and probably *did* not do) these things. Whether he did or not, Mrs. Gamp would be called "Mrs. Gamp." Therefore, such an utterance on Dickens's part (if it occurred) was not an act of dubbing, and had nothing in particular to do with the fact that it is proper for us to call the important female character introduced in Ch. 19 of *Martin Chuzzlewit*, "Mrs. Gamp." Moreover, it is obvious that our ability to refer to this character as "Mrs. Gamp" does not derive from some early Dickens critic's having said, "I hereby dub the main satiric villainess of *Martin Chuzzlewit*, 'Sarah Gamp.'"

*Martin Chuzzlewit,*" for this is a quite straightforward definite description that names what we also call "Mrs. Gamp" for the same reason that "the tallest structure in Paris in 1905" names what we also call "the Eiffel Tower": in each of these cases, a definite description denotes a certain object in virtue of a certain property that that object has uniquely. I think that if we are to have a satisfactory theory of how it is that we manage to refer to particular creatures of fiction, this theory will have to treat such *descriptions* as "the main satiric villainess" as the *primary* means of reference to these objects, and *proper names* as a secondary (though more common) means of reference. I would suggest that the *only* reason "Mrs. Gamp" denotes a certain creature of fiction is that that creature of fiction satisfies the open sentence "A (being named 'Mrs. Gamp,' *x Martin Chuzzlewit*)."[8] Thus, any such explanation of "A(*x,y,z*)" as the one we are considering must be circular, for the fact that a certain creature of fiction (such as the main satiric villainess of *Martin Chuzzlewit*) is denoted by a "fictional proper name" (like "Mrs. Gamp") can be explained only in terms of the ascription relation. Moreover, even if such an explanation were not circular, it would not show us how to understand instances of "A(*x,y,z*)" in which the "*y*"-position is filled by a definite description involving a uniquely exemplified "literary" property, such as "the character introduced in Ch. 19."

It is because of these difficulties that I am content to take "A(*x,y,z*)" as primitive. (But one small stipulation: let us say that a property *entails* a second property if it is not possible that something have the former and not have the latter; then ascription is "closed" under entailment. That is, ($\forall x$) ($\forall y$) ($\forall z$) ($\forall w$)[A(*x,y,z*) & *x* entails *w*. ⊃ A(*w,y,z*)].)

This, in essence, is the theory of creatures of fiction I want to present. To recapitulate:

(a)  Sentences like (2), (3), (4), (5), and (6) are about characters in novels. Characters in novels belong to a class of entities I call "creatures of fiction," which class is a sub-class of the class of theoretical entities of criticism.

---

[8]  That is, we have embodied in our rules for talking about fiction a convention that says that a creature of fiction *may* be referred to by what is (loosely speaking) "the name it has in the story." It is owing to a similar convention that we use *personal* pronouns in connection with entities that are literally *not* persons: we call Mrs. Gamp "she" because, though she is not a woman, the property of being a woman is ascribed to her. (Cf. the Cartesian's explanation of how it is we are able to use demonstrative pronouns and adjectives in referring to substances that are *literally* non-spatial.) Once we have grasped the ascription relation, it is easy enough to explain and analyze our use of "mixed" descriptions like "the fat old nurse introduced in Ch. 19." (Cf. the Cartesian's explanation of our use of "the fattest person thinking of Vienna.")

(b) Sentences like (1), that is, typical narrative or descriptive sentences taken from works of fiction, are not about creatures of fiction. They are not about anything. They are not used by their authors as the vehicles of assertions.

(c) Creatures of fiction exist and obey the laws of logic, just as everything else does.

(d) Creatures of fiction *have* or *exemplify* only "literary" properties such as *being introduced in Ch. 19* and "high-category" properties like self-identity. They do not have such properties as being human or being fat, despite the fact that ordinary-language sentences like "Mrs. Gamp is fat" can be used to express true propositions about them. (We call the relation that, I claim, is asserted by sentences like this to hold between creatures of fiction and such everyday properties as you or I might have, "ascription.")

I shall conclude by showing how three problems about fictional entities can be easily solved on the present theory.

v

The first problem: How should we deal with questions like "Has Mrs. Gamp an even number of hairs on her head?"? The Meinongian, remember, says that Mrs. Gamp neither has nor lacks the property of having an even number of hairs on her head. The typical anti-Meinongian says (roughly) that "she" is not "there" either to have or to lack such a property. I say she simply lacks it, just as she lacks the properties of being material, being human, having hair, and being bald. Moreover, for any property whatever, Mrs. Gamp either has that property or lacks it.

But what is *not* true is this:

$$(\forall x)\,(\exists y)[A(x, \text{Mrs. Gamp}, y) \veebar A(\text{not having } x, \text{Mrs. Gamp}, y)].$$

(Here "$\veebar$" represents exclusive disjunction.) And, in particular, *this* is not true.

> A(having an even number of hairs on one's head, Mrs. Gamp, *Martin Chuzzlewit*) $\veebar$ A(not having an even number of hairs on one's head, Mrs. Gamp, *Martin Chuzzlewit*).[9]

This disjunction is false simply because Dickens was noncommittal about the oddness or evenness of the number of Mrs. Gamp's hairs. It is these facts, I think, that the Meinongian perceives through a glass darkly when he says that a creature of fiction is an incomplete object.

---

[9] But the proposition that A(having or not having an even number of hairs on one's head, Mrs. Gamp, *Martin Chuzzlewit*) is true, owing to the fact that ascription is closed under entailment.

The second problem: Mrs. Gamp appears to have incompatible properties. For consider the properties

being a woman
having been created by Dickens.

Now, since Dickens was not God, it would seem that nothing could have both these properties. To this the Meinongian will reply that I am mistaken in thinking that only God can create things that fall within the extension of the property *being a woman*; what only God can do, the Meinongian will tell us, is to create things that fall within this extension and which are also *existent*. Dickens is perfectly capable of creating women (the Meinongian holds); he is, however, incapable of creating *existent* women. (Or perhaps, the Meinongian will want to say that Dickens did not *create* Mrs. Gamp, but did something more like *discovering* her in the realm of *Sosein*. I shall not explore the ramifications of this thesis, except to point out that it makes the creativity of the novelist seem very like the "creativity" of the flower-arranger.) This reply seems to me to be unsatisfactory. What reason do we have for saying that Mrs. Gamp has the property *being a woman*? Only that she "has it in the story." Well, "in the story" she also has the property of existence, at least if existence *is* a property (but this the Meinongian assumes).[10] Therefore, I submit, if the Meinongian has any good reason for saying that the extension of *being a woman* includes Mrs. Gamp, he has an equally good reason for saying that the extension of *being existent* includes her.

This problem is, of course, trivial on the theory I am proposing: Mrs. Gamp *has* only the second of these properties; the first is not *exemplified* by her, but is, rather, ascribed to her.

The third problem: Consider the definite descriptions, "the main satiric villainess of *Martin Chuzzlewit*" and "the character in *Martin Chuzzlewit* who appears in every chapter." Since no character in *Martin Chuzzlewit* appears in every chapter, there seems to be an important difference between these two descriptions. I can describe this difference very simply. The first of these descriptions denotes something (Mrs. Gamp), and the second does not: there *is* no character in *Martin Chuzzlewit* who appears in every chapter; no such character *exists*. The Meinongian will want to say that each of these descriptions denotes

[10] Note that "in the story" Mrs. Gamp's imaginary friend Mrs. Harris, unlike Mrs. Gamp herself, does *not* exist.

55

something, and that what each denotes fails to exist. But there is obviously an important ontological difference between the ways in which these two descriptions relate to the world. I leave it to the Meinongian to explain how this difference is to be spelled out in his terms.[11]

---

[11] A little reflection on this problem should show that what I call creatures of fiction cannot be or be among the "merely possible individuals" the existence of which is assumed in most informal explanations of Kripke's and others' systems of formal semantics for quantified modal logic. Creatures of fiction could not serve as merely possible objects because, for one thing, they are *actual* objects. But then what of the sentence with which we began, "Mr. Pickwick does not exist," and our concession that it could be used to express a truth? This is a very complicated question. Part of the answer is this. The utterer of such a sentence would probably be addressing himself to someone who had mistaken discourse about Pickwick for discourse about a *man*, owing to the fact that the ascription relation is expressed in English by what sounds like the apparatus of predication. He would probably be expressing the proposition that there is no such *man* as Pickwick, or, more precisely, the proposition that nothing *has* all the properties *ascribed to* Pickwick.

# 4

## *Why is there anything at all?*

The question that is my title is supposed to be the most profound and difficult of all questions. Some, indeed, have said that it is a dangerous question, a question that can tear the mind asunder. But I think we can make some progress with it if we do not panic.

Let us begin by asking what would count as an answer to it. One sort of answer, the best if we could get it, would consist in a demonstration that it was impossible for there to be nothing.[1] Or so I would suppose: if showing that it is impossible for a certain state of affairs to obtain doesn't count as answering the question why that state of affairs does not obtain, I don't know what would count.

How would one go about proving that it was impossible for there to be nothing? One way would be to prove the existence of a necessary being. By a "being" I mean a concrete object – whatever *that* may mean – and, therefore, by a necessary being I mean a necessarily existent concrete object. I will assume that at least some abstract objects – numbers, pure sets, "purely qualitative" properties and relations, possibilities, possible worlds themselves – exist in all possible worlds. I do not think that the question that people have actually intended to ask when they ask

First published in *Proceedings of the Aristotelian Society* (1996), pp. 95–110.
[1] Most of the arguments of this essay will be modal arguments of one sort or another. In presenting these arguments, I am going to assume that David Lewis's metaphysics of modality – "Genuine Modal Realism" – is wrong, and that the "abstractionist" modal metaphysic of Kripke and Plantinga and Stalnaker is right. Problems about the validity and cogency of modal reasoning are normally not particularly sensitive to how one answers the question whether possible worlds are what Lewis says they are or what his opponents say they are. The arguments we shall be considering, however, are exceptions to this generalization. The question "Why should there be anything at all?" looks very different when viewed from the perspective provided by Lewis and from the perspective provided by Kripke *et al.* I am sorry to have to begin this essay by simply assuming without argument that Lewis is wrong about the metaphysics of modality, but I can't address every question in one essay. I discuss Lewis's "Genuine Modal Realism" in "Two Concepts of Possible Worlds," *Midwest Studies in Philosophy* 11 (1986), pp. 185–213 (Chapter 12 of the present volume).

why anything at all should exist could be answered by pointing out – I will take this statement to be true for the sake of the illustration; *I* certainly think it's true – that the number 510 would exist no matter what. If the notion of an abstract object makes sense at all, it seems evident that if *everything* were an abstract object, if the *only* objects were abstract objects, there is an obvious and perfectly good sense in which there would be nothing at all, for there would be no physical things, no stuffs, no events, no space, no time, no Cartesian egos, no God . . .[2] When people want to know why there is anything at all, they want to know why *that* bleak state of affairs does not obtain.

It is by no means a trivial assertion that a demonstration of the impossibility of there being nothing must take the form of a demonstration that there is a necessary being. If one could do it, it would certainly suffice to show that it was a necessary truth that there were some beings, and that proposition does not formally entail the proposition that there is a necessary being. (It might be that there is at least one being in every possible world, even if there is no being that exists in every possible world.) I can say only that it seems to me hopeless to try to devise any argument for the conclusion that it is a necessary truth that there are beings that is not also an argument for the conclusion that there is a necessary being. I simply have no idea of how one might even attempt that. It is at any rate true that showing that there is a necessary being would do the trick: if there is a necessary being then it is impossible for there to be nothing.

But can it be done? Is it possible to show that there is a necessary being? The friends of the ontological argument (if there are any) will no doubt remind us that showing that there is a necessary being is just what their argument claims to be particularly good at. Let us see whether the ontological argument can help us with our question. Of all the versions

---

[2] Suppose there were *pure stuffs*: stuffs whose presence in a region of space did not require any being to be wholly or partly present in that region. (Butter would be a pure stuff if butter existed but, (i) nothing was made of butter, and (ii) some regions of space were filled with butter without there being any quarks, electrons, atoms, or other concrete things in those regions.) Then it would be possible for there to be no beings – and yet not *nothing*. Or suppose that there were *pure events*: events whose occurrence did not consist in a change in the intrinsic properties of any being or a change in the external relations that held among two or more beings. Then, again, it would be possible for there to be no beings – and yet not *nothing*. In my view, however, pure stuffs and events are metaphysically impossible. If I were to be convinced otherwise, certain aspects of the language of this essay would have to be revised, but not, I think, in any way that affected any of its central theses.

of the ontological argument, the version I have called the Minimal Modal Ontological Argument is the one that can be most profitably studied by the philosopher who wants an argument whose conclusion is the existence of a necessary being. (The argument is indisputably logically valid; it has just the desired conclusion; every other version of the ontological argument that is indisputably logically valid will have a premise or premises that it would be harder to defend than the premise of the Minimal Modal Argument.) The argument is easy to state:

> Consider the two properties, necessity (that is, necessary existence or existence in all possible worlds) and entity or concrescence (the property of being a being or concrete object). These two properties are compatible – it is not absolutely or metaphysically or intrinsically impossible for something to have both of them. Therefore, there *is* something that has both of them; that is, there is a necessary being.[3]

But why should we accept the premise of the argument – that necessity and entity are compatible? I know of only one argument for the compatibility of these two properties that is even superficially plausible. This argument is a version of the cosmological argument. It has three premises:

> Every fact has an explanation
> If a property *F* has, as a matter of contingent fact, a non-empty extension, then any explanation of this fact must somehow involve beings (concrete things) that do *not* have *F*
> Contingency (the property of being a contingent being) has, as a matter of contingent fact, a non-empty extension.

It obviously follows from these three premises that if there are, as a matter of contingent fact, contingent beings, there are also non-contingent beings – that is, necessary beings. But we know by observation that there are beings, and every being is either contingent or necessary. If, therefore, this version of the cosmological argument is sound, the observed fact that there are beings entails that there is at least one necessary being, and hence entails that it is impossible for there to be nothing. (This conclusion depends on our assumption that if there are contingent beings this state of affairs obtains only as a matter of contingent fact. But if there were contingent beings of necessity, it would also follow that it was impossible for there to be nothing.)

We can, in fact, reach this conclusion without any appeal to observa-

---

[3] For a discussion of the Minimal Modal Ontological Argument, a discussion that includes a demonstration of its validity, see my "Ontological Arguments," *Noûs* 11 (1977) pp. 375–395. This essay is reprinted in Peter van Inwagen, *God, Knowledge, and Mystery: Essays in Philosophical Theology* (Ithaca, NY: Cornell University Press, 1995).

tion. We can show that it is impossible for there to be nothing without using any observed fact as a premise, even the fact that there are some beings. If the first two premises of our argument are true at all, then, surely, they are necessarily true, and the argument is therefore sound in any world in which it is a contingent truth that there are contingent beings. Therefore, if our first two premises are true, and if the existence of beings, any beings at all, beings of any sort, is a possible state of affairs, then it is possible for there to be a necessary being – that is to say, necessity and entity are compatible properties. And, as we have learned from our examination of the Minimal Modal Ontological Argument, if necessity and entity are compatible properties, there is a necessary being. Therefore, if the first two premises of our version of the cosmological argument are true, it is a necessary truth that there are beings if there could be beings. In other words, given that the first two premises of our version of the cosmological argument are true, it is *possible* for there *not* to be anything only if it is *impossible* for there to *be* anything. And one could hardly be expected to do better with the question "Why is there anything at all?" than to establish this conclusion. Unfortunately, however, we have *not* established this conclusion. We have failed to establish it because the first premise of our cosmological argument – a variant on the Principle of Sufficient Reason: that every fact has an explanation – is wholly unbelievable. It is unbelievable because it has an absurd consequence: that all truths are necessary truths. Or so, at least, it seems to me, and so I have argued elsewhere. The general form of my argument was this: Suppose "Alpha" is a proper name of the actual world; if every fact has an explanation, the fact that Alpha is actual has an explanation; but if this fact has an explanation, then every truth is a necessary truth.[4]

In my judgment, there is no known argument that can plausibly be said to show that there is a necessary being, and there is therefore no known argument that can plausibly be said to show that it is impossible for there to be nothing.

I propose, therefore, to try another sort of approach to the question, "Why is there anything at all?" In the sequel, I will not try to show that it is impossible for there to be nothing. Rather I will argue that if there being nothing is not impossible, it is at any rate *improbable* – as improbable as anything can be. If something is as improbable as anything can be,

---

[4] For a demonstration, see my *Metaphysics* (London: Oxford University Press, 1993), pp. 104–107.

its probability is, of course, 0: I am going to argue that the probability of there being nothing is 0.[5]

I confess I am unhappy about the argument I am going to present. Like Descartes's ontological argument, with which it shares the virtue of simplicity, it seems a bit *too* simple. No doubt there is something wrong with it – it may share that defect with Descartes's argument – but I should like to be told what it is.[6]

The argument has four premises:

(1) There are some beings
(2) If there is more than one possible world, there are infinitely many
(3) There is at most one possible world in which there are no beings
(4) For any two possible worlds, the probability of their being actual is equal.

Now let *Spinozism* be the thesis that there is just one possible world. We proceed by cases.

If Spinozism is true, then, by premise (1), it is a necessary truth that there are some beings, and the probability of there being no beings is 0.

If Spinozism is false, then, by premise (2), logical space comprises infinitely many possible worlds. If logical space comprises infinitely many possible worlds, and if any two worlds are equiprobable – premise (4) – then the probability of every world is 0. If a proposition is true in at most one world, and if the probability of every world is 0, then the probability of that proposition is 0. But then, by premise (3), the probability of there being no beings is 0.

Hence, the probability of there being no beings is 0.

[5] The probability of any impossible event is 0, but not all events whose probability is 0 are impossible. (For example – at least if we allow ourselves a little harmless idealization – the probability of a dart's hitting any particular point on a dart board is 0.) Or, at any rate, this is true if probabilities are real numbers, which is what I shall assume in this essay. I am not going to defend my assumption that probabilities are real numbers. The primary reason is that if I were to reject this assumption and to assume that there were infinitesimal probabilities (probabilities greater than 0 but less than any real number greater than 0) the effect of this assumption on the argument would be mainly verbal: I'd have to word some of the things I say a bit differently.

[6] Robin Collins has called my attention to the fact that a brief statement of the essence of the argument occurs in Robert Nozick's *Philosophical Explanations* (Cambridge, Mass., 1981), pp. 127–128. I had read Nozick's book when it first appeared – in fact, I had taught a graduate seminar on it – but, as far as I can tell, I had entirely forgotten this feature of it. I do not recall having seen the argument elsewhere in the philosophical literature, but it is so simple that it can hardly be unobvious. (Jim Holt, a science writer, has a version of the argument in his article "Nothing Ventured" in the November 1994 *Harper's*; he seems to have got the argument from Nozick. Robin Collins has shown me a paper he wrote as a first-year graduate student that contains a version of the argument that is certainly independent of Nozick.)

It is important not to confuse the conclusion of this argument with various superficially similar propositions. The conclusion of the argument is consistent with the following proposition: the probability that God (or whatever factor produces physical universes) will produce a physical universe is much greater than 0 – say, 0.8. The conclusion of the argument is not about the probability of there being no physical beings, but about the probability of there being no beings of any sort. If "whatever factor produces physical universes" existed but had not produced a physical universe, it would still be true that there was at least one being. (If God had not produced a physical universe, and if God was a necessary being, then the probability of there being beings would be 1 – as high as a probability gets.) At any rate, I do not see how a "factor" that might (but in fact does not) produce a physical universe could exist if there were no beings. Such a factor – at least this seems evident to me – would have to be "embodied" in the properties of one or more beings or in the relations that held among two or more beings. (John Leslie, I suppose, would disagree. I should be interested to know whether anyone else would.)

Let us examine the premises of the argument.

The truth of premise (1) seems a safe enough assumption.

In defense of premise (2), it may be pointed out that if there is more than one possible world, then things can vary; and it seems bizarre to suppose, given the kinds of properties had by the things we observe, properties that *seem* to imply a myriad of dimensions along which these things could vary continuously, that there might be just 2 or just 17 or just 510 worlds.

Premise (3) can be defended as follows: there is nothing in virtue of which two worlds that contained only abstract objects could be different. If two worlds are distinct, there must be some proposition that is true in one and false in the other. If, therefore, there are *two* worlds in which there are no beings, there must be some proposition such that both that proposition and its denial are consistent with there being no concrete beings. (It would, of course, have to be a contingent proposition, since a necessary proposition and its denial can't both be consistent with anything.) But it's very hard to see how there could be a proposition that met this condition – much less to come up with a (possible) example of one.

Premise (4) is the one that people are going to want to dispute. Why should the probability of any given world's being actual be equal to the probability of any other given world's being actual?

Well, this seems very plausible to me. I have an a posteriori argument for the conclusion that I find this premise plausible independently of its consequences for answering the question, Why should there be anything at all? In a recent essay, I have outlined a way of looking at objective probabilities.[7] That is, in this essay I was concerned to outline a view of probability according to which every proposition has, as one of its essential features, a probability – according to which each proposition has a probability in much the same sense as that in which each proposition has a modal status – or each set a cardinality. (Well, that's an exaggeration. Those who know something about the philosophy of probability will know that when I say this I must be either confused or exaggerating. I hope only the second disjunct holds. It can't be true that *every* proposition has a probability, for reasons connected with the fact that it can't be true that every set of points on the line has a measure. What I was aiming at was a way of looking at probability such that a very large class of propositions had "intrinsic" probabilities, a class I hoped would include all those propositions we could single out or name.) My purposes were unconnected with ontological questions. I was concerned to try to show that the concept of subjective probability made sense only on the assumption that objective probabilities of the kind I was trying to describe existed – and that project was in its turn connected with an attempt to clarify the so-called probabilistic argument from evil. In constructing this philosophical picture of objective probability, I unhesitatingly built into the picture I was drawing the following feature: on the assumption that there are infinitely many possible worlds, the probability of any world's being actual is 0. I did not in that paper attempt to defend that aspect of my picture because it seemed to me to be so obvious as to need no defense. I suppose that the argument I'm now considering must have occurred to me when I reflected on the fact that it follows from this feature of the picture (together with the assumption that there is at most one possible world in which there is nothing) that the probability of there being nothing is 0. But what had seemed trivial can come to seem less trivial after it has been seen to have important philosophical consequences. I must therefore raise the question: What argument can be given in support of the thesis that any two possible worlds are of equal

---

[7] "Reflections on the Chapters by Draper, Russell, and Gale" in Daniel Howard-Snyder (ed.), *The Evidential Argument from Evil* (Bloomington and Indianapolis: Indiana University Press, 1996), pp. 219–243.

probability? (My allegiance to this thesis rests on my interior manipulations of the mental picture of probabilities that I use. I find these manipulations hard to articulate and I find it hard to arrange the results of my attempts at articulation into an argument. The sequel is my best effort.)

Suppose we think of a fictitious object called Reality. Possible worlds are to be thought of as maximally specific (and hence mutually inconsistent) states of this Reality – logical space, or the set or class of all worlds, is the ensemble of all these maximally specific states that Reality could be in. If a Tractarian ontology were correct – if there were the same fundamental concrete objects in every possible world – and if the fundamental objects had the same mereological sum in every possible world, then Reality would not be a fictitious object: it would be the mereological sum of all the fundamental things, and a possible world would be any consistent and fully specific description of it. But I am not willing to grant any of these things, and I therefore call Reality a fictitious object. Still, I find it a useful fiction for reasons that will transpire.

When we think about an object or system of objects, it is hard to reason probabilistically about this object or system unless we are able to partition the possible states of the object or system into sets of states of equal probability – the partition being sufficiently fine-grained that each proposition to which we want to assign a probability be identifiable with a particular set of these states. For example, we can reason probabilistically about dice to very good effect on the assumption that if a die is thrown, the probabilities that any two of its faces will come up are equal – provided that every proposition about the dice we want to assign a probability to is such that its truth-value is determined by which dice fall with which faces up.

It would seem that we can sometimes find reasons for such assignments of equal probability. Suppose we think about dice, either dice in the abstract, or particular dice that have never been thrown (and thus have no "track record"). If we want to know whether the above assumption is true, whether it is indeed true that the probabilities are equal that any two faces of a die will come up, it is obviously relevant to raise the question whether the die is of homogeneous density. I give this example simply to illustrate the fact that we can sometimes identify factors that are relevant to the question whether two possible states of a system of objects are of equal probability.[8] No doubt my confidence that

[8] But see Ian Hacking, *The Emergence of Probability* (Cambridge, 1975), pp. 51–52. My answer: the intuitions operating in this case relate to (idealized) material objects – "mid-

the question whether a die is of homogeneous density is relevant to the question whether each of its faces is equally likely to come up when it is thrown is partly due to my knowledge of the existence of loaded dice and of how dice are loaded. But I think there is an a priori element in my confidence that this factor is relevant. We do seem to have some capacity for determining a priori that some states of some systems are of equal probability. Perhaps I am absurdly overconfident about the reliability of this capacity, but I am going to try to exercise it in application to a very abstract case indeed. I am going to propose a sufficient condition for the states belonging to certain partitions of the states of a system being of equal probability. The condition I propose will, I argue, have the consequence that all possible worlds are of equal probability.

Let us consider some system of objects. We suppose that associated with the system are certain abstracta called "states." For each of these states the system is, without qualification, either "in" that state or not "in" that state. States behave logically very much like propositions. (They may even *be* propositions, propositions, perhaps, about the intrinsic properties of the objects that make up the system and the relations they bear to one another.) States, that is, can be conjoined or disjoined, and they have negations or complements, and so on. The conjunction of two states will not necessarily be a state, however, for I will take "state" to mean the same as "possible state." We call a state $x$ of a system *maximal* if, for every state $y$, either, necessarily, if the system is in $x$ it is in $y$, or, necessarily, if the system is in $x$ it is in the complement of $y$. Or, what is the same thing, a state $x$ of a system is maximal if, for every state of the system $y$ such that $x$ is not the conjunction of $y$ and some other state(s), the conjunction of $x$ and $y$ is not a state.

Let us say that a system of objects is *isolated* if no facts about objects external to the system could in any way influence the system. More exactly, a system is isolated *with respect to a certain set of its states* if no facts about objects external to the system could in any way have any influence on which of those states the system was in. In the sequel, I will mostly ignore this bit of fine-tuning and will speak of a system's being isolated *simpliciter*.

---

sized specimens of dry goods." There *is* an unreliable intuition that tends to be at work when we think about partitions of the state-space of systems composed of small numbers of photons or small numbers of electrons, but it has nothing in particular to do with probability; it is that these systems can be thought about as if they were spatial ensembles of tiny material objects, objects that retain their identities under spatial translation.

I propose: for any system of objects (that has maximal states) the maximal states of the system should be regarded as equally probable, provided that the system is isolated.

Consider my computer. Suppose we accept some programmer's definition, some software definition, of the states of this system (as opposed, say, to a definition based on the states of the elementary particles that physically compose it). It is no doubt false that the maximal states of my computer are equally probable. No doubt a state that includes a novel written in Urdu stored on the hard disk is less probable than the actual state of the computer. But we make this judgment because we know that the computer is not an isolated system. I, who am external to the computer, am to a certain degree responsible for its states, and we know that I am unlikely put it into a state in which it contains a novel written in Urdu. But what should we expect of a computer that was an isolated system? How might we imagine something that at least approximated an "isolated" computer?

Well, suppose that a computer like mine came flying out of an "evaporating" black hole. (We have Stephen Hawking's word for it that an evaporating black hole might produce a grand piano.) We'd then expect a hard disk that contained novels written in English, French, Urdu, and Esperanto to be about equally probable.[9] (We'd expect the probabilities of each to be very close to 0, but not quite there, and very close to one another.) And, surely, we'd expect this because we think that in the space whose points are maximal software states, blobs of about equal volume represent hard disks containing novels in French and Urdu (simply because the number of the maximal states of the system is finite, and about the same number of states includes a disk that contains a novel in either language) – and, we think, the black hole is equally likely to produce any of the maximal states. (Of course, we haven't really imagined an "isolated" computer; but the black hole on which the computer depends for its existence cannot easily be supposed to "prefer" any of the possible software states of the system to any of the others. Thus we have captured an important and relevant feature that an isolated computer would have. It should be noted, however, that what the black hole is really indifferent about is what possible *physical* state the computer it produces will be in. We have done nothing to rule out this epistemic possibility: some of the maximal software states of the computer correspond

---

[9] I ignore Kripke-style questions about whether the novels would actually *be* in these languages.

to blobs of significantly different volume in the space of possible physical states of the system. That would be a case in which the computer was not even "for all practical purposes" isolated with respect to its software states; that would be a case in which we should be unable to ignore the fact that the software state of the computer is determined by its hardware state.)

The principle I have suggested seems, therefore, to have some plausibility: If a system is isolated, then any two of its maximal states are of equal probability. But then we have an argument for the conclusion that any two possible worlds are of equal probability: "Reality" is an isolated system, and possible worlds are maximal states of Reality.

There are, however, intuitions that oppose the thesis that the "empty world" is no more probable than any other world, and we must examine them. Consider, for example, the famous passage in *Principles of Nature and Grace* in which Leibniz argues that it is necessary to search for an explanation of there being something rather than nothing, since "nothing is simpler and more easy [*facile*] than something." If "nothing" is indeed simpler than "something," might not the simplicity of "nothing" at least suggest that "nothing" is *more probable* than "something" – or at least more probable than any *given* arrangement of "somethings"?

In what sense is "nothing" *simpler* than "something"? The only sense I can make of this idea is contained in these two statements: "There being nothing" is – provided it is indeed possible for there to be nothing – a complete specification of a way Reality could be (note that it settles the truth-value of every proposition); it is a very simple specification indeed, for any other complete specification of a way Reality could be would be of very great, perhaps of infinite, complexity.[10]

Does the fact that "nothing" is in this sense simpler than "something" give any support to the thesis that "nothing" is more probable than "something" – or to the thesis that nothing is more probable than any given arrangement of "somethings"? Suppose, *per impossibile*, that there are exactly two possible worlds, the empty world and ours. Consider the following two theses:

- The probability of the empty world's being actual is $\frac{2}{3}$; the probability of ours being actual is $\frac{1}{3}$ (So we're lucky in the way a man would be lucky if he

---

[10] Any other complete specification besides "Things being as they actually are", that is. But this specification contains no information; one cannot deduce from it the truth-value of any contingent proposition.

survived his turn at Russian Roulette in a match played with four rounds in the six chambers of the revolver.)

- The probability of the empty world's being actual is $\frac{1}{2}$; the probability of ours being actual is $\frac{1}{2}$. (So we're lucky in the way a man would be lucky if he survived his turn at Russian Roulette in a match played with three rounds in the six chambers of the revolver.)

Suppose that we somehow knew that one of these two probability-assignments was true. Would the fact that the empty world is vastly, even infinitely, easier to describe than our world give us any reason to prefer the first probability assignment to the second? I have a hard time seeing why anyone should think that it did. It seems to me that one can find this plausible only if one is covertly thinking that there is something that is outside the "Reality" of which possible worlds are maximal states, something by whose operations actuality is conferred on whatever world it is that enjoys that status. One might, for example, believe that the greater simplicity of the empty world made it more probable than ours if one believed that there was a "pre-cosmic selection machine," not a part of Reality, the operations of which select a maximal state for Reality to be in, and that something about the not-fully-deterministic workings of this machine made it more probable that it would select a state that could be simply described than one that required a very complicated description.

Leibniz believed something like this, although his selector was God, not a machine. But only something *like* this. Leibniz's "possible worlds" are not possible worlds in the current sense of the term. They are rather possible Creations. They are not therefore maximal states of Reality but only of the created part of it. And, of course, simplicity might well be a factor that would recommend a particular possible Creation to a potential Creator contemplating the question, "Which possible Creation shall I cause to be actual?"

Something very similar can be said about ease. Suppose, for example, that it is *easier* for God to bring about the actuality of the state of affairs *There being nothing besides God* than the state of affairs *There being something besides God* – perhaps He has to do nothing to produce the former and something rather difficult to produce the latter; something that would require, say, six days of work and a day of recuperation afterwards – and if God, like most of us, preferred not to expend effort without good reason, then it might be more probable that there not be any created beings than that there be any.

Whatever merit these speculations may have, they are of no use to someone who wants to know about the probability of there being nothing at all: they are relevant only to a question of conditional probability: What is the probability of there being nothing created, given that there is an uncreated being capable of creation?

Let me suggest an example that may militate against the intuition that the simplicity of the empty world entails that that world is more probable than any other world. Recall, if you are old enough, those political rallies in China in the 1960s when thousands of people would produce an enormous portrait of Chairman Mao by holding up big sheets of cardboard. At some signal, everyone on one side of an arena would hold up either a red or a white sheet, and instantly a portrait of the Great Helmsman would appear, in red against a white background. We can look upon the participants in and paraphernalia of this system of portraiture (on a particular occasion of its use) as constituting a system of objects, a system each maximal state of which corresponds to an assignment of either "red" or "white" to the position of each participant. Such a system, of course, is not isolated and cannot be regarded as isolated even as an idealization, for each participant is given, along with his red or white cardboard sheet, a seat number, and is instructed to take great care to sit in the seat with that number. (I suppose that's how it's done.) Now suppose that on one of these occasions, counter-revolutionary saboteurs had garbled the assigned seat numbers – totally randomized them, in fact. What should we expect those present to see when the signal was given and they looked at the area in which a portrait was supposed to appear? No doubt what they would observe would be a pink expanse of pretty close to uniform saturation. The following argument has no force at all: pure white (or pure red) is the *simplest* of the maximal states of the system, so it's more probable that we'd see pure white (red) than pink or a portrait of Mao or a diagram of the structure of a paramecium. It is, in fact, false that "pure white" is more probable than any other particular maximal state of the system: all are of exactly equal probability (now that the seating assignments have been randomized) and whichever one of them turns up will have had exactly the same chance of turning up as one of them that displays a portrait of Chiang Kai-shek. (Any *one* of them; of course a portrait of Chiang would be billions of times more likely to turn up than "pure white," since there are billions of maximal states that would count as portraits of Chiang.)

69

I conclude – tentatively – that the simplicity of the empty world provides us with no reason to regard it as more probable than any other possible world. One's feeling that the empty world must somehow be the most probable of all worlds – that it must have a greater-than-zero probability – seems to depend on one's smuggling into one's thinking the assumption that there is something that is somehow outside the "Reality" of which possible worlds are maximal states, something that would be more likely to put Reality into the state *There being nothing,* or, it may be, something that determines that *There being nothing* is the "default setting" on the control-board of Reality. But there could be no such thing, for nothing is outside Reality.

So I conclude. But have I really said anything that supports this conclusion? Whether I have depends on the answers to two questions:

- Is the principle "The maximal states of an isolated system are of equal probability" true in the cases in which it applies?
- Is the case in which I have applied it really one of the cases in which it applies?

As to the latter question, perhaps one might argue that the principle is applicable only to "Tractarian" systems, systems in which the same "fundamental objects" are present no matter what state the system is in – the maximal state of the system being defined by the various possible arrangements of the fundamental objects. It could be argued that the "Chinese Arena" case – which I used to argue against the thesis that the simplest maximal state of a system should be regarded as its most probable maximal states – is convincing only in application to Tractarian systems. (The Chinese Arena is, of course, a Tractarian system.) And, it could be argued, no conclusion that applies only to Tractarian systems supports the conclusion I have been arguing for, since *There being nothing* is not a possible state of a Tractarian system. A Tractarian system may have states that are in a sense counterfeits of *There being nothing.* For example, the state of the Chinese Arena in which only white sheets are showing is a sort of counterfeit "nothing." Perhaps my use of the (acknowledged) fiction of a Reality of which possible worlds are maximal states shows that on some level I am thinking of logical space as a space of states of a Tractarian system; perhaps on some level, despite my official denials, I am thinking of possible worlds in a way that implies that the same fundamental objects are present in each world; perhaps I am thinking of worlds as being a kind of concrete analogue of the "ersatz worlds" Lewis describes in *Counterfactuals.* In that case, the fundamental objects present in each world would be something like points in space, and each of them would have two possible states: "on" and "off" or "occupied" and "unoccupied." Am I thinking of the empty world as the world in which all the fundamental objects are in the "off" or "unoccupied" state? It may be that I am. I try not to use that sort of picture, but it is a powerful and seductive picture and it is possible that, on some level, I have been seduced by it.

*Is* the principle "The maximal states of an isolated system are of equal probability" applicable to non-Tractarian systems? Is it, in particular, applicable to a system if one of the states of that system is *There being nothing* – a real "nothing," not a counterfeit nothing like a vast space composed entirely of unoccupied but potentially occupied points? I am inclined to think so. But I am unable to convince myself that this inclination is trustworthy.

# PART II

## *Identity*

# 5

# The doctrine of arbitrary undetached parts

## I

Many philosophers accept what I shall call the Doctrine of Arbitrary Un-detached Parts (DAUP). Adherents of this doctrine believe in such objects as the northern half of the Eiffel Tower, the middle two-thirds of the cigar Uncle Henry is smoking, and the thousands (at least) of over-lapping perfect duplicates of Michelangelo's *David* that were hidden inside the block of marble from which (as they see it) Michelangelo lib-erated the *David*. Moreover, they do not believe in only *some* "unde-tached parts"; they believe, so to speak, in *all* of them. The following statement of DAUP, though it is imperfect in some respects, at least cap-tures the *generality* of the doctrine I mean to denote by that name:

> For every material object[1] M, if R is the region of space occupied[2] by M at time *t*, and if sub-R is *any* occupiable[3] sub-region of R *whatever*, there exists a material object that occupies the region sub-R at *t*.

First published in *Pacific Philosophical Quarterly* 62 (1981), pp. 123–137.

[1] I shall not define *material object*.

[2] I shall assume that the space we inhabit is a three-dimensional continuum of *points*. A *region* is any set of points. Suppose we agree that we know what it means to say that a given point in space *lies within* a given material object at a given moment. Then an object *occupies* a certain region at a certain moment if that region is the set containing all and only those points that lie within that object at that moment.

[3] A region of space is *occupiable* if it is possible (in what Plantinga calls "the broadly logical sense") for it to be occupied by a material object. Presumably not all regions of space are occupiable. Consider a ball-shaped region S; consider that sub-region of S that consists of just the points within S that are at distances from the center of S that have irrational measures: it is certainly hard to see how this sub-region could be occupied by a material object. I shall not discuss occupiability further, however, since its exact nature is not relevant to the issues that we shall be taking up. For an interesting proposal about occupiable regions, see Richard Cartwright's fine paper "Scattered Objects" in *Analysis and Metaphysics*, ed. Keith Lehrer (Dordrecht, 1975). If we accept Cartwright's account of what it is for a region to be occupiable (to be what he calls a "receptacle"), then DAUP is an immediate consequence of (though it does not entail) what he calls the *Covering Principle*.

(It should be obvious that DAUP, so defined, entails the existence of the northern half of the Eiffel Tower[4] and the other items in the above list.) This definition or statement or whatever it is of DAUP has, as I have said, certain imperfections as a statement of the doctrine I wish to describe certain philosophers as holding. One was mentioned in footnote 4. Another is this: there are philosophers who hold what is recognizable as a version of DAUP who would not be willing to admit regions of space into their ontologies.[5] Here is a third: this statement entails that material objects have boundaries so sharp that they occupy regions that are sets of points; and no adherent of DAUP that I know of would accept such a thesis about material objects. But these defects are irrelevant to the points that will be raised in the sequel and I shall not attempt to formulate a statement of DAUP that remedies them. For our purposes, therefore, DAUP may be identified with my imperfect statement of it.

What I want to say about DAUP involves only two components of that doctrine: (i) the arbitrariness of the parts − a *part* of an object is of course an object that occupies a sub-region of the region occupied by that object − whose existence it asserts (". . . *any* occupiable sub-region of R *whatever* . . .") and (ii) the concreteness and materiality of these parts. The second of these features calls for a brief comment. A philosopher might hold that, e.g., the northern half of the Eiffel Tower exists, but identify this item in his ontology with some *abstract* object, such as the pair whose first term is the Eiffel Tower and whose second term is the northern half of the region of space occupied by the Eiffel Tower. (If this idea were to be applied to moving, flexible objects or to objects that grow or shrink, it would have to be radically elaborated; I mean only to provide a vague, general picture of how one might identify parts with

---

[4] More precisely: DAUP entails that, for any time *t*, if the Eiffel Tower exists at *t*, and if the northern half of the space it occupies at *t* is then occupiable − and I think no one would want to deny *that* − then there exists an object at *t* that occupies that space, an object it would certainly be natural to call "the northern half of the Eiffel Tower."
There is a thesis that DAUP intuitively "ought" to entail that my statement of it does *not* entail. Consider two times *t* and *t'*. Suppose that the Eiffel Tower exists and has the same location and orientation in space at both these times. Suppose that at both these times it consists of the same girders, struts, and rivets, arranged in the same way. The thesis: the thing that is the northern half of the Eiffel Tower at *t* is identical with the thing that is the northern half of the Eiffel Tower at *t'*. I regard the failure of my statement of DAUP to entail this thesis as a defect in that statement. (I *think* this entailment fails to hold. It certainly cannot be shown formally to hold. For all I know, however, there may be some feature of the concept of a material object in virtue of which it *does* hold.)

[5] Argle for example. See "Holes" by David and Stephanie Lewis, *The Australasian Journal of Philosophy* 48 (1970).

abstract objects.) This paper is not addressed to that philosopher's doctrine. It is addressed to DAUP, which holds that, e.g., the northern half of the Eiffel Tower is a concrete material particular in the same sense as that in which the Eiffel Tower itself is a concrete material particular.

## II

The Doctrine of Arbitrary Undetached Parts is false. It is also mischievous: it has caused a great deal of confusion in our thinking about material objects. But I shall not attempt to show that it is mischievous. I shall be content to show that it is false.

As a first step towards showing this, I shall show that DAUP entails a thesis very close to *mereological essentialism*: it entails the thesis that it is impossible for an object to lose any of its parts; that is, it entails the thesis that if a part is removed from an object, and no new part is added to the "remainder," then that object must therewith cease to exist. This is a weaker thesis than mereological essentialism proper, which entails that if a part is removed from an object, then that object must therewith cease to exist *whether or not* any part is added to the remainder.[6] We may call this weaker doctrine *Mereological Near-Essentialism* (MNE). I shall not raise the question whether DAUP entails mereological essentialism proper; it will do for my purposes to show that it entails MNE. (A parenthetical note. We are speaking at a very high level of abstraction. I have not said what it would be for an object to "lose" a part. An adherent of DAUP may very well believe in the existence of "scattered objects," that is, objects that are not "in one piece."[7] Whether he does will depend on which regions he takes to be occupiable in the sense of · footnote 3. Someone who accepts the existence of scattered objects might very well accept the following account of cutting a cake. If I cut a cake and separate the newly cut piece from the remainder, I have not caused anything to "lose a piece"; I have merely changed a certain cake from a non-scattered to a scattered object. Thus, in this context and at this level of generality, it is not clear just what "losing a part" may come

---

[6] Mereological essentialism proper also entails that a thing could not have "started out with" different parts, which is not a consequence of the weaker thesis. For general discussions of mereological essentialism, see Roderick M. Chisholm, "Parts as Essential to Their Wholes," *The Review of Metaphysics* 26 (1973) and *Person and Object: A Metaphysical Study* (La Salle, Wisc., 1976), Appendix B.

[7] "Scattered objects" is Cartwright's term. See his article of that title (cited in fn. 3, above) for a precise definition of "scattered object."

down to. Still, the *annihilation* of a part would seem to be sufficient for the losing of it. In any case, the loss of parts is possible or it isn't. If it is, then MNE refers to just those possible cases that count as losses of parts, whether by separation or annihilation. If it isn't, MNE is a vacuously necessary truth and is thus entailed by DAUP.)

I shall now show that DAUP entails MNE. Assume that DAUP is true and MNE false. It follows from the falsity of MNE that there is a time (which for simplicity's sake I shall assume to be the present) such that there could be objects O and P such that P is a part of O at that time and such that O could survive the subsequent loss of P. Suppose such objects exist. By DAUP there is an object that occupies just that region of space that is the set-theoretical difference between the region occupied by O and the region occupied by P.[8] Call this object O-minus. O-minus is numerically diverse from O, since they occupy different regions of space and have different parts. Now suppose O were to lose P; for good measure let us suppose P to be annihilated, all other parts of O remaining unchanged, except for such changes in them as may be logically necessitated by the annihilation of P. It would seem that O-minus would still exist. Admittedly, this is not a formally demonstrable consequence of DAUP. Nevertheless, the proposition that a thing cannot cease to exist *simply* because something that was *not* a part of it is "detached" from it seems to be a sufficiently obvious conceptual truth that we may in good conscience use it as a premise. We have seen that O could (logically) have survived the annihilation of P. Let us suppose it has. What is the relation (now) between O and O-minus? Only one answer would seem to be possible: identity. "Each" is a material object, after all, and "they" now have the same boundaries, and, in fact, share all their "momentary" physical properties. Someone *might* say that O and O-minus are two material objects that now have the same size, shape, position, weight, or-

---

[8] Here I assume the following principle: if A is a material object and B is (a material object that is) a part of A and if $R_A$ is the region occupied by A and $R_B$ is the region occupied by B, then $R_A$ minus $R_B$ is occupiable. If there is any doubt about this principle, it could be proved as follows. Imagine that B was annihilated and that all else remained the same. Then $R_A$ *would be* occupied by a material object (even if it hadn't been before the annihilation of B). This principle is, strictly speaking, false if certain views about occupiability are correct, since it assumes that both "closed" and "open" regions are occupiable. (This is an implicit assumption of our little proof.) Those who care about such things will see that this assumption could be removed at the cost of a little elaboration that would not materially affect the use made of the principle in the body of the essay. Those who wish to deny the existence of "scattered objects" may wish to append the clause "if topologically connected" to the principle.

ientation in space, linear velocity, angular velocity, and so on, these two objects being numerically distinct simply in virtue of their having different histories. But this *I* cannot conceive of; if the meaning of "material object" is such as to allow the conceptual possibility of this, then I do not understand "material object" and therefore do not understand DAUP. We have reached the conclusion that O is now O-minus. But O and O-minus were once diverse (when P was a part of O) and thus we have arrived at a violation of the principle of the transitivity of identity. Hence we must reject our assumption that MNE is false, and we have shown that DAUP entails MNE.[9]

I should be the last to deny that there are disputable steps in this argument. In the next section we shall apply this general argument to a particular case, and I shall try to leave no disputable contention undefended. What I shall say may, I hope, be applied to the general case.

Let us agree for the nonce that I have shown that DAUP entails MNE. So what? Why shouldn't the proponent of DAUP simply accept MNE? No reason, I suppose. Unless there is some object that is known to be capable of surviving the loss of a part.

### III

There is. We ourselves, we men and women, are such objects. Or at least we are if we *have* parts; whether or not we have parts is a question the correct answer to which depends on the correct answer to the general, theoretical questions raised in this paper. But, at any rate, we all

---

[9] A very similar argument can be found in Cartwright, "Scattered Objects," pp. 164–166. Someone might argue that if the above argument is sound, then it can be extended in the following way to prove not simply that MNE follows from DAUP but that MNE is true *simpliciter*: Either there are undetached parts or there aren't; if there aren't, then MNE is vacuously true; if there are, then our argument can be used to show that MNE is true. This reaction conflates DAUP with the thesis that there are undetached parts. Any argument like the one I have presented in the text would have to employ some principle that allowed the arguer to pass from the existence of the object O and the part P to the existence of the object O-minus. This is just what DAUP allows one to do. (Of course there are weaker principles that would legitimize this inference.) Therefore, if one rejects DAUP (and if one accepts no other principle that would legitimize the inference of the existence of O-minus from the existence of O and P), one can consistently believe in the existence of undetached parts that are not essential to their wholes. I, for example, believe that there exists a cell in my right hand that is an undetached part of me and such that I could survive the loss of it. I can consistently believe this because I do not think that there is any such object as "I-minus-that-cell"; that is, if R is the region of space I occupy and r is the region of space that cell occupies, I do not think that there exists any object that occupies the region R − r.

too frequently undergo, and often survive, episodes of the sort that it is correct to describe in ordinary speech as "losing a finger" or "losing a leg." I wish to examine in detail one such episode – a fictional one involving a real person – on the assumption that DAUP is true. (We shall reach an absurd result – that identity is not transitive – and we shall therefore have to conclude that DAUP is false.) We have already seen, in the preceding section, in abstract outline, what our examination of this episode will reveal.

Consider Descartes and his left leg.[10] (The adherent of DAUP is going to have a certain amount of trouble with Descartes's left leg: there are, according to DAUP, an enormous number of objects that are equally good candidates for the office of "Descartes's left leg." I shall not address this problem. I shall assume in the sequel that some one of these candidates has been chosen, by fair means or foul, to fill this office.) If DAUP is true, then at any moment during Descartes's life, there was a thing (problems of multiplicity aside) that was his left leg at that moment. Let us pick some moment, call it $t_0$, during Descartes's life, and let "L" designate the thing that was his leg at the moment. There *also* existed at that moment, according to DAUP, a thing we shall call *D-minus*, the thing that occupied at $t_0$ the region of space that was the set-theoretic difference between the region occupied by Descartes and the region occupied by L. Obviously, Descartes and D-minus were not the same thing (at $t_0$), since, at $t_0$, they were differently shaped. Now suppose that at $t$ (shortly after $t_0$), L and D-minus became separated from each other; for good measure, let us suppose that L was then annihilated.

It would seem that after this episode – which I assume could be correctly described in the idiom of everyday life like this: Descartes's left leg was cut off and then destroyed – D-minus still existed. The survival by D-minus of its separation from L is not a formal consequence of DAUP. Still, how can we avoid this conclusion? It seems simply *true*, an inescapable consequence of the requirement of DAUP that the undetached parts of material objects be themselves, in the same sense, material objects. What "material objects" are may not be altogether clear. But if you can cause a thing to cease to exist by detaching from it (or even by destroying) something that was *not* one of its parts but simply part of its *environment*, while leaving the arrangement of all *its* parts wholly un-

---

[10] The following reflections on Descartes and his left leg supersede those contained in my essay "Philosophers and the Words 'Human Body,'" in *Time and Cause: Essays Presented to Richard Taylor*, ed. Peter van Inwagen (Dordrecht, 1980).

changed, if you can do *that*, then, I maintain, you have not got anything that can properly be called a material object.

It would seem that after this episode, Descartes still existed. One can, after all, survive the loss of a leg.

But if both Descartes and D-minus survived the severance of L from D-minus at *t*, what was the relation between them immediately after *t*? Only one answer is possible: they were then identical. If they were not, then we should have to admit that there was a time at which there were two material objects having the *same* size, shape, position, orientation, attitude, mass, velocity (both linear and angular), and color. Someone *might* say this, I suppose, but I should not understand him and I suspect that no one else would either.

We may also reach the conclusion that Descartes and D-minus were identical after *t* by a slightly different route. Before *t*, D-minus was *ex hypothesi* a part of Descartes. At *t*, Descartes lost L and lost no other parts (save parts of him that overlapped L). Therefore, after *t* Descartes had D-minus as a part. But, clearly, after *t*, no part of Descartes was "larger" than D-minus – that is, no part of Descartes had D-minus as a *proper* part. Therefore, Descartes (after t) had D-minus as an improper part. Therefore, after *t*, Descartes and D-minus were identical.

Our argument has led us to this conclusion: that there was a time at which Descartes and D-minus were identical. And, as we have noted, there was an earlier time at which they were *not* identical. But if this is correct, then there was once an object that had earlier been two objects, which is a plain violation of the principle of the transitivity of identity. I mean it is a violation of the principle of the transitivity of identity *simpliciter*, by the way, and not of a principle that claims transitivity for some "specialized" version of identity like "identity through time." So far as I can see, there is no relation called "identity through time," unless those words are simply another name for identity *simpliciter*. We may represent explicitly the violation of the transitivity of identity I contend we have arrived at as follows. If our argument is correct then all four of the following propositions are true:

> The thing that was D-minus before *t* =
> the thing that was D-minus after *t*
>
> The thing that was D-minus after *t* =
> the thing that was Descartes after *t*
>
> The thing that was Descartes after *t* =
> the thing that was Descartes before *t*

81

The thing that was D-minus before $t \neq$
the thing that was Descartes before $t$.[11]

Thus our *reductio* has been accomplished, and we must conclude that there was never any such thing as D-minus. Therefore, DAUP is false, for DAUP entails that there was such a thing as D-minus.

We can, in fact, easily reach an even more striking conclusion: L does not exist either: there was never any such thing as Descartes's left leg. We need only one premise to reach this conclusion, namely that if L existed, D-minus did too. And this premise seems quite reasonable, for it would seem wholly arbitrary to accept the existence of L and to deny the existence of D-minus. In more senses than one, L and D-minus stand or fall together. If these things existed, they would be things of the same sort. Each would be an *arbitrary* undetached part of a certain man.[12] This fact may be disguised by our having (problems of multiplicity and vagueness aside) what is a customary and idiomatic name for L if it is a name for anything: "Descartes's left leg." But this is a linguistic accident that reflects our interests. (We may imagine a race of rational beings who raise human beings as meat animals. Suppose these beings, for religious reasons, never eat left legs. They might very well have in their language some customary and idiomatic phrase that stands to D-minus in the same relation as that in which the English phrase "Descartes's left leg" stands to L.)

If our argument against DAUP also leads to the conclusion that there never was any such thing as Descartes's left leg (which I am willing to grant), this may lead some people to think that there *must* be something wrong with the argument. Here is a leg (one is tempted to say) and here is another leg, and therefore van Inwagen is wrong. I am not entirely out of sympathy with this reaction. If a philosophical argument leads us to

[11] The first and third of these four propositions I take to be trivial logical truths. Or, at least, to follow trivially from the propositions that D-minus existed before and after $t$ and that Descartes existed before and after $t$.

[12] Perhaps I am wrong about this. If I am, if a leg is like a cell (say), and unlike the left half of a cell, in being a non-arbitrary part of a human being, then I am wrong about something that is of no great import, since I am not saying that there are *no* undetached parts (cf. fn. 9). But whether or not there was such a thing as L, there was certainly no such thing as D-minus. And the non-existence of D-minus is sufficient to refute DAUP. Nevertheless, I think I am right and that L did not exist. I will assert this rather than suspend judgment because I think that if my thesis about parts entails that L did not exist, then my thesis has an extremely counter-intuitive consequence and I do not wish to make my thesis look more plausible than it is by glossing over its more implausible consequences.

deny something that every human being in history has believed, then it is a pretty good bet that something is wrong with the argument. But I doubt whether in saying that there never was any such thing as Descartes's left leg[13] I am denying anything that has been believed, as the Church says, *ubique et ab omnibus*.[14] The proposition I mean to express by the words "There never was any such thing as Descartes's left leg" does not, as I see it, entail the falsity of, e.g., the proposition that Descartes scratched his left leg on the morning of his eleventh birthday. I think I could show this. To make good this claim, I should at least have to provide some reason for thinking that sentences that apparently involve reference to or quantification over the limbs of animals can be translated into sentences that don't even apparently involve such reference or quantification. I believe I could do this, but this is not the place for it. My purpose in the present paragraph is to explain what sort of position my position on the nonexistence of Descartes's left leg is, and not to defend that position. (My position is comparable to that of many other philosophers who have denied the existence of various objects in order to escape the paradoxical consequences that they thought, rightly or wrongly, would follow from the existence of such objects. Philosophers who have denied the existence of the material substrate have not, in general, denied the existence of tables and chairs; philosophers who have denied the existence of sense-data have not, in general, denied the existence of perception or even the existence of a distinction between appearance and reality; philosophers who have denied the existence of pains have not, in general, denied the existence of pain.)

Nonetheless, an argument that leads to the conclusion that there never was any such thing as Descartes's left leg is at least *prima facie* objectionable. But all the objections to this argument I know of involve principles or lead to conclusions that, in my view at least, are more objectionable than the proposition that Descartes's left leg did not exist. In the remainder of this section and in the two sections that follow I shall examine these objections.

There are four objections, or types of objection, that I shall simply dismiss.

I shall simply dismiss any objection that involves a denial of the principle of the transitivity of identity. People who take this line are, as Professor Geach would say, "not to be heard." Anyone who rejects the

---

[13] There's the bit where you say it.
[14] There's the bit where you take it back.

principle of the transitivity of identity simply does not understand the difference between the number one and the number two.

I shall simply dismiss any objection that involves the contention that it would have been logically impossible for Descartes to survive the loss of a leg.[15] I do not know if anyone would say this, but if anyone would, he too is not to be heard.

I shall simply dismiss any objection that involves the contention that it would have been impossible for D-minus to survive being separated from L.

I shall simply dismiss any objection that involves the contention that it was possible for Descartes and D-minus to have been numerically distinct material objects having the same momentary physical properties. (I would not go so far as to say that such objections are not to be heard. I dismiss them because I cannot understand them and therefore have nothing to say about them.)

I know of two objections to my argument that are worthy of extended consideration. I shall call them the *Chisholm Objection* and the *Lewis Objection*. I will discuss them in the two sections that follow.

## IV THE CHISHOLM OBJECTION

It will not have escaped the reader's attention that my argument assumes that Descartes was a flesh-and-blood object that, when unmutilated, was shaped like a statue of Descartes. Many philosophers, including Descartes, would reject this assumption. Though I am myself convinced of its truth beyond all doubt and beyond all possibility of conversion by philosophical argument, I admit that it is highly controversial. To be sure, few philosophers would deny either that there was once a flesh-and-blood object shaped like a statue of Descartes or that that object was somehow intimately related to Descartes. But many philosophers would deny what seems evident to me: that he (that thing that thought) *was* that object. These philosophers would say that that object was not Descartes but rather his *body*. The philosopher who thus distinguishes between Descartes and his body and who wishes to accept the existence of D-minus may reply to the argument of Section III as follows:

---

[15] Some philosophers distinguish between survival and identity. I have no idea what they mean by this. When I say that a certain person survived a certain adventure, what I say entails that a person who existed before the adventure and a person who existed after the adventure were the same person.

> I can accept the existence of D-minus, and I can accept the proposition that Descartes was capable of surviving the loss of a leg, and I can accept the principle of the transitivity of identity, and your arguments do not show that my acceptance of these things forces upon me the desperate expedient of admitting that it is conceptually possible for there to be two conterminous material objects. I need only say – and I *do* say it – that D-minus was not a part of Descartes but only a part of Descartes's *body*.

And this response is perfectly proper. But this is not the end of the matter, for certain consequences follow upon it.

First, though my imaginary philosopher has escaped the consequences of the assumption that D-minus was a part of Descartes, he must nonetheless face the consequences of conceding that D-minus was a part of Descartes's body. Here is one: that Descartes's body (that is, the thing that at any given moment was the body Descartes had *then*) could not have survived the loss of a part. This could be easily shown by a trivial modification of the argument of Section III. Moreover, since, as a matter of empirical fact, human bodies are (to speak with the vulgar) constantly exchanging matter with their surroundings, he must concede that Descartes is continually "changing bodies"; and not just every now and then, but hundreds of times every second. Well, perhaps he will be willing to say this. We have shown independently of any considerations involving persons and their bodies that DAUP entails MNE, and the continual changing of one's body is a consequence of the proposition that at any given time one has some body or other, together with MNE and certain empirical facts about the human organism.

There is, however, a much more serious and far-reaching consequence of our imaginary philosopher's objection to the argument of Section III. Of those philosophers I know of who have thought about these matters, only Roderick Chisholm has seen the inevitability of this consequence.[16] I therefore call the above objection to the argument of Section III the *Chisholm Objection*, provided that it is understood to include the consequence I shall set forth in the following paragraphs.

If DAUP is true, then a human being, if he lasts from one moment to the next, cannot during that interval lose any parts. This is simply a consequence of the fact that DAUP entails MNE. Now there may be some "everyday" material objects that endure for appreciable periods of time

---

[16] My knowledge of Chisholm's views on this question comes entirely from a paper I heard him read in 1978. He has recently told me, however, that I have not misrepresented him.

according to the strict standards of endurance entailed by MNE. The Hope Diamond, say, or a fly in amber. But none of these observable, enduring material things is you or I. Therefore, if DAUP is true, and if you and I last from one moment to the next, we cannot be everyday material objects. I concede that there are observable material things other than the statue-shaped flesh-and-blood objects that *I* think you and I are that, according to reputable philosophers, are what you and I are. For example, some reputable philosophers think that you and I are living human brains. But such views are no more consistent with DAUP than is my own, for no such view is consistent with MNE and, therefore, no such view is consistent with DAUP. (Suppose for example that I am a brain. Surely I can survive the loss of some part of myself; a single cell, say. Let P be a part of me I can survive the loss of. Let B-minus be the object that occupies the region that is the set-theoretic difference between the region occupied by my brain – that is, by me – and the region occupied by P . . .)

It would seem, therefore, that (given our persistence through time, the transitivity of identity, and so on) it follows from DAUP that we are not observable material things, or, at any rate, that we are not material things of any sort that *has* so far been observed. Therefore, anyone who accepts DAUP must either accept the thesis that we are not material things or else accept the thesis that we are material things of a kind very different from any kind that has ever been observed.

The difficulties with the thesis that we are, contrary to all appearances, immaterial things, are well known.

Let us examine the thesis that we are material things of a sort that has never been observed. Anyone who accepts this may reasonably be expected to answer the question, *Why* have we so far gone unobserved? It cannot be for want of people's poking and prying inside human bodies. There are, I think, three possible answers.

(i)   We have gone unobserved because we are very small; perhaps as small as or smaller than a single cell. Presumably an object that small, or even a bit larger, might be located inside our bodies – inside our brains if anywhere, I should think – and have escaped the attention of the most assiduous physiologists.

(ii)  We have gone unobserved because we are made of some sort of subtle matter (the "nameless and unknown" soul-stuff of Epicurus and Lucretius) that can affect gross, everyday matter – or else we should not have charge of our bodies – but which affects it to such a small degree that physicists have not yet taken note of its effects.

(iii) We have gone unobserved because we are far from our bodies, with which we interact at a distance.

We may note that (i), (ii) and (iii) are not exclusive alternatives: perhaps we are at once tiny, subtle, and far away.

Let us call an object a *Chisholm Object* if it is a concrete particular that thinks and wills and is the cause of the voluntary movements of a human body and is in practice unobservable, either because it is immaterial (a Cartesian ego) or, if material, tiny or made of subtle matter or remote from the human body it controls.

We may now state the Chisholm Objection more adequately:

> Your argument has a false premise: that D-minus was a part of Descartes. Moreover, there is no true proposition that you could use in place of the proposition that D-minus was a part of Descartes in some reconstructed argument against DAUP, for Descartes was a Chisholm Object; if he ever lost a part, he lost it in 1650 (the year of his death) or later. Moreover, in the strict, philosophical sense (to borrow Bishop Butler's fine phrase) of *same* it is very unlikely that there was any appreciable interval throughout which Descartes had the same body.

I think that this is the only possible objection to my argument that is not demonstrably wrong. I have nothing to say against it except that I do not believe a word of it. But that is a psychological report, not an argument. Doubtless there are philosophers who find equally incredible my contention that, in the strict, philosophical senses of *was* and *thing*, there never was any such thing as Descartes's left leg.

I think that the arguments of this section and the preceding section show that anyone who accepts DAUP should also accept the proposition that every person is a Chisholm Object. For my part, I say so much the worse for DAUP. At any rate, I am fairly sure that few philosophers would find acceptance of the propositions the Chisholm Objection commits its adherents to an acceptable price to pay for DAUP.

## V THE LEWIS OBJECTION

One philosopher who balks at paying this price and who is nevertheless attracted to DAUP is David Lewis.[17] Lewis argues, *à la* Gaunilon, that

---

[17] Lewis holds that "persons and their bodies are identical." See his "Counterparts of Persons and Their Bodies," *The Journal of Philosophy* 68 (1971).

my reasoning must be faulty since parallel reasoning leads to an obviously false conclusion.[18]

Consider the Austro-Hungarian Empire in, say, 1900. In 1900, Austria existed and Hungary existed and these two countries composed the Empire. That is, they did not overlap and the portion of the earth's surface occupied by one or the other was just exactly the portion of the earth's surface occupied by the Empire. Thus in a very obvious sense, these two countries stood to the Empire as L and D-minus (if such there were) stood to Descartes. Now (the Lewis Objection runs) consider the following argument:

> Suppose that the Martians had totally destroyed Hungary and had left the territory occupied by Austria untouched. We can only suppose that Austria would have survived this destruction of Hungary. We can only suppose that the Austro-Hungarian Empire (whose capital at Vienna of course escaped destruction) would also have survived the destruction of Hungary. (True, "the Austro-Hungarian Empire" might not have been a very good *name* for it thereafter; but the example of the Holy Roman Empire shows that the name of an empire need not be a *good* name.) Empires and other states can increase and decrease in extent and can gain and lose parts without losing their identities (consider, for example, the fact that the United States survived the admission into the Union of Alaska and Hawaii). The act we have supposed the Martians to have performed would have caused the Empire to lose a part without causing it to cease to exist. Now what would have been the relation between Austria and the Empire after the destruction of Hungary? We can only suppose that it would have been identity, for what distinction would there have been between them? Moreover, Austria would have been the largest part of the Empire, and, according to any acceptable mereology, the largest part of a thing is its sole improper part, itself. But this is to suppose that the Empire might have been Austria at one time and not at another, which would be a violation of the principle of the transitivity of identity. Since the principle of the transitivity of identity is a necessary truth, only one conclusion is possible: Austria did not exist in 1900. Moreover, since Hungary existed in 1900 if and only if Austria did, Hungary did not exist in 1900 either.

Since the conclusion of this argument is absurd, there must be something wrong with the argument. But the argument is sound if and only if our earlier *reductio* arguments are sound. Therefore they are not sound.

I reject the Lewis Objection. I believe it contains a false premise: that

---

[18] This argument was communicated to me in a letter. The wording of the argument in the text is mine. It is my fault and not Lewis's that the political details of the example are inaccurate. I should like to apologize to anyone who cares about the constitution of the Dual Monarchy.

after the destruction of Hungary, Austria and the Empire would have been identical. I say they would merely have occupied the same territory. They would have differed in many of their properties. Two examples would be historical properties (the Empire would have had the property *having had Hungary as a part*; Austria would not have had it) and modal properties (the Empire would have had the property *possibly having Bavaria as a part*; Austria would not have had it).

As to the "largest part" argument, though one politico-geographical entity may correctly be said to be "part" of another, "part" in this sense does not obey the laws of any mereology I know of.[19] Call this relation the *PG-part relation*. It would seem that it should be defined as follows: A is a PG-part of B if the territory occupied by A is a part (in the standard, spatial sense) of the territory occupied by B. If this definition is accepted – and what are the alternatives? – then there would seem to be only one natural definition of "A is a larger PG-part of B than C is" and only one natural definition of "A is a proper PG-part of B"; in fact, these definitions are so natural it would be pedantic to state them. But it follows from these natural definitions that there need be no such thing as the largest PG-part of the politico-geographical entity, and, moreover, that a politico-geographical entity may have improper PG-parts other than itself. Take, for example, the City of Washington and the District of Columbia. Each of these is an improper PG-part of the other, and yet, by the principle of the non-identity of discernibles, they are numerically diverse. For example, the District of Columbia has the properties *having been the same size throughout its existence*, *not being a city*, and *having had Georgetown as a PG-part in 1850*; Washington has none of them. If matters had gone as we imagined with Austria and the Austro-Hungarian Empire, then this would have been just their situation: each would have been an improper PG part of the other.

Therefore, the Lewis Objection fails, since the "parallel" argument Lewis produces, though it indeed has an absurd conclusion, is not really parallel to the *reductio* arguments of Sections II and III. In a nutshell, the

---

[19] By a "politico-geographical entity," I mean an entity that (i) is a political entity – is brought into existence by human beings' entering into political relations with one another – and (ii) extends over part of the Earth's surface. (Strictly speaking, this is a definition of a *terrestrial* politico-geographical entity.) Thus the Caspian Sea is not a politico-geographical entity because it fails to satisfy condition (i). The Congress of the United States fails to satisfy condition (ii). The United States, the British Commonwealth, Paris, Nova Scotia, and the territorial waters of Peru are politico-geographical entities.

reason is this: "parts" of material objects and "parts" of politico-geographical entities do not work the same way. If an "improper part" of a material object is a material object that occupies the same region of space as that object, then every material object has exactly one improper part: itself. If an "improper part" of a politico-geographical entity is a politico-geographical entity that occupies the same territory as that entity, then every politico-geographical entity has *at least* one improper part: itself; but some have more.

<h2 style="text-align:center">VI</h2>

The Chisholm Objection I cannot accept. The Lewis Objection fails. I therefore find no reason to doubt the soundness of our *reductio* arguments, and I conclude that, though (I have no doubt) there are un-detached parts, there are not "just any" undetached parts. That is, I conclude that DAUP is false. In this, the final section, I will show how what has been said in the earlier sections may be applied to another sort of "part."

Some philosophers would call "parts" of the sort we have been talking about, "spatial parts." They would oppose them to *temporal* parts. I fully accept the arguments of Chisholm and Geach for the conclusion that the idea of a temporal part is incoherent.[20] I simply do not understand what these things are supposed to be, and I do not think this is my fault. I think that no one understands what they are supposed to be, though of course plenty of philosophers think they do. (If anyone who thinks he does understand temporal parts feels inclined to charge me with conceptual arrogance, I invite him to consider the following list: the Absolute Idea; impossible objects; Cartesian egos; bare particulars; things-in-themselves; pure acts of will; simple, non-natural properties; logically perfect languages; sense-data. I think it very likely that he will find that there is at least one item on this list that he has no glimmering of an understanding of. Yet each of them has been believed in by great philosophers. Anyone, therefore, who fails to understand some item on this list is no less conceptually arrogant than I.) But if I do not understand temporal parts, I at any rate understand what parameters are supposed by most philosophers who say they believe in them to individuate them: to each persisting object and each occupiable interval of time such that that object exists at every

---

[20] See Geach's British Academy Lecture "Some Problems about Time," reprinted in *Logic Matters* (Oxford, 1972) and Appendix A to Chisholm's *Person and Object*.

moment in that interval, there corresponds a *concrete* particular that is a temporal part of that object.[21] (Of course if some philosopher wishes to call an object-interval pair a "temporal part" of its first term, I have no objection.) So far as I know, no philosopher who believes there are *any* temporal parts thinks that there could be some occupiable sub-interval of the interval during which a given object exists that is *not* occupied by a temporal part of that object. That is to say, all philosophers who accept the existence of (proper) temporal parts, would accept what might be called the Doctrine of Arbitrary Temporal Parts (DATP):[22]

> For every persisting object P, if I is the interval of time occupied by P and if sub-I is *any* occupiable sub-interval of I *whatever*, there exists a persisting object that occupies the interval sub-I and which, for every moment *t* that falls within sub-I, has at *t* exactly the same momentary properties[23] that P has.

This doctrine is formally very similar to DAUP. (The differences in structure can, I think, be traced to the fact that there are three spatial dimensions and only one temporal dimension.)

There is at least one philosopher, the author of this paper, who thinks that while there *are* undetached spatial parts, comparatively few of the occupiable regions that fall wholly within a given material object are occupied. (See footnote 9.) *I* think this because I think that the cells living things are made of are, in a sense I cannot here explore, *unitary* things, things having an entelechy; in this respect they are like the men, women, and dogs (Thurber's list) of which they are parts. It is very hard to see how anyone could take a similar attitude toward temporal parts. I reject the Doctrine of Undetached Arbitrary (Spatial) Parts. But if there were temporal parts, then they would *all* be "arbitrary": there are no temporal analogues of cells.

Or perhaps this is wrong. Perhaps there is one sort of temporal part such that one could affirm the existence of parts of this sort and, without

---

21 An object *occupies* a set of moments of time if it exists at every moment in that set and at no other moments. A set of moments of time is an *occupiable interval* if it is possible in the broadly logical sense for there to be some object that occupies it. Presumably not all sets of moments of time are occupiable intervals. Cf. fn. 3.

22 I do not say "*undetached* temporal parts." A detached temporal part of a thing, presumably, would be something that *used to be* a temporal part of that thing. None of the friends of temporal parts, so far as I know, has found any use for such a notion.

23 It is well known that grave difficulties attend the notion of a "momentary" property. But I do not see how to state DATP without using it. I shall not exploit these difficulties in what follows, however, and thus *I* am under no obligation to explain momentary properties.

appearing to be placing wholly arbitrary restrictions on one's ontology, deny the existence of all other (proper) temporal parts. I am thinking of *instantaneous* temporal parts, those that occupy a mathematical instant of time, an interval of measure 0. In what follows, I am going to adopt the arguments that were employed earlier in this paper against DAUP to the task of showing that DATP is false. I think that anyone who, perhaps impressed by my argument, rejects DATP and who wants to believe in *some* temporal parts has only one possibility open to him: he must believe in the improper temporal part of an object (i.e., the object itself) and he must believe in all the instantaneous parts of the object and in no other parts. He must, for example, believe in Descartes and he must believe in the part of Descartes that occupied *t*, where *t* is any *instant* of time at which Descartes existed, and he must *not* believe in the part of Descartes that occupied the year 1625. I shall offer no arguments against *this* doctrine of temporal parts.

I said in the preceding paragraph that I should argue that DATP was false, I spoke loosely. DATP is not false. It is meaningless because the notion of a temporal part is meaningless. Or, at any rate, *I* don't understand it. But I *can* give an argument that *would* be an argument for the falsity of DATP if that doctrine made any sense. I can do this because, as I said above, though I do not understand the notion of a temporal part, I know what parameters are supposed to individuate temporal parts. Moreover, I can justifiably assume that discourse about temporal parts must satisfy certain formal constraints that I am familiar with from my understanding of parts *simpliciter*. But this self-justification is too abstract to convey much. Let us turn to the argument.

Our argument against DAUP depended on its being possible for a thing to lose its parts, or, more accurately, for its parts to become separated or to be annihilated. Nothing like this can figure in an argument about temporal parts: no one would suppose that two "adjoining" temporal parts of a thing might become separated or that a temporal part of a thing might cease to exist. (I *think*. I'm feeling my way about in the dark, you understand. The chair I'm sitting on is supposed to be a temporal part of itself and *it* could cease to exist.) At any rate, I won't assume this is possible. But one can assume, I think, that adjoining temporal parts of a thing might not have been in "contact"; not, perhaps, that there might have been an interval between them, but, at any rate, that one of them might not have existed. Take Descartes, for example. Let L be the temporal part of Descartes that occupied the last year of Descartes's existence.[24] Let D-minus be the temporal part of Descartes that occupied the interval from Descartes's birth (or conception or whenever it was he began to exist) to the moment exactly one year before Descartes ceased to exist. Though L and D-minus were in fact "joined" to each other, there would not seem to have been any necessity to this: there are surely possible worlds in which D-minus exists and L does not, either because *no* temporal part of Descartes adjoins D-minus or because some part other than L does.

Now if this is so, then it is easy to adapt our earlier methods to the task of deducing an absurdity from the proposition that there was such a thing as D-minus. If there was such a thing as D-minus, then there was such a thing as L, and the relations that held between D-minus, L, and Descartes are those that were described in the preceding paragraph. In that case, obviously, D-minus and Descartes were not identical. But suppose, as seems possible, that Descartes had ceased to exist exactly one year earlier than he in fact did; or, if you like, suppose, as seems possible, that D-minus had not been "attached to L" or "continuous with L" (or however one should put it). What then would have been the relationship that held between D-minus and Descartes? What could it have been but identity? To suppose otherwise is to suppose that a thing might have had two improper temporal parts. But if D-minus and Descartes could have been identical, then there are two things that could have been one thing. This is not only a violation of an obvious *modal* principle about identity ("$x \neq y \supset \Box x \neq y$"), it is a violation of the principle of the transitivity of identity *simpliciter*. This may be seen from inspection of the following four propositions (in which "$t$" denotes the moment exactly one year before the moment at which Descartes ceased to exist):

> D-minus = the thing that would have been D-minus if Descartes had ceased to exist at $t$
> The thing that would have been D-minus if Descartes had ceased to exist at $t$ = the thing that would have been Descartes if Descartes had ceased to exist at $t$
> The thing that would have been Descartes if Descartes had ceased to exist at $t$ = Descartes
> D-minus $\neq$ Descartes.[25]

---

[24] Some people believe that Descartes has never ceased to exist. The argument I shall present does not really require that we assume that Descartes has ceased to exist but only that we assume that it is *possible* for him to cease to exist.

[25] The first and third of these four propositions I take to be trivial logical truths. Or, at least, to follow trivially from the propositions that D-minus existed and would have

I have not presented any explicit argument for the conclusion that all four of these propositions can be derived from the assumption that D-minus exists (and would have existed if Descartes had ceased to exist at *t*). I should do so if this paper consisted solely of an attack on DATP. But I have devoted a good deal of space to an argument showing that DAUP entails a violation of the principle of the transitivity of identity, and I believe the reader will find it an easy task to construct the arguments I *would* give (if pressed) for the conclusion that DATP entails a violation of that principle.

I conclude that DATP fails for much the same reason that DAUP fails. More exactly, I conclude that if anyone ever does provide some explanation of the notion of a temporal part (thus bringing DATP into existence: at present there is no such doctrine), then DATP *will* fail for much the same reason that DAUP fails.[26]

existed if Descartes had ceased to exist at t and that Descartes existed and would have existed if he had ceased to exist at *t*. Cf. fn. 11.

[26] This paper was read at philosophy colloquia at the University of Western Ontario, Brown University, Rutgers University, and New York University. I should like to thank the audiences at these colloquia for their stimulating objections and comments. I have benefited from criticism of this paper by David Armstrong, Mark Brown, Roderick Chisholm, Richard Feldman, Eli Hirsch, Jennifer Hornsby, Michael Levin, David Lewis, Stephanie Lewis, Lawrence Brian Lombard, Philip Quinn, Michael Tye, James Van Cleve, and, especially, Peter Unger.

# 6

# Composition as identity

Let us say that $x$ is a *part of* $y$ just in the case that $x$ is either a part of $y$ in the ordinary sense of the English word "part" or is identical with $y$. (I leave it an open question whether the ordinary sense of the word "part" is consistent with a thing's being a part of itself.) Then:

$x$ is a proper part of $y$ $=_{df}$ $x$ is a part of $y$ but is not identical with $y$.

$x$ overlaps $y$ $\qquad =_{df}$ Some one thing is a part of both $x$ and $y$.

$y$ is a fusion of the $x$s $=_{df}$ A thing overlaps $y$ if and only if it overlaps one or more of the $x$s.[1]

And let us call the "multigrade" relation expressed by "$y$ is a fusion of the $x$s" *composition*.[2]

### I

*Mereology* is a theory about parts and wholes, and, more generally, about composition. If it is formulated in terms of plural variables and plural

First published in *Philosophical Perspectives* 8: *Logic and Language* (1994), pp. 207–220.

[1] For an account of "plural variables" ("the $x$s," "the $y$s" . . .), and the plural quantifiers ("for some $x$s," "for any $y$s") that bind them, see my *Material Beings* (Ithaca, NY, 1990), pp. 23–27. See also David Lewis, *Parts of Classes* (Oxford, 1991), pp. 62–71. The mereological terminology of the present paper is that of *Parts of Classes* and not that of *Material Beings*.

[2] For a discussion of "multigrade" relations, see van Inwagen, *Material Beings*, pp. 27–28. In *Parts of Classes*, Lewis sometimes calls the multigrade relation of composition a "many–one" relation. By this he means simply that composition holds between a plurality of objects on the one hand (the planks, say) and a single object on the other (the ship). It should be noted that he is not using this term in its standard sense, according to which a many–one relation is a binary relation (a relation that holds between a single object and a single object) such that an object cannot bear it to each of two objects. (Denotation, for example.) Lewis also describes the part–whole relation and the overlap relation as "one–one," meaning simply that they are ordinary and not multigrade relations. It should be noted that in the standard sense of the term, these two relations are not one–one but, so to speak, many–many. (Each of the planks bears both of them to the ship; and not to the ship alone but to itself and various other proper parts of the ship.)

quantifiers (in addition to ordinary variables and quantifiers), it consists of the logical consequences of the following two axioms:

- Parthood is transitive
- For any *x*s, those *x*s have one and only one fusion.

The range of the variables of Mereology is usually taken to be unrestricted, but in this essay I shall consider only material objects (whatever those are) and their parts – if material objects can have parts that are not themselves material objects. (Some people would not be comfortable with the idea that, say, quarks and electrons are "material objects"; but most people would want to say that material objects have quarks and electrons as parts. And then, of course, there are – or, rather, in my view, there *aren't* – "tropes" and "immanent universals" and various other things that some people think are parts of material objects and yet are not themselves material objects.)

David Lewis has recently advanced the thesis that Mereology is "ontologically innocent."[3] One can well imagine this thesis being received with incredulous stares. There might be speeches behind some of these stares. Here are two speeches that I can imagine.

I believe only in metaphysical simples, things without proper parts. This makes for a neat, manageable ontology of the material world, although (I concede) I have to do a lot of hard philosophical work to explain what's "good" about typical utterances of "There are three apples in the bowl" and "bad" about typical utterances of "There are three pixies in the bowl." (For, by my lights, the world is, in the strict and philosophical sense, as empty of apples – which would be composite objects if they existed – as it is of pixies.) If I were to accept Mereology, I'd have to believe in all sorts of things I don't believe in now. I'd have to believe that all sorts of properties that I now believe have empty extensions had non-empty extensions. I'd face all sorts of philosophical problems that I don't face now – problems about the identities of composite objects across time or across worlds, for example. Tell me that if I accept Mereology I'll end up with a more satisfactory metaphysic, and I'll listen. Tell me that the new problems I'll face have solutions or are more tractable than the problems I currently face, and I'll listen. But don't tell me that Mereology is *innocent*. If you tell me that, you're no better than the salesman who tells me that a new Acme furnace is free because the

---

[3] Lewis, *Parts of Classes*, pp. 81–87.

money it saves me will eventually equal its cost. "Innocent" is like "free," and "free" does not mean the same as "well worth it."

I believe that the statue and the lump of gold that constitutes it are numerically distinct. I believe this because I believe that the statue and the lump have different properties. Even if God created the statue (and, of course, the lump) *ex nihilo*, and the statue remained in existence and unchanged for a year, after which God annihilated the statue (and the lump), the lump had the property "could survive radical deformation" and the statue did not have that property. And the statue had the property "is necessarily conterminous with a statue," and the lump did not have this property. But there are certain gold atoms such that the statue was one fusion of those gold atoms and the lump was another. My thesis (I concede) faces philosophical problems. Ask me how each of the two properties I've mentioned manages to get associated with one of the fusions of the gold atoms and not with the other, and I'll agree that I need to address that very serious question. But don't tell me that any theory that – like Mereology, with its unique fusions – is incompatible with my ontology of the material world is *innocent*.

II

Lewis has an argument for the innocence of Mereology. Sometimes he puts the argument like this: Composition is a kind of identity. Therefore, in accepting fusions, you are accepting only something that is identical with what you have already accepted, and nothing could be more ontologically innocent than that. And Mereology asks you to accept nothing more than fusions of what you already accept. Lewis eventually qualifies the thesis that composition is a kind of identity, and his qualifications seem to me to be significant enough that I should want to call the argument based on the qualified premise a statement of a new and different argument. For the present, I shall consider only the unqualified argument.

Whatever the larger merits of this argument may be, there is a minor hole in it. I think, however, that this hole can be fairly easily plugged. Here is the hole: A theory that tells you to accept only things that are identical with things you already accept is not necessarily a theory that you will happily regard as "ontologically innocent," for it may tell you that there are *fewer* things than you were inclined to believe in. (It would be odd to argue that atheism or materialism or nominalism was an ontologically innocent theory on the ground that it asked you to believe only in things you already believed in: finite things, as it may be, or material things or individual things.) This is the complaint of the believer in the distinct statue and lump: Mereology entails that either the statue does not exist or the lump does not exist or the statue and the lump are identical. In the present case, however, one can point out that if composition is indeed a kind of *identity*, there can hardly be two fusions of the same gold atoms: if something bears identity both to $x$ and to $y$, then $x$ and $y$ must be, well, identical. The oncoiconists, so to call them, may complain that Mereology is not ontologically innocent, but their position can be compared with that of the philosopher (if there is such a philosopher) who believes that the statue is identical with the lump and that the statue and the lump have different properties. That philosopher may complain if you tell him that the standard account of identity is ontologically innocent, but the principles endorsed by the standard account are pretty uncontroversial, and we can't be expected to use "ontologically innocent" so scrupulously as to avoid giving offense to those who deny the indiscernibility of identicals. Nor can we, even in these days of rampant pluralism, be expected to be so scrupulous in our use of this term as to avoid giving offense to those who deny the transitivity of identity – which is, after all, a consequence of the indiscernibility of identicals. (Indeed, if composition is a kind of identity, then it would seem that the oncoiconists might as well say that the statue and the lump are identical and yet the bearers of different properties as say that they are composed of the same atoms and yet not identical; if composition is a sort of identity, then the two theses are equally grave violations of the principles normally supposed to govern identity.)

The philosopher who made the first of our imaginary speeches is a different case, and is the sort of philosopher to whom Lewis's argument is, in intention, addressed. (He is the most extreme case of this sort of philosopher: he believes that the $x$s *never* have a fusion – or, more exactly, he believes that the $x$s have a fusion if and only if there is exactly one of them.) If he comes to agree with Lewis, he will describe his conversion in some such words as the following: "I thought that I believed only in simples. I was blind but now I see. I see that *in* accepting the existence of simples, I accepted the existence of the fusion of any simples. I see that, in accepting the thesis that any simples have a fusion, I

98

accept only things that are (in a sense, to be sure) identical with what I have already accepted."

### III

In a sense. But in *what* sense does Lewis believe that if *y* is a fusion of the *x*s, then *y* is identical with the *x*s? And will it be evident that his thesis is true, once its meaning has been spelled out, or will some further argument be required to show that it is true? On these points I am unclear. I am unclear because there are a great many things that Lewis says that I am unable to make any real sense of. I am going to quote, from the relevant sections of *Parts of Classes*, a fairly large number of sentences that seem to me to be the main vehicles of Lewis's attempts at an informal, intuitive explanation of the sense in which composition is a kind of identity. I say I am unable to make "any real sense" of what Lewis says on this topic because, although many of the sentences I am going to examine *seem* to mean something true and important when one first encounters them, this apparent meaning becomes very elusive when one tries to pin it down. That, at least, has been my experience. When I try carefully to spell out what these sentences mean, I discover a growing conviction (which I by no means regard as infallible) that they do not mean anything at all. In addition to quoting the sentences, I make will some remarks about them that are intended as a record of my failure to make sense of them. The sentences that I list below are in most cases not exact quotations. I have, for example, often replaced pronouns in Lewis's sentences both with variables and noun-phrases, as it seemed good to me. The number after each sentence refers to the page of *Parts of Classes* where the original occurred.

- A fusion is nothing over and above its parts. (80)

But what does "nothing over and above" mean? This slippery phrase has had a lot of employment in philosophy, but what it means is never explained by its employers. Sometimes it needs no explanation, for it sometimes has a straightforward mereological sense. (Think of the materialist who says "I am nothing over and above my body"; presumably he means that he has no part that is not a part of his body.) If Lewis is using "nothing over and above" in this straightforward mereological sense, then the quoted sentence means that a fusion has no parts other than its parts. But this, surely, is not what Lewis intended to convey by this sentence. It would be interesting to see an example of a thing that Lewis thinks *is* something over and above its parts; it would be interesting to see an example of something that had this feature according to some philosophical theory that Lewis rejected.

- The fusion of the *x*s just *is* the *x*s (81)
- The *x*s just *are* the fusion of the *x*s. (81)

There is the "is" of (singular) identity. This word makes syntactical sense when it is flanked by singular terms and variables: Tully is Cicero; $x$ is the successor of 0; $x$ is $y$. There is the "are" of (plural) identity. This word makes sense when it is flanked by plural terms (or "plural referring expressions") and plural variables: Locke, Berkeley, and Hume are the British Empiricists; The *x*s are the Mortons and the Hanrahans; The *x*s are the *y*s. But what kind of syntactical sense is there in taking either "is" or "are" and putting a singular term or variable on one side of it and a plural term or variable on the other? Both singular and plural identity can be defined in terms of "is one of" or "is among" (as, Berkeley is one of the British Empiricists):

$x$ is $y$        $=_{df}$ For any $z$s, $x$ is one of the $z$s if and only if $y$ is one of the $z$s

The *x*s are the *y*s $=_{df}$ For all $z$, $z$ is one of the *x*s if and only if $z$ is one of the *y*s.

But the "hybrid" is/are cannot be defined in terms of "is one of", or in any other way that I can see.

- The "are" of composition is, so to speak, the plural form of the "is" of identity. (82)

I am not sure what the force of "so to speak" is, but, whatever the "are" of composition may be, it cannot be the plural form of the "is" of identity, for that office is already filled: the plural form of the "is" of "identity" is the "are" of identity.

- The whole is the many parts counted as one thing. (83)

(This sentence occurs in a quotation from an article by Donald Baxter.[4] But Lewis does not seem to regard the sentence as at all puzzling; the quotation is presented in support of Lewis's position.) This sentence contains the is/are hybrid, but it has another feature that I find puzzling. What does "counted as one thing" mean? What does it mean to count,

---

[4] Donald Baxter, "Identity in the Loose and Popular Sense," *Mind* 97 (1988), pp. 575–582.

say, the British Empiricists as one thing? "She's only interested in one thing in philosophy." "What's that?" "The British Empiricists." Well, that means one *topic* of conversation or contemplation or research, the topic that is constituted by the writings of, careers of, and issues addressed by the British Empiricists. "For Heidegger, there's no difference between the British Empiricists. They all exemplify Forgetfulness of Being to the highest possible degree, and are really the same philosopher." No comment needed. Probably there are lots of ways to "count several things as one," but none of them really has much to do with the ideas suggested by the word "whole."

- Take the *x*s together or take them separately, the *x*s are the same portion of Reality either way. (81)

What is it to take things together and to take them separately? And haven't we got that hybrid is/are in the second clause? Could the following be the proposition that makes this sentence seem intelligible, owing to the fact that this sentence sort of looks as if it might, in a way, express something not too unlike it – I mean if you didn't look too closely?

> The fusion of the *x*s is the fusion of certain simples, the *y*s; the simples that are parts of any of the *x*s are the *y*s.

Or could it be the following proposition (if material things are not ultimately composed of simples but are rather ultimately constituted of continuous stuff)?

> The fusion of the *x*s is constituted by a certain quantity of stuff *y*; the total quantity of stuff such that any of it constitutes any of the *x*s is *y*.[5]

Or this one?

> The fusion of the *x*s occupies (fits exactly into) a certain region of space *y*; the region of space that is collectively occupied by the *x*s is *y*.

Or this one?

> The same spatial distribution of shape and color and other "local" properties is determined by the way the *x*s are and by the way the fusion of the *x*s is; start with the fusion and determine the distribution without taking into account the fact that it has proper parts, or start with the *x*s and determine the distribution without taking into account the fact that they have a fusion, and you'll get the same distribution.

[5] "Quantity" is to be understood not in the sense of "amount" but in the Russell/ Cartwright sense. (In Russell's words, "A quantity is anything which is capable of quantitative equality with something else.") See Helen Morris Cartwright, "Heraclitus and the Bath Water," *Philosophical Review* 74 (1965), pp. 466–485.

Could the fact that a picture (or mental image) of a plurality of objects and a picture of their fusion are the same – the fact that one cannot distinguish pictorially between objects and their fusion – be a part of what causes us to regard this sentence as expressing something true and important? (I mean, just look at the picture. Here they are; here their fusion is. You don't do something different to draw them and to draw their fusion. Drawing them *is* drawing their fusion.)

- Commit yourself to the existence of the *x*s all together or one at a time, it's the same commitment either way . . . the new commitment is redundant, given the old. (81)

"I hereby commit myself to the existence of the Continental Rationalists." That's committing myself to the existence of the Continental Rationalists all together. "I hereby commit myself to the existence of Descartes. I hereby commit myself to the existence of Spinoza. I hereby commit myself to the existence of Leibniz." That's committing myself to the existence of the Continental Rationalists one at a time. Or, at any rate, these commitments are what "committing oneself to the *x*s all together" and "committing oneself to the *x*s one at a time" suggest to *me*. Lewis, it would appear, agrees about "one at a time," but not about "all together." For Lewis, to commit oneself to the Continental Rationalists all together is to commit oneself to the existence of an object such that a thing overlaps that object if and only if it overlaps one or more of the Continental Rationalists. This seems to me to be an odd use of "committing oneself to the existence of the Continental Rationalists all together," one that is in as much need of explanation as the thesis that composition is a kind of identity. It does not explain the sense, if any, in which the Rationalists are identical with their fusion, or why commitment to their fusion is not a new commitment for someone who already believes in Descartes, Spinoza, and Leibniz.

- If you draw up an inventory of Reality . . . it would be double counting to list the fusion of the *x*s and also list the *x*s. (81)

Double-counting? Counting the same thing twice? Why so? "An example should make my point clear. If you boast that you own one large parcel of land and six small ones, and if it turns out that the six small parcels of land *compose* the one big one, you're exaggerating your holdings. You're exaggerating them because the big parcel *is* the small parcels, and in listing it you've already listed them. Your boast is like this boast: I am one of the most erudite of students of American letters, for I am an expert not only on the writings of Mark Twain but on those of Samuel Clemens as well." (Cf. *Parts of Classes*, pp. 81–82. Lewis uses the "parcels of land" example – which he borrows from Baxter – to illustrate a different point, but I think it provides a particularly good illustration of the intuitive force of the idea that there is some sense in which including both the $x$s and their fusion as separate items in the same list is "double-counting.")

But consider. Suppose that there exists nothing but my big parcel of land and such parts as it may have. And suppose it has no proper parts but the six small parcels. (I have not forgotten that the Mereologist will want to say that any two, three, four, or five of the small parcels will compose a piece of land that is a proper part of the big parcel. If you want to complicate the argument I am about to give by including the composite proper parts of the big parcel, go ahead: you will do no more than complicate it.) Suppose that we have a batch of sentences containing quantifiers, and that we want to determine their truth-values: "$\exists\, x\, \exists\, y\, \exists\, z$ ($y$ is a part of $x$ & $z$ is a part of $x$ & $y$ is not the same size as $z$)"; that sort of thing. How many items in our domain of quantification? Seven, right? That is, there are seven objects, and not six objects or one object, that are possible values of our variables, and which we must take account of when we are determining the truth-values of our sentences. Or suppose that we are evaluating a batch of quantificational sentences in relation to a universe in which there are aleph-zero simples and only such other things as have them as parts. What (given the two axioms of Mereology) is the cardinality of our domain of quantification? The power of the continuum, right? Not aleph-zero? But if counting both the $x$s and their fusion is "double-counting," then why are our domains respectively seven- and $c$-membered, rather than six- and aleph-zero-membered?

## IV

The following quotation – we have already looked at one of the sentences it contains – is a nice summary of Lewis's position on composition, identity, and the ontological innocence of Mereology:

I say that composition – the relation of part to whole, or, better, the many-one relation of many parts to their fusion – is like identity. The "are" of composition is, so to speak, the plural form of the "is" of identity. Call this the thesis of *Composition as Identity*. It is in virtue of this thesis that mereology is ontologically

103

innocent: it commits us only to things that are identical, so to speak, to what we were committed to before. (*Parts of Classes*, p. 82)

Lewis goes on to say, "In endorsing Composition as Identity, I am following the lead of D. M. Armstrong and Donald Baxter." I have already examined a crucial sentence from Baxter ("The whole is the many parts counted as one thing"). No one will be able to get anything out of Baxter unless he understands this sentence, and I, as I have said, do not understand it. Armstrong is another story. He has advanced a different thesis from Baxter's concerning the relation between composition and identity. Lewis describes Armstrong's position in these words:

Armstrong takes strict identity and strict difference as the endpoints of a spectrum of cases, with cases of more or less extensive overlap in between. Overlap subsumes part–whole as a special case: it may be $x$ itself, or $y$ itself, that is a common part of $x$ and $y$. Two adjoining terrace houses that share a common wall "are not identical, but they are not completely distinct from each other either. They are partially identical, and this partial identity takes the form of their having a common part. Australia and New South Wales are not identical, but they are not completely distinct from each other. They are partially identical, and this partial identity takes the form of the whole–part 'relation' . . . Partial identity admits of at least rough-and-ready degree. Begin with New South Wales and then take larger and larger portions of Australia. One is approaching closer and closer to complete identity with Australia." (*Parts of Classes*, pp. 82–83)[6]

What exactly is Armstrong saying? I suggest that the best way to interpret the quoted passage is as an argument for the thesis that it is philosophically instructive to read "$x$ overlaps $y$" as "$x$ is partly identical with $y$".[7] And there does seem to be some sort of insight to be gleaned from thinking of overlap as partial identity. If $x$ overlaps $y$, then a part of $x$, something that partly contains the *being* of $x$, is such that it, that very same thing, also partly contains the being of $y$. For something to happen to that thing (for it to be touched or struck, say) is for something to happen to both $x$ and $y$ – in a large class of cases the same thing that happens to the common part of $x$ and $y$. For that thing to instantiate a local property at point $a$ is for both $x$ and $y$ to instantiate that property at point $a$. Both parthood and identity, moreover, can be defined in terms of overlap, and calling overlap "partial identity" is a perspicuous way of calling attention to the fact that the roots of both parthood and identity are contained in

---

[6] The quotation is from David Armstrong, *Universals and Scientific Realism*, 2 vols. (Cambridge, 1978), vol. II, pp. 37–38.

[7] I have changed Armstrong's "partially identical" to "partly identical." Here I follow Fowler: see the article "partially" in *Modern English Usage*.

the overlap relation. Here are the definitions, with "partial identity" replacing "overlap" ("$\leq$" represents parthood and "$=_p$" partial identity):

$$x \leq y \quad =_{df} \quad \forall z \, ( z =_p x \rightarrow z =_p y)$$
$$x = y \quad =_{df} \quad \forall z \, ( z =_p x \leftrightarrow z =_p y).$$

The formal similarity between these two definitions may be some sort of argument for a close relation between parthood and identity. (Both partial identity and identity can be defined in terms of parthood, but neither partial identity nor parthood can be defined in terms of identity. I'm not sure whether the force of the argument is weakened by the observation that partial identity and identity can be defined in terms of parthood.)

Let's suppose that all this is right: there *is* a close relation between parthood and identity, and thinking of overlap as partial identity is a good device for making this close relation evident. What follows about the ontological innocence of Mereology?

You believe in the "automatic" fusions of Mereology. I believe in the *x*s. You tell me that there is a *y* such that a thing is partly identical with y if and only if it is partly identical with one or more of the *x*s. What makes this assertion of yours "ontologically innocent"? We suppose that there is an intimate relation between parthood and identity, one that is displayed by thinking of what we used to call overlap as partial identity. Does this intimate relation between parthood and identity show that the assertion of the existence of a fusion of the *x*s is ontologically innocent? I don't see why it should. You have asserted that an object having certain properties exists. Why should I believe you? "Well, it's identical with what you already believe in, the *x*s." But that's neither true nor false. That doesn't make any sense. That's just the hybrid is/are, and thinking of overlap as partial identity is not going to be of any help in making sense of *that* notion.[8] It is true that if *y* exists, it is partly identical with lots of things I believe in, and each of them is partly identical with it. But

---

[8] Lewis talks as if Armstrong, who says that overlapping objects are partly identical, and Baxter, who says that the whole is the parts counted as one thing, were saying the same thing, or at least closely related things. Lewis links his quotation from Armstrong to a quotation from Baxter, which begins with the sentence I have examined above, with the words, "Baxter puts it this way" (*Parts of Classes*, p. 83). But what is this "it" that Armstrong is putting one way and Baxter another? Apparently, "it" is supposed to be the thesis of Composition as Identity. It is certainly true that Armstrong and Baxter have both put forward theses that could be called "the thesis of Composition as Identity"; but they are hardly the *same* thesis. For one thing, Baxter's thesis depends on the intelligibility of the is/are hybrid, and Armstrong's does not.

why should I believe that $y$ exists? All sorts of objects can be specified by stipulating the partial identity relations that they (supposedly) bear to objects whose existence is uncontroversial, but that does not mean that anything answers to those specifications. I do not believe that there is anything that satisfies the open sentence "For some $x$, $x$ is an electron and $y$ is partly identical with $x$ and for some $z$, $z$ is partly identical with $x$ and $z$ is not partly identical with $y$," since I do not believe that electrons have proper parts. No one would tell me that the assertion that something satisfied this sentence was ontologically innocent. I do not believe that there is anything that satisfies the open sentence "For all $x$, $x$ is partly identical with $y$ if and only if, for some $z$, $z$ is an electron and $x$ is partly identical with $z$," since I do not believe that there is such a thing as the fusion of all the electrons. Why, then, would someone tell me that the assertion that something satisfied this sentence was ontologically innocent?

It would seem, therefore, that someone could accept Armstrong's thesis about the intimate relation between overlap and identity without being in any way moved to regard Mereology as ontologically innocent. If we decide to label Armstrong's position "the thesis of Composition as Identity," then the thesis of Composition as Identity in *this* sense does not support the ontological innocence of Mereology.

v

We have been considering Lewis's argument for the Composition as Identity thesis, and his argument for the conclusion that this thesis entails that Mereology is ontologically innocent. More exactly, we have been considering various theses to the effect that composition and identity are in some sense intimately linked, and the argument that, because they are thus intimately linked, Mereology, which commits one only to things that bear the relation *composition* to things one already believes in, is ontologically innocent. But this is not exactly the argument that Lewis, in the end, officially and definitively accepts. In Section II, I said, "Lewis eventually qualifies the thesis that composition is identity, and his qualifications seem to me to be significant enough that I should want to call the argument based on the qualified premise a statement of a new and different argument. For the present, I shall consider only the unqualified argument." It is now time to turn to the qualified argument. The qualification consists in a weakening of the Composition as Identity thesis. (Or so I would describe it; Lewis might resist this description.) Lewis's considered or official position is that, while it is instructive to think of composition as a form of identity, this cannot be, strictly speaking, maintained:

> . . . even though the many and the one are the same portion of Reality, and the character of that portion is given once and for all whether we take it as many or take it as one, still we do not really have a generalized principle of indiscernibility of identicals. It does matter how you slice it – not to the character of what's described, of course, but to the form of the description. What's true of the many is not exactly what's true of the one. After all, they are many while it is one. (*Parts of Classes*, p. 87)

(I will remark parenthetically that, while I am not sure I understand everything Lewis says in this passage, I do understand its final sentence. It is an excellent epitome of my difficulties with what I have called the hybrid is/are.) The relation between composition and identity is not, as Baxter thinks, identity. It is, rather, analogical:

> Mereological relations . . . are strikingly analogous to ordinary identity. So striking is this analogy that it is appropriate to mark it by speaking of mereological relations – the many–one relation of composition, the one–one relations of part to whole and overlap – as kinds of identity. Ordinary identity is the special limiting case of identity in the broadened sense. (*Parts of Classes*, p. 83)

The sense of this passage seems to be this: our present vocabulary does not reflect the striking analogy between composition and identity; it is, therefore, philosophically appropriate to expand the meaning of "identity" to cover both composition and identity, and to regard what used to be called "identity" as the "special limiting case" of what is now to be called "identity."

And what is this striking analogy? "The analogy," Lewis tells us, "has many aspects" (p. 85). They are as follows.

First, just as it is redundant to say that $x$ and $y$ exist when $x$ is identical with $y$, so it is redundant to say that $x$ and the $y$s exist, when $x$ is a fusion of the $y$s.

Secondly, just as, given that $x$ exists, it is automatically true that something identical with $x$ exists, so, given that the $x$s exist, it is automatically true that a fusion of the $x$s exists.

Thirdly, just as there cannot be two things both of which are identical with $x$, so there cannot be two things both of which are fusions of the $x$s. There is something analogous to the transitivity of identity in this feature of composition: if $x$ is the $y$s, and the $y$s are $z$, then $x$ is $z$.

Fourthly, just as fully to describe $x$ is fully to describe the object that is identical with $x$, so fully to describe the $x$s is fully to describe their fusion.

Fifthly, just as $x$ and $y$ must occupy the same region of spacetime if the former is identical with the latter, so $x$ and the $y$s must occupy the same region of spacetime if the former is the fusion of the latter.

These statements explain what is meant by saying that composition and identity are strikingly analogous. It would seem, then, that Lewis's thesis of Composition as Identity could be put as follows:

> Since composition and identity are analogous in these five respects, it is philosophically appropriate to expand the meaning of "identity" to cover both composition and identity, and to regard what used to be called "identity" as the "special limiting case" of what is now to be called "identity."

At any rate, that is how I will understand the thesis.

*Are* composition and identity alike in these five ways?

Not everyone is going to accept all five of the above "just as" statements. I myself accept only the third and the fifth without qualification. I definitely reject the second, and that leads me to reject the first as well, since it is, surely, not redundant to say that the $y$s and the fusion of the $y$s exist if it is not automatically true that just any objects have a fusion. (And I am not sure what even the believer in "automatic fusions" means by saying that it is redundant to say that the $y$s and the fusion of the $y$s exist. Recall our "domain of quantification" point: if there are $n$ simples ($n > 1$) and they have a fusion, then there must be at least $n + 1$ items in the list of objects to be checked in the course of determining the truth-values of statements containing quantifiers; but if that is so, in what sense is it redundant to say that the $y$s and the fusion of the $y$s exist?) I accept the fourth statement only with a serious qualification (as, indeed, Lewis himself must, since he believes that "what's true of the many is not exactly what's true of the one"): "fully to describe $x$ [the $y$s]" must mean something like "fully to describe the distribution of local properties in the smallest spacetime region that includes the events that make up the career[s] of $x$ [the $y$s]."[9] Furthermore, although I accept the third statement, not everyone will: the oncoiconist will not.

---

[9] It is instructive to contrast the "$n > 1$" with the "$n = 1$" case. If there is only one simple, it is identical with the fusion of all the simples, and there is therefore only one object – not two objects – to be taken account of in determining the truth-values of statements containing quantifiers in a one-simple universe. In the "$n = 1$" case, it really *is* redundant to say that the $y$s exist and the fusion of the $y$s exists.

From my point of view, therefore, the analogy between composition and identity is so weak as really not to be much of an analogy at all.[10] Even from the point of view of the Mereologist, the analogy is not quite so strong as Lewis suggests. (This is the burden of my parenthetical comments, in the preceding paragraph, on the first and fourth sentences.) But let us grant that, from the Mereologist's point of view, the analogy is still strong enough to be compelling. (It does not seem that there is any *other* point of view from which it would be strong enough to be compelling.) *If* Mereology is a correct theory of composition, therefore, Lewis's Composition as Identity thesis (in its considered, analogical form) would appear to be correct – and otherwise not. And if the Composition as Identity thesis is correct, then Mereology is ontologically innocent.[11] What Lewis's argument would appear to establish, therefore, is that if Mereology is correct, then it is ontologically innocent. There would seem to be no way to find out whether Mereology is innocent than this: find out whether it is true.

Those who begin by believing that Mereology is false will not accept Lewis's argument for the ontological innocence of Mereology (and they are hardly likely to accept this thesis on some other ground). Whatever reasons persuade them that Mereology is false will persuade them that composition lacks many of the features Lewis claims for it, and will therefore persuade them that composition is not strongly analogous to identity. They will, therefore, reject Lewis's considered, analogical version of the Composition as Identity thesis, and that thesis is the main premise of his argument for the ontological innocence of Mereology.

The Composition as Identity thesis may perhaps provide a reason for someone who accepts Mereology to be pleased with Mereology, but it will not be recognized as an advantage of Mereology by those who do not adhere to its tenets. The theist may regard the fact that theism provides an explanation for the existence of the cosmos as a reason to be pleased with theism, but the atheist who believes – and who believes that he has reasons for believing – that the cosmos does not require an explanation, or that it requires an explanation of a sort that is incompatible

---

[10] Nevertheless, similarities between parthood and identity remain. If an explanation of these similarities is required, perhaps it could be supplied by Armstrong's thesis that overlap is partial identity.

[11] Or so Lewis argues, and let us suppose he is right. But if composition is not really identity, but only very strongly analogous with identity, then what is the force of the argument that, in accepting fusions, we are accepting only what we already believe in? Is the force of this argument not at least somewhat diminished?

with theism, will regard the fact that theism provides an explanation for the cosmos as a defect in theism, an additional reason for rejecting theism. "Genuine Modal Realists" may regard the fact that Genuine Modal Realism provides a reductive analysis of modality as a reason to be pleased with Genuine Modal Realism, but those who reject Genuine Modal Realism will regard this reductive analysis of modality (which they see as assigning the wrong truth-values to modal sentences) as a defect in Genuine Modal Realism.[12] Similarly, those who reject Mereology will regard the strong analogy between composition and identity that is a consequence of Mereology as a defect in Mereology, since (they will say) composition lacks many of the features that a statement of the analogy attributes to it.

[12] See my "Two Concepts of Possible Worlds," *Midwest Studies in Philosophy*, 11 (1986), pp. 185–213, pp. 194–199 in particular.

# 7

# Four-dimensional objects

It is sometimes said that there are two theories of identity across time. First, there is "three-dimensionalism," according to which persisting objects are extended in the three spatial dimensions and have no other kind of extent and persist by "enduring through time" (whatever exactly that means). Secondly, there is "four-dimensionalism," according to which persisting objects are extended not only in the three spatial dimensions, but also in a fourth, temporal, dimension, and persist simply by being temporally extended.

In this paper, I shall argue that there are not two but three possible theories of identity across time, and I shall endorse one of them, a theory that may, as a first approximation, be identified with what I have called "three-dimensionalism." I shall present these three theories as theories about the ways in which our names for persisting objects are related to the occupants (or the alleged occupants) of certain regions of spacetime.

I

Let us begin by considering some object that persists or endures or exhibits identity across time. I will use Descartes as an example of such an object. Let us draw a spacetime diagram (Figure 7.1) that represents Descartes's "career." In order to confer on this diagram maximum powers of accurate representation, let us pretend two things: (1) that the diagram is three-dimensional – made of wire, say, with the z-axis perpendicular to the page – and (2) that Descartes was a "flatlander," that he had only two spatial dimensions.

The outlined three-dimensional region in the diagram – or, since we are imagining that the "diagram" sticks out of the page and is made of wire, let us call it a model – represents a 2 + 1-dimensional region of

First published in *Noûs* 24 (1990), pp. 245–255.

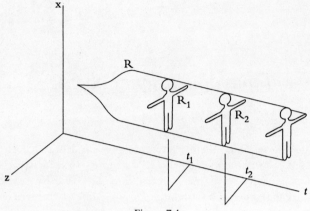

Figure 7.1

spacetime called R. (We represent the dimensionality of regions of
spacetime, and of objects that are extended in time as well as in space, by
expressions of the form "n + 1". In such expressions, "n" represents the
number of spatial dimensions included in the region or exhibited by the
object.) R is the region that some will say was occupied by the $2 + 1$-di-
mensional Descartes; others will call it the union of the class of regions
successively occupied by the always two-dimensional Descartes in the
course of his career. $R_1$ and $R_2$ are subregions of R of zero temporal
extent. Some will describe $R_1$ as the region occupied by the largest part
of Descartes that is wholly confined to $t_1$; others will say that $R_1$ is the
region that Descartes occupied at $t_1$. But, however R, $R_1$, and $R_2$ are to
be described in terms of their relations to Descartes, it's clear which
spacetime regions – that is, which sets of spacetime points – they *are*.

We may now present three theories about how the name "Descartes"
is semantically related to the occupants of R and of subregions of R like
$R_1$ and $R_2$. (Two of these theories, the second and the third, are reflected
in the disagreements I have noted about how to describe R and $R_1$.)

### Theory 1

If you say, "Descartes was hungry at $t_1$," you refer to, and ascribe hunger
to, a two-dimensional object that occupies (fits exactly into) $R_1$ and no
other spacetime region. If you say, "Descartes was thirsty at $t_2$," you
refer to a *distinct* two-dimensional object, one that occupies $R_2$, and

ascribe thirst to it. Let us suppose that both the descriptions "the philosopher who was hungry at $t_1$" and "the philosopher who was thirsty at $t_2$" denote something. It is evident that they cannot denote the *same* thing. It is therefore evident that the sentence "the philosopher who was hungry at $t_1$ = the philosopher who was thirsty at $t_2$" cannot be true. Thus, if those sentences of ordinary English that *appear* to assert that one and the same person (building, river . . .) existed at two different times are ever to be true, what looks like the "is" of identity in them must be interpreted as standing for some other relation than identity – call it gen–identity.

## Theory 2

When you use the name "Descartes" you always refer to the $2 + 1$-dimensional whole that occupies R. When you say "Descartes was hungry at $t_1$," you are referring to this whole and ascribing to it the property of having a $t_1$-part that is hungry. Thus, this sentence is exactly analogous to "Water Street is narrow at the town line": in saying *that*, you refer to the whole of Water Street and ascribe to it the property of having a narrow town-line-part. What occupies $R_1$ is not what anyone, ever, even at $t_1$, refers to as "Descartes"; it is, rather, a proper temporal part of the single referent that "Descartes" always has.

## Theory 3

All the regions like $R_1$ and $R_2$ – instantaneous "slices" of R – are occupied by the very same two-dimensional object. When we say that Descartes was hungry at $t_1$, we are saying either (take your pick) that this object bore the relation *having* to the time-indexed property *hunger-at-$t_1$*, or else that it bore the time-indexed relation *having-at-$t_1$* to hunger.

The proponent of Theory 3, then, agrees with the proponent of Theory 2 that "The philosopher who was hungry at $t_1$ = the philosopher who was thirsty at $t_2$" can be a genuine identity-sentence and be true; and he agrees with the proponent of Theory 1 that each of the terms of this sentence refers to a two-dimensional object – or, in the real world, a three-dimensional object. (But this second parallel should not be pressed too far. The "Oneist" holds that the terms of this sentence refer to objects that have non-zero extent in the spatial dimensions, but zero temporal extent: in *that* sense they are two-dimensional in our imaginary world, and three-

113

dimensional in the real world. The "Threeist," on the other hand, is probably not going to want to talk about temporal extent at all, not even temporal extent of zero measure. I shall presently return to this point.)

I am a proponent of Theory 3. In this paper, I can't hope to say even a fraction of what there is to be said about the questions raised by these three theories. I want to do just two things. First, to address some arguments for the conclusion that Theory 3 is incoherent, and, secondly, to present an argument for the conclusion that Theory 2 commits its adherents to a counterpart-theoretical analysis of modal statements about individuals. That hardly constitutes a refutation of Theory 2, of course, but, if true, it is an important truth; and it does seem that most philosophers, including, I suppose, many adherents of Theory 2, find counterpart theory rather unattractive. (I will not further discuss Theory 1, except in relation to one very special point. I doubt whether anyone would prefer Theory 1 to Theory 2.)

## II

In this section, I shall reply to four arguments for the conclusion that Theory 3 is incoherent. I shall also attempt to answer two pointed questions that my replies to these arguments are likely to raise.[1]

*Argument A*  What exactly fills one region of spacetime cannot be what exactly fills another.

*Reply*  Any plausibility that this assertion may have arises from an illegitimate analogy with the clearly true principle:

> What exactly fills one region of *space* at a given time cannot be what exactly fills a distinct region of *space* at that time.

This is valid for a space of any number of dimensions. Suppose spacetime is $9 + 1$-dimensional, as in "superstring" theories. Then space is nine-dimensional and what occupies any, e.g., four-dimensional region of

---

[1] Three of the arguments – A, B, and D – and the pointed questions are taken from letters I have received from, and conversations I have had with, various philosophers. I am particularly grateful to David Armstrong, Mark Heller, Frances Howard-Snyder, Michael Levin, David Lewis, and Michael Patton. Argument C is an adaptation of some points that have been made by David Lewis. See his discussion of "the problem of temporary intrinsics" in *On the Plurality of Worlds* (Oxford, 1986), pp. 202–204, and 210.

space at t is not what occupies any other four-dimensional region at t – or any two- or seven-dimensional region. But the corresponding *spacetime* principle is wrong, or at least not self-evident, and would be wrong, or not self-evident, for any number of dimensions.

The spacetime principle may get an illusory boost from our three-dimensional physical model of a $2 + 1$-dimensional spacetime. The two-dimensional region of space that represents $R_1$ in the physical model, and the two-dimensional region of space that represents $R_2$ in the model, cannot, of course, be simultaneously occupied by the same two-dimensional physical object. But it no more follows that $R_1$ and $R_2$ must have different occupants than it follows from the fact that two photographs are in different places at the same time that they are not photographs of the same object. Our model occupies a three-dimensional region of space; one axis of the model has been arbitrarily assigned the task of representing the temporal dimension of a $2 + 1$-dimensional spacetime. But this three-dimensional region of space is simply *not* a $2 + 1$-dimensional region of spacetime, and the properties of a $2 + 1$-dimensional region of spacetime can be read from the model only with caution. In my view, at least, any support that the physical model seems to give to the spacetime principle is an "artifact of the model." We could perhaps imagine a universe – call it Flatland – associated with a $2 + 1$-dimensional spacetime, a universe whose spatial dimensions at different times coincided with those of appropriate cross-sections of the model. If the speed of light in Flatland were low enough, time-like intervals in the spacetime of Flatland might even be made to coincide in a non-arbitrary way with appropriate spatial intervals in the model. Nevertheless, the space the model occupies would not be a *duplicate* of the spacetime of Flatland, but only a representation of it.

*Argument B* (The "Twoist" speaks.) "Do you say that only a part of Descartes occupies $R_1$, or that all of him does? In the former case, you agree with me – in the latter, well it's just obvious that you haven't got all of him in there."

*Reply* I cannot yet answer this question because the appropriate senses of "part of" and "all of" have not yet been defined. I shall return to this question. For the nonce, I will say that my position is that *Descartes* occupies both $R_1$ and $R_2$, and that if you understand "part of Descartes" and "all of Descartes," then you understand "Descartes."

*Argument C* Theory 3 must employ either time-indexed properties or the three-term relation "x has F at *t*." But how are these properties, or this relation, to be understood? Take the case of the relation. We are familiar with the relation "x has F," the relation that holds between an object and its properties. If we are to understand the three-term relation, we must be able to define it using the two-term relation and other notions we understand. (We cannot simply take "x has F at *t*" as primitive, for that would leave the logical connections between the two-term and the three-term relation unexplained.) The "Twoist" has such a definition:

> x has F at *t* = $_{df}$ the *t*-part of x has F.

But the "Threeist" has no such definition. He must leave the relationship between *has-at-t* and *has* a mystery – and a wholly unnecessary mystery, at that. One might as well postulate a mysterious, inexplicable connection between "x has F" and "x has F at the place p." Just as it is obvious that "The US is densely populated in the Northeast" means "The northeastern part of the US is densely populated", it is obvious that "The US was sparsely populated in 1800" means "The 1800-part of the US was sparsely populated".

*Reply* One may say both that the relation "x has F at t" is primitive and that its connection with "x has F" is not inexplicable. One need only maintain that "x has F" is the defined or derived relation, and "x has F at t" the undefined or primitive relation. (Such cases are common enough. Consider, say, "x is a child of y" and "x is a child of y and z.") And I do maintain this. To say that Descartes had the property of being human is to say that he had that property at every time at which he existed. To say that he had the property of being a philosopher is to say that he had that property at every member of some important and salient class of moments – his adult life, say. I concede that "x has F" is primitive and "x has F at the place p" is derived (or, more exactly, that "x has F at *t*" is primitive and "x has F at *t* at p" is derived). But I see no reason why I should take the interaction of place and predication as a model for the interaction of time and predication. It may be that both space and time are abstractions from the concrete reality of spacetime. But they are *different* abstractions, and may be differently related to many things, including predication.

*Argument D* What occupies $R_1$ – call it $D_1$ – is clean-shaven. What occupies $R_2$ – call it $D_2$ – is bearded. Hence, $D_1$ is not identical with $D_2$.

*Reply*  $R_1$ and $R_2$ are *indices*. Descartes is clean-shaven at $R_1$ and bearded at $R_2$. Let $R_3$ be a region of spacetime that was occupied by Mark Brown at some instant in 1973. I could point at Brown and say (correctly), "See that bearded man over there? He is clean-shaven at $R_3$."

*Pointed Question 1*  So "that man over there" occupies $R_3$, a region that fell within 1973. *When* does he occupy it?

*Answer*  When is the proposition that Descartes was born on March 31, 1596 true? Say what you like: that it's timelessly true, that the question is meaningless, that it's always true, that, strictly speaking, there is no *time* at which it's true . . . and I'll obligingly adopt the corresponding answer to your question.

*Pointed Question 2*  So Descartes occupies both $R_1$ and $R_2$. What occupies $R$? And what properties does it have? Please describe them carefully.

*Answer*  Well, it's not clear that I'm forced to say that *anything* occupies R. But let's assume that something does. It seems plausible to suppose that if something occupies $R_1$ and $R_2$ then, if anything occupies $R_1 \cup R_2$, it must be the mereological sum of what occupies $R_1$ and what occupies $R_2$. And it seems plausible to generalize this thesis: if something occupies the union of a class of regions of spacetime, and if each member of that class is occupied by something, then the thing that occupies the union must be the mereological sum of the things that individually occupy the members of the class.

Now the region R is the union of an infinite class of regions that includes $R_1$ and $R_2$ and indenumerably many other regions much like them. Each of these regions, *I* say, is occupied by, and only by, Descartes. It follows from this and our "plausible supposition" that it is *Descartes* that occupies R.

You ask me to describe carefully the properties of this object. An historian of early modern philosophy could do this better than I, but I can certainly tell you that it was human, that it was French, that it was educated by the Jesuits, that it wrote *Meditations on First Philosophy*, that it believed that its essence was thinking, that it died in Sweden, and many things of a like nature.

Of course, the question is a little imprecise, since the occupant of R had different properties at different indices – it was, for example, hungry at $R_1$ and full at many other regions. If you insist on treating $R$ as an index, and ask what properties the occupant of $R$ had *at R*, it seems most reasonable to say: only those properties that it had at *all* the "momentary" indices like $R_1$ and $R_2$: *being human*, say, or *having been born in 1596*.

We may note that if Descartes occupies $R$ as well as $R_1$ and $R_2$, this explains why the adherent of Theory 3 and the adherent of Theory 1 cannot mean quite the same thing by saying that the referent of, e.g., "the philosopher who was hungry at $t_1$" is – in the real world and not in our simplified $2 + 1$–dimensional world – a three-dimensional object. The "Oneist" means by a three-dimensional object (at least in this context) one that has a greater-than-zero extent in each of the three spatial dimensions, and zero extent in the temporal dimension. But the "Threeist," if he takes the option we are now considering, believes that Descartes occupied $R_1$, which is of zero temporal extent, and also occupied $R$, which has a temporal extent of fifty-four years – and, presumably, that he occupies regions having extents whose measures in years correspond to every real number between 0 and 54. Therefore, in his view, Descartes did not have a unique temporal extent. That is to say, he didn't have a temporal extent at all; the concept of a temporal extent does not apply to Descartes or to any other object that persists or endures or exhibits identity across time. Thus, in saying that the philosopher who was hungry at $t_1$ was a three-dimensional object, the "Threeist" means that he had a greater-than-zero extent in each of the three spatial dimensions – and that's all.

This completes my attempt to meet the most obvious arguments for the incoherency of Theory 3. I now turn to the promised argument for the conclusion that Theory 2 commits its adherents to a counterpart-theoretical understanding of modal statements about individuals.

### III

Theory 2 entails that persisting objects, objects like Descartes, are sums of *temporal parts*. That is, the "Twoist" holds that persisting objects are extended in time, and are sums of "briefer" temporally extended objects. Descartes, for example, extended from 1596 to 1650, and, for any connected sub-interval of that fifty-four-year interval, that sub-interval was occupied by a temporal part of Descartes. (He may also have had discontinuous or "gappy" temporal parts, but, if so, we shall not need to consider them.)

118

Now it does not seem to be the case that Descartes had a temporal
extent of fifty-four years essentially: his temporal extent might have been
one year or fifty-five years or even a hundred years. But how will the
Twoist understand this modal fact, given his thesis that Descartes is an
aggregate of temporal parts? He will almost certainly not say *this*: If Descartes had had a different temporal extent from his actual temporal
extent, he would have been composed of exactly the same temporal parts
that composed him in actuality, but some or all those parts would have
had a different temporal extent from their actual temporal extent. For
example, it is not likely that the Twoist will say that if Descartes had had
a temporal extent of eighty-one years, he would have been composed of
exactly the same temporal parts, each of which would have had a temporal extent half again as great as its actual temporal extent. No, the
Twoist will want to say that if a temporally extended object like Descartes has different temporal extents in different possible worlds, it must
accomplish this feat by being the sum of different (although perhaps
overlapping) sets of temporal parts in those worlds. And the Twoist will
want to say this because he will want to say that temporal parts (i.e.,
objects that are temporal parts of something) have their temporal extents
*essentially*. The Twoist will want to say that it would make no sense to
say of the temporal part of Descartes that occupied the year 1620 that it
might have had an extent of a year and a half: any object in another possible world that has a temporal extent of a year and a half is some other
object than the object that in actuality is the 1620-part of Descartes. We
may summarize this point by saying that the Twoist will want to maintain that temporal parts are "modally inductile" (and "modally incom-
pressible" as well). And I am sure that the Twoist is right to want to say
these things. If there are objects of the sort the Twoist calls temporal
parts, then their temporal extents must belong to their essence.

But then the argument against Theory 2 is almost embarrassingly
simple. If Theory 2 is correct, then Descartes is composed of temporal
parts, and all temporal parts are modally inductile. But Descartes himself
is one of his temporal parts – the largest one, the sum of all of them. But
then Descartes is himself modally inductile, which means he could not
have had a temporal extent greater than fifty-four years. But this is obviously false, and Theory 2 is therefore wrong.

We may also reach this conclusion by a slightly different route. If
Theory 2 is correct, then there is an object, a temporal part of Descartes,
that we may call his "first half." Now suppose that Descartes had been

119

annihilated halfway through his actual span: then Descartes would have *been* the object that is in actuality his "first half." (At least I think so. In a possible world in which Descartes ceased to exist at the appropriate moment, Descartes would have existed – we have so stipulated – and so would the object that is, in actuality, his first half. At least I *think* it would have. How not? But if they both existed in such a world, what could the relation between them be but identity?) But if Descartes and a numerically distinct object could have been identical, then they conspire to violate the very well established modal principle that a thing and another thing could not have been a thing and itself.

There seems to me to be only one way for the Twoist to reply to these arguments. The Twoist must adopt a counterpart-theoretical analysis of modal statements about individuals. And he must suppose that there are two different counterpart relations that figure in our modal statements about the object X that is both the person Descartes and the largest temporal part of Descartes: a *personal* counterpart relation and a *temporal-part* counterpart relation. According to this view of things, an object in some other world will count as a temporal-part counterpart of X only if it has the same temporal extent as X – anything that lacks this feature will be *ipso facto* insufficiently similar to X to be a counterpart of X under that counterpart relation. But an object in another world will count as a personal counterpart of X only if, like X, it is a maximal aggregate of temporal parts of persons. (That is, only if it is a temporal part of a person and its mereological union with any temporal part of a person that is not one of its own parts is not a temporal part of a person.) This device will allow us to say that X, which is both a temporal part and a person, could not have had a greater temporal extent *qua* temporal part and could have had a greater temporal extent *qua* person. That is: while every temporal-part counterpart of X has the same temporal extent as X, some personal counterparts of X have greater temporal extents than X. (As to the second argument: (i) counterpart theory allows world-mates to have a common counterpart in another world; (ii) this liberality is irrelevant in the present case, for if an object Y in another world is a maximal aggregate of temporal parts of persons that is an intrinsic duplicate of the first half of X, Y will not be a counterpart of *both* X and the first half of X under either counterpart relation.)

This reply to our two arguments is certainly satisfactory – provided that one is willing to accept counterpart theory. (It is important to realize that, as Stalnaker has pointed out, one can accept counterpart theory without accepting the modal ontology – David Lewis's "extreme" or "genuine" modal realism – that originally motivated it.[2] I can see no other satisfactory reply to these arguments. I conclude that the proponents of Theory 2 are committed to a counterpart-theoretical analysis of modal statements about individuals.[3]

[2] Robert Stalnaker, "Counterparts and Identity," *Midwest Studies in Philosophy* 11 (1986), pp. 121–140.

[3] Versions of this essay were read at departmental colloquia at the University of Massachusetts, Amherst, Virginia Polytechnic Institute and State University, Wayne State University, and York University. I am grateful to the audiences at these colloquia for their useful comments and questions. Special thanks are due to David Cowles, Fred Feldman, Edmund Gettier, Toomas Karmo, Cranston Paul, Larry Powers, and Jonathan Vogel.

# 8

# *Temporal parts and identity across time*

Many philosophers think that "What is identity across time?" is an important and meaningful question. I have a great deal of trouble seeing what this question might be. But, very often, if one cannot understand a philosophical question, one's best course is to look at some alleged answers to it; sometimes these answers enable one to see what question it is that they are offered as answers to. The following passage by Michael Tooley is supposed to provide an answer to the question we are trying to get at.

[W]hat does it mean to say, for example, that the book on the table at time $t$ is identical with the book on the chair at time $t^\star$? One answer is that it means that the object referred to by the expression "the book on the table at time $t$" is the same object as that referred to by the expression "the book on the chair at time $t^\star$." But one need not rest with this superficial account, since one can go on to ask what is meant by "the object referred to by the expression 'the book on the table at time $t^\star$'". And one very natural answer is this. The expression "the book on the table at time $t$" picks out a certain spatially and temporally limited part of the world, and it does so either by picking out an instantaneous slice, of the book variety, which exists at time $t$, or else by picking out a relatively small non-instantaneous temporal part, of the book variety, which occupies a small interval containing time $t$ and then by linking this up with all other slices (or parts) of the relevant sort which stand in a certain causal relation to the slice (or part) existing at (or around) time $t$.[1]

Let us examine this answer carefully. I shall write as if Tooley accepted his "one very natural answer," since this answer encapsulates a point of view I wish to examine and it will be convenient to have someone to at-

First published in *The Monist* 83/3 (2000), pp. 437–459.

[1] Michael Tooley, critical notice of Alvin Plantinga's *The Nature of Necessity*, *Australasian Journal of Philosophy* 55 (1977), pp. 91–102. The quoted passage occurs on pp. 97–98.

tribute it to; if Tooley is not fully committed to this answer, I apologize to him for taking this liberty.[2]

There are two important theses on display in this passage. One is a thesis about the existence of certain objects, and the other is a thesis about the relation of certain phrases in our language to those objects. The first thesis is that there are such things as "temporal parts" or "temporal slices." (The difference between very "thin" temporal parts and temporal slices does not matter much in the present context. I shall talk mainly of "slices," but what I shall say could be applied to "thin parts" easily enough.) The second thesis is that the way in which "time-involving" definite descriptions of physical objects like "the book on the table at *t*" relate to their referents should be analyzed or explained in terms of slices.

One thesis about the referents of time-involving descriptions that Tooley clearly does *not* hold is this: that phrases like "the book on the table at time *t*" actually denote slices; that "the book on the table at time *t*" denotes the "*t*-slice" of the book. Philosophers who hold *this* view must either say that sentences like "The book on the table at time *t* is identical with the book on the chair at time *t★*" must always express propositions that are, strictly speaking, false, or else they must say that in such sentences "is identical with" does not express the idea of numerical identity – two slices being *two* slices – but rather some relation of causal or spatiotemporal continuity.[3]

Tooley's view of the matter is more artful and does not confront this awkward dilemma. As Tooley sees it, "the book on the table at *t*" is a name for a certain four-dimensional object, one having slices "of the book variety" as parts, these parts being bound together into a whole by (again) some relation of causal or spatiotemporal continuity. As Tooley sees it, the phrase "the book on the table at *t*" means something like "the four-dimensional book the *t*-slice of which is on (the *t*-slice) of the table" and, similarly, "the book on the chair at *t★*" means "the four-dimensional book the *t★*-slice of which is on (the *t★*-slice) of the chair." And, of course, no particular problems are raised by the assertion that two such descriptions as these might be names for a single object.

Both these theories about the way in which time-involving definite

---

[2] The theory I am ascribing to Tooley is very like the theory I called "Theory 2" in "Four-dimensional Objects," *Noûs* 24 (1990), pp. 245–255 (Chapter 7 of the present volume).

[3] This is the theory I called "Theory 1" in "Four-dimensional Objects."

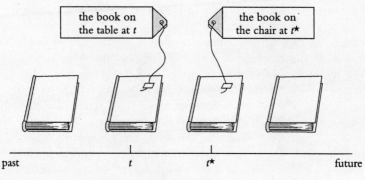

Figure 8.1

descriptions are related to the world can be represented pictorially. The first theory can be represented as shown in Figure 8.1. The line drawn beneath this figure is a "time-axis": each point on it represents a point in time, the left-to-right arrangement of the points representing the past-to-future arrangement of points in time. The "books" drawn above the time-axis represent slices "of the book variety." I have, of course, been able to represent only a few such slices: the viewer must somehow contrive to imagine that the sequence of book-drawings is continuous, just as the sequence of points on the line is. Each book-slice-representation is drawn directly above the point that represents the point in time it "occupies." Finally, the description–referent relation is represented by labels bearing the description and attached to the referent. (I don't mean this device in any sense to represent the "mechanics" of securing reference. It is meant to be neutral with respect to theories of what reference is and how it is established. It is used merely to display the fact that certain phrases denote certain objects.)

The second theory, Tooley's theory, may be represented by the picture shown in Figure 8.2. In this picture, the time-axis and the books mean what they meant in Figure 8.1. The rectangle represents the boundary of the four-dimensional object that is what the book really is. The description–referent relation is again represented by labels, but the labels are fixed to the "whole" book and not to slices of the book. More-over, each of the cords attaching the labels to the "whole" book passes through a book-slice – the same slice it is attached to in Figure 8.1 – on its way to its point of attachment to the book. This feature of the picture is intended to represent Tooley's idea that a description like "the book

124

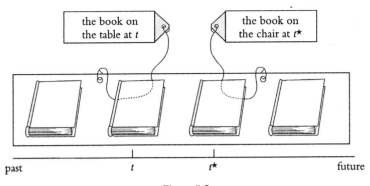

Figure 8.2

on the chair at *t*" gets "linked up with" the book *via* the *t*-slice of the book. (The points of attachment of the labels have no significance; I have to draw them as attached *somewhere*.)

In my view, these pictures embody grave illusions about the nature of enduring objects and about the way in which time-involving descriptions apply to their referents and about the kind of facts expressed by sentences formed by flanking the identity sign with time-involving descriptions. (Let us call such sentences "temporal identity-sentences.") I believe it is a grave illusion to suppose that there are four-dimensional objects or that things are somehow composed of "temporal parts" or "slices" or that the facts represented by temporal identity-sentences even look as if they were facts about such objects. I believe that people who suppose such things as these are the victims of seductive but incoherent pictures – pictures like Figure 8.1 and Figure 8.2, in fact. In the previous essay, "Four-dimensional Objects," I presented arguments for the following conclusion: the thesis that an enduring object is composed of temporal parts has unacceptable modal consequences. But these arguments were far from conclusive. For one thing – not the only thing – , they presupposed that a counterpart-theoretical account of modality *de re* was unacceptable. I might in this essay try to plug some of the holes in the argument of "Four-dimensional Objects." I might, for example, try to show why I believe a counterpart-theoretical account of modality *de re* to be unacceptable. I will not do this. I propose instead first to explain why I find temporal parts hard to understand, and, secondly, to describe how identity across time "looks" to someone who has no grasp of temporal parts – to provide a "picture" of identity across time that is a rival

125

to the pictures presented in Figures 8.1 and 8.2. Finally, I shall show how to draw a third picture, for Figures 8.1 and 8.2 have at least one rival, a rival that is far more different from them than they are from each other.

II

What are temporal parts supposed to be? – or, if you like, What is "temporal part" supposed to mean? Many philosophers find these things, and this phrase, wholly unproblematic. They construct elegant solutions to various philosophical problems by appealing to temporal parts, and they seem to assume that these objects enjoy the same methodological rights as numbers or sets: although there are philosophical problems that could be raised in connection with them (I daresay they will be willing to concede that much), temporal parts are well enough understood that philosophers can appeal to them without incurring any obligation to interrupt their discussions of personal identity – or whatever – to explain them. (The most celebrated example of this sort of appeal to temporal parts would probably be Quine's "Identity, Ostension, and Hypostasis."[4])

Well, isn't it pretty clear what they are? We have, after all, perfectly intelligible *names* for them. For example: "St. Paul's in 1850" and "Philip drunk." (The second of these is presumably a name for a non-connected part of Philip.) And we understand these names perfectly well, because we understand perfectly well the sentences in which they occur: "St. Paul's in 1850 was dingier than St. Paul's last year"; "Philip drunk is rash, but Philip sober is crafty." And if we understand the names, we understand the things: "temporal part" is merely the general term that covers objects like St. Paul's in 1850 and Philip drunk.

I do not think this is right, for I do not think that "St. Paul's in 1850" and "Philip drunk" are names at all. Let us look at some sentences in which these phrases occur. To start with, let us look at "St. Paul's in 1850 was dingy." In this sentence, "in 1850" is an adverbial phrase modifying "was": When was St. Paul's dingy?; In 1850, at any rate.[5] It is,

---

[4] *From a Logical Point of View* (Cambridge, Mass., 1953), pp. 65–79.

[5] Achille Varzi has asked me several questions about my analysis of the role of "in 1850" in the sentence "St. Paul's in 1850 was dingy." They could be summed up in this question: "Granted, 'in 1850' is not an adjective modifying 'St. Paul's'; but is the only alternative that it is an adverb modifying 'was'? – are there not other possibilities?" According to the traditional grammar I was taught in school, the copula "was" is "the verb of" the sentence, "St. Paul's in 1850 was dingy" and "in 1850" modifies it. But a

therefore, a mistake to think of this sentence as having a structure like this:

| *St. Paul's* | *in 1850* | *was* | *dingy* |
|---|---|---|---|
| substantive | attributive adjective | copula | predicate adjective |

| subject | | predicate | |

Its structure is rather this:

| *St. Paul's* | *in 1850* | *was* | *dingy* |
|---|---|---|---|
| substantive | adverb | copula | predicate adjective |

| subject | | predicate | |

Philosophers who do not recognize the adverbial function of phrases like "in 1850," and who treat them as if they were adjectives modifying the subjects of the verbs they in fact modify, are guilty of a fallacy I like to call adverb-pasting. If the adverb-pasters were given free rein, all manner of fascinating philosophical problems would be created. Consider, for example, the sentence

> Alice, viewed full-face, is strikingly beautiful, but Alice, viewed in profile, is aesthetically unremarkable.

Here we have the germ of the problem of cross-perspectival identity: what is the relation between the strikingly beautiful Alice-viewed-full-face and the aesthetically unremarkable Alice-viewed-in-profile? And

more up-to-date grammar might tell us that when "to be" functions as a copula, it does not belong to the grammatical category "verb" (despite the fact that "to be," whatever its function, displays the grammatical accidence traditionally definitive of the category "verb": tense, voice, mood, aspect), but rather to the category "takes an adjective and makes a verb." According to this view of the matter, the simplest verb in "St. Paul's in 1850 was dingy" is "was dingy" – the past tense of the verb "to be dingy" – and "in 1850" modifies "was dingy" (applies to it to produce the complex verb "was dingy in 1850'). Another up-to-date view of the function of "in 1850" in this sentence is this: "in 1850" is not an adverb (a "takes a verb and makes a verb") at all, but a sentence-modifier, a representative of the grammatical category "takes a sentence and makes a sentence"; in the present case, it modifies "St. Paul's was dingy." Which of these three accounts of the function of "in 1850" is correct – if there is indeed a fact of the grammatical matter – makes no difference for our purposes, for each account has the consequence that "St. Paul's in 1850" is not a noun-phrase and hence does not represent itself as denoting an object. In the text, I presuppose the traditional view, but the correctness of the traditional view is in no way essential to my arguments. My arguments could easily be expressed in the terms provided by either of the "up-to-date" accounts of the function of "in 1850."

127

there is the problem of cross-evaluational identity: what is the relation between the brilliant Hume-according-to-Professor-A and the doltish Hume-according-to-Professor-B?

More or less the same points (to revert to the case of temporal adverbs) apply to more complicated sentences, like our "St. Paul's in 1850 was dingier than St. Paul's last year." The grammatical structure of this sentence may be compared with the grammatical structure of "Condorcet as representative figure of the Enlightenment is more interesting than Condorcet as original thinker." ("Condorcet is interesting." "How? In what respects?" "Well, as a representative figure of the Enlightenment; less so as an original thinker." "St. Paul's was dingy." "When? At what times?" "Well, in 1850; less so last year.") I trust that no one will want to say that "Condorcet as representative figure of the Enlightenment" is a name of a certain temporal part of Condorcet, a part that comprises just those moments at which he was engaged in representing the Enlightenment, while "Condorcet as original thinker" is a name of the part of Condorcet that comprises those moments at which he was engaged in original thought.

A similar account applies to "Philip drunk." As a first approximation to a correct account of the sentences in which this phrase figures, we may say that a sentence like "Philip drunk is rash" is just a fancy way of saying "Philip, when he is drunk, is rash," or – even less fancy – "Philip is rash when he is drunk." (We may compare "Philip drunk is rash, but Philip sober is crafty" to "Philip the man is rash, but Philip the politician is crafty." Lest someone argue that "Philip the politician" is a name for a temporal part of Philip, the part comprising just those moments at which he was engaged in politics, we may stipulate that all Philip's actions had both a personal and a political component, and that the utterer of our sentence means by it that Philip rarely thought about the consequences of his acts for himself and his friends and family, but always thought carefully about their political consequences.) I say "as a first approximation" because the rhetoricians have been at "Philip drunk." Availing themselves of the fact that "Philip drunk" can look rather like a substantive, they have produced conceits like this: "Macedon has two kings, Philip drunk and Philip sober." But this sort of trope (doubtless the Greeks had a word for it) is of no ontological interest. We should remind ourselves that it may have influenced our thinking and then turn our attention to more profitable matters.

We cannot, therefore, explain "temporal part" by saying that it is "merely the general term that covers objects like St. Paul's in 1850 and Philip drunk." What other explanations are available? I know of only one. It is due to David Lewis, and, as one might expect, it repays close attention.

Some would protest that they do not know what I mean by "more or less momentary person-stages, or times-slices of continuant persons, or persons-at-times." Others do know what I mean, but don't believe there are any such things.

The first objection is easy to answer, especially in the case where the stages are less momentary rather than more. Let me consider that case only; though I think that instantaneous stages also are unproblematic, I do not really need them. A person-stage is a physical object, just as a person is. (If persons had a ghostly part as well, so would person-stages.) It does many of the same things that a person does: it talks and walks and thinks, it has beliefs and desires, it has a size and shape and location. It even has a temporal duration. But only a brief one, for it does not last long. (We can pass over the question how long it can last before it is a segment rather than a stage, for that question raises no objection of principle.) It begins to exist abruptly, and it abruptly ceases to exist soon after. Hence a stage cannot do everything that a person can do, for it cannot do those things that a person does over a longish interval.

That is what I mean by a person-stage. Now to argue for my claim that they exist, and that they are related to persons as part to whole. I do not suppose the doubters will accept my premises, but it will be instructive to find out which they choose to deny.

First: it is possible that a person-stage might exist. Suppose it to appear out of thin air, then vanish again. Never mind whether it is a stage of any person (though in fact I think it is). My point is that it is the right sort of thing.

Second: it is possible that two person-stages might exist in succession, one right after the other but without overlap. Further, the qualities and location of the second at its appearance might exactly match those of the first at its disappearance. Here I rely on a *patchwork principle* for possibility: if it is possible that X happen intrinsically in a spatiotemporal region, and if it is likewise possible that Y happen in a region, then also it is possible that both X and Y happen in two distinct but adjacent regions. There are no necessary incompatibilities between distinct existences. Anything can follow anything.

Third: extending the previous point; it is possible that there might be a world of stages that is exactly like our own world in its point-by-point distribution of intrinsic local qualities over space and time.

Fourth: further, such a world of stages might also be exactly like our own in its causal relations between local matters of particular fact. For nothing but the distribution of local qualities constrains the pattern of causal relations. (It would be simpler to say that the causal relations supervene on the distribution of local qualities, but I am not as confident of that as I am of the weaker premise.)

Fifth: then such a world of stages would be exactly like our own simpliciter. There are no features of our world except those that supervene on the distribution of local qualities and their causal relations.

Sixth: then our own world is a world of stages. In particular, person stages exist.

Seventh: but persons exist too, and persons (in most cases) are not person-stages. They last too long. Yet persons and person-stages, like tables and table-legs, do not occupy spatiotemporal regions twice over. That can only be because they are not distinct. They are part-identical; in other words, the person-stages are parts of the persons.

Let me try to forestall two misunderstandings. (1) When I say that persons are maximal aggregates of person-stages, I do *not* claim to be reducing "constructs" to "more basic entities." (Since I do not intend a reduction to the basic, I am free to say without circularity that person-stages are aggregates of shorter person-stages.) Similarly, I think it is an informative necessary truth that trains are maximal aggregates of cars interrelated by the ancestral of the relation of being coupled together (count the locomotive as a special kind of car). But I do not think of this as a reduction to the basic. Whatever "more basic" is supposed to mean, I don't think it means "smaller." (2) By a part, I just mean a subdivision. I do not mean a well-demarcated subdivision that figures as a unit in causal explanation. Those who give "part" a rich meaning along these lines should take me to mean less by it than they do.[6]

In a way this is all very straightforward. In another way, it puzzles me deeply. Let me try to explain my puzzlement. I shall begin by restating (I hope that is what I am doing) Lewis's explanation. I shall, as Lewis does, speak here only of the stages or parts of *persons*, but what I shall say, like what he says, is easily generalized.

We could easily devise some sort of set-theoretical object to play the role of the "career" of a person: perhaps a function from moments of time to sets of momentary properties[7] could be called a *career*, and a given career could be said to be the career *of* a given object if its domain is just the set of moments at which the object exists and it assigns to any moment just the set of momentary properties that object has at that moment. A *part* of the career of a person or other object would then be a function whose domain is a subset of the career's domain and which, in its domain, takes on the same values as the career. It follows from our definition of "career" that a part of a career is itself a career, though not necessarily the career of anything. A *Lewis-part* of a given person is an object whose career is part of the career of that person.[8]

[6] David Lewis, "In Defense of Stages," Appendix B to "Survival and Identity," in *Philosophical Papers I* (New York, 1983), pp. 76–77.

[7] A momentary property is a property an object could have at one time and lack at another – like "being seated" and "being Socrates' widow," and unlike "being descended from King David."

[8] This definition leaves open the question whether there may be parts of a person's career that are "topologically unsuited" to being the careers of objects. Suppose, by suitable

Since I understand all these words, I understand "Lewis-part" and know what Lewis-parts are. In a way. In the same way as the way in which I should understand talk of "propertyless objects" if I were told that "propertyless object" meant "object of which nothing is true"; in the same way as that in which I should understand talk of "two-dimensional cups" if I were told that "two-dimensional cup" meant "cup that lies entirely in a plane." These phrases would not be what one might call "semantical nonsense" for me; they would not be like "abracadabra" or "machine that projects beams of porous light" or "Das Nichts nichtet." But I should hardly care to say that I understood what someone was talking about (even if it were he who had given me these definitions) who talked of propertyless objects or two-dimensional cups, and who, moreover, talked of them in a way that suggested that he supposed there *were* such things. For I cannot see how there could be any such things. In fact, I think I can see clearly and distinctly why there could not possibly be any propertyless objects or two-dimensional cups (so defined). And this is very nearly the position I am in with respect to Lewis-parts. I say "very nearly" because the idea of a Lewis-part is obviously not an impossible idea, not an idea that could correspond to no possible reality, for each of us obviously has at least one Lewis-part: himself. (So much is immediately evident from the definition.) But what about the "other" temporal parts of persons, their *proper* temporal parts, the objects whose careers are proper parts of the careers of persons? How can I say I can't see how there could be any such things in the face of Lewis's argument? I say this because I do not understand the step in his argument labeled "second." The pivotal sentence in the step "second" is: "It is possible that two person-stages might exist in succession, one right after the other but without overlap." I cannot see how two person-stages could exist "in succession, one right after the other but without overlap." I will try, in Quine's words, to evoke the appropriate sense of bewilderment. God could, I suppose, create *ex nihilo*, and annihilate a year later, a human

correlation of numbers with moments of time, we associate the domain of Descartes's career with the real numbers 0 through 1, inclusive (we should be able to do this if there was both a first and a last moment of Descartes's existence). Could the part of Descartes's career whose domain is the rational numbers between 0 and 1 be the career of an object? A part whose domain is a set that has no Lebesque measure? How about some relatively well-behaved (topologically speaking) but non-connected set? — say, one corresponding to March 1610 and Good Friday, 1633? These are questions that we can leave to the friends of temporal parts. How they are answered is irrelevant to our argument.

being[9] whose intrinsic properties at any instant during the year of its existence were identical with the intrinsic properties of, say, Descartes at the "corresponding" instant in, say, the year 1625. And if God could do that, he could certainly create and annihilate a second human being whose one-year career corresponded in the same way to the 1626-part of Descartes's career. But could God, so to speak, lay these two creations end-to-end? (I ignore nice points about open and closed intervals of time.) Well, he could create, and two years later annihilate, a human being whose two-year career corresponded to the 1625/1626-part of Descartes's career. He could do this, but I don't see what else, what more, he could do to accomplish the goal of "laying these two creations end-to-end." What I cannot see is how, if God did this, it could be that the "two-year-man" would have first and second "halves." More exactly, I don't see how it could be that the first half of the two-year-man's career could be the career of anything, and I don't see how it could be that the second half of the two-year-man's career could be the career of anything. When I examine the story of the creation and annihilation of the two-year-man, I don't find anything in it that comes to the end of its existence after one year: the only thing "there" (as I see matters), the two-year-man, will *not* come to an end after one year; he will, rather, continue to exist for another year. And, in the same way, when I examine the story, I don't find anything in it that begins to exist halfway through the story.

These remarks are not meant to be a refutation of Lewis's argument. They are meant only to identify the point in the argument at which one philosopher, myself, parts company with Lewis. In identifying this point, I am merely accepting Lewis's invitation: "I do not suppose the doubters will accept my premises, but it will be instructive to find out which they choose to deny."

To recapitulate: in virtue of Lewis's explanation of what temporal parts are, I understand the term "temporal part," but I do not see how (in the sense of "temporal parts" Lewis's explanation has supplied) a thing could have temporal *proper* parts. And this is not the end of my difficulties with proper parts – my difficulties, that is, with understanding how temporal parts (understood as "Lewis parts") could have the features that those who appeal to temporal parts in their philosophical work suppose them to have. When I look at temporal parts through the lens

---

[9] I ignore Kripkean scruples about whether what was apparently a human being that was created *ex nihilo* would really be a human being.

Lewis's explanation supplies, I see things that seem to me obviously to have modal properties at variance with the modal properties that are commonly ascribed to temporal parts. It seems to me to be obvious that the one temporal part of a thing must be "modally ductile" and "modally compressible." Consider, for example, Descartes and his one temporal part, himself. Descartes's one temporal part – Descartes – existed from 1596 to 1650. The object that is called both "Descartes" and "Descartes's only temporal part" might have existed for twice as long as it did (it is modally ductile), and it might have existed for only half as long (it is modally compressible). It seems obvious to me, moreover, that this object might have had entirely different momentary properties at the corresponding points in its career. Suppose, for example, that Descartes had been stolen by Gypsies shortly after he was born; if that had happened, then the object that is in actuality Descartes's one temporal part would still have existed but might well never have acquired the property "is able to speak French." These modal propositions about Descartes's single temporal part seem to be inconsistent with the modal properties that are ascribed to temporal parts by those philosophers who believe that there is useful philosophical work for temporal parts to do, for these philosophers, or most of them, seem to treat temporal parts as things that have their "temporal extensions" and their careers essentially. Now I may be wrong about this. I am doing no more than recording an impression. I can't point to any passage in which a philosopher has said in so many words that temporal parts have either their temporal extensions or their careers essentially. My point is only this: if there are philosophers who think that temporal parts have their temporal extensions and their careers essentially, I can't see how what they believe could be true.

Let us now return to the topic of identity across time. If there are, as I believe, no temporal parts, or if each enduring thing has only one, where does this leave us with respect to this notion? Surely it is temporal parts (or stages, or phases, or whatever) that are the *terms* of the cross-time identity relation? If a thing has no temporal parts, or has only one, what can be meant by the assertion that it exists at different times?

### III

These questions conflate several issues.

First, whether or not there is such a thing as "identity across time," there are certainly what I have called temporal identity-sentences: sentences that consist of "is identical with" flanked by time-involving definite descriptions. Tooley's sentence "The book on the table at $t$ is identical with the book on the chair at $t^\star$" is an example of a temporal identity-sentence, though, as we shall see, it is a rather special one. And, of course, what we say when we utter temporal identity-sentences is often true. Therefore, there are facts that we may call "facts of temporal identity." Does the existence of these facts entail that there is such a relation as "identity across time"? Well, that all depends on what one means by "identity across time." These words are sometimes used as a name for a relation that is not identity and which takes proper temporal parts of enduring things as its terms. This conception is illustrated in Figure 8.1. (But the content of Figure 8.1 is not exhausted by the proposition that there is such a relation. Figure 8.1 also illustrates a semantical thesis: that the time-involving definite descriptions that figure in temporal identity-sentences denote proper temporal parts.) The words "identity across time" are sometimes used as a special name for identity, a name we call identity by when its terms are the four-dimensional wholes that some philosophers take enduring objects to be – rather as "equality" is a name we call identity by when its terms are numbers. This conception is illustrated in Figure 8.2. (But the content of Figure 8.2 is not exhausted by the trivial thesis that four-dimensional objects are identical with themselves. Figure 8.2 also illustrates a semantical thesis: that the time-involving definite descriptions that figure in temporal identity-sentences denote four-dimensional wholes and apply to them only *via* their proper temporal parts.)

If "identity across time" means, as the theory represented by Figure 8.1 says it does, a relation that takes proper temporal parts as its terms, then there is no such thing, for there are no proper temporal parts. But whether or not there is such a thing as "identity across time," there are facts of temporal identity. (Moreover, if there are no proper temporal parts, then the account of facts of temporal identity represented by Figure 8.2 is incorrect, since that account essentially involves proper temporal parts.)

How, then, should we understand facts of temporal identity? I believe that the first step towards understanding these facts must be to dispense with pictures that depict enduring objects as being composed of parts that are distributed along a time-axis. The next step is to replace such pictures with the very simple-minded picture shown in Figure 8.3. In

the book that was
on the table at *t*

the book that was
on the chair at *t*★

Figure 8.3

this picture, as in the others, the "book-drawing" represents a three-dimensional object. (But this is dangerously close to a pun. "Slices" are three-dimensional in the sense that they have an extension of measure zero along one dimension and a non-zero extension in three others. The book-drawing in Figure 8.3 has a non-zero extension in three dimensions *tout court*. "Slices" do not *endure* through time – this is what Wittgenstein would call a grammatical proposition – but are located at a time; books endure.) As in Figure 8.1, each label is attached to a three-dimensional object. As in Figure 8.2, each label is attached to the *same* object. (Thus temporal identity sentences, according to the theory represented in Figure 8.3, are straightforward expressions of numerical identity.) Figure 8.3, unlike its two rivals, assimilates temporal identity-sentences to other identity-sentences. "The book that was on the table at *t* is identical with the book that was on the chair at *t*★" differs from "The book that Bill is reading is identical with the book that Tom is looking for" in only one interesting respect: in the former sentence, "is identical with" is flanked by descriptions whose verbs are in the past tense, and in the latter sentence it is flanked by descriptions whose verbs are in the present tense. (Both sentences, of course, are equally well represented by pictures showing one book twice labeled, which is what would intuitively seem right for a sentence that pivots about "is identical with.")

The acute reader will have noticed the transition in the preceding paragraph (and in Figure 8.3) from Tooley-style time-involving descriptions like "the book on the chair at *t*" – verbless ones, that is – to the time-involving descriptions containing tensed verbs that are the normal time-involving descriptions of everyday discourse. In some simple cases, the verb in such descriptions can be dropped: "The book on the table at noon was red," is good English, though, I would point out, a "that was" is present "in spirit" in this sentence, even if it is unpronounced, for the adverbial phrase "at noon" modifies an understood "was." (Philosophers who suppose that such phrases as "at noon" and "in 1850" are adjectives describing the location of temporal slices or whatnot are, as we have seen, mistaken.) In more complicated cases, there is no possibility of wholly eliminating tensed verbs from time-involving descriptions, as is shown by "the car that used to be owned by the man who will marry the woman who had been the first woman President."

There is one sort of temporal identity-sentence that cannot be represented in any very straightforward way by a picture in the style of Figure 8.3. I have in mind temporal-identity sentences containing so-called phase-sortals. (A phase-sortal is a count-noun such that a given object may fall within its extension at one time but not at another.) Consider, for example

> The surgeon who removed the tumor from my brain is the boy who once shined my shoes.

Obviously (one might argue) we cannot represent a fact of the sort this sentence purports to express by a picture of someone twice labeled, for no one is simultaneously a boy and a surgeon. And it will do the friends of Figure 8.3 no good to protest that the "is" in this sentence is a rhetorical conceit, the strictly correct copula being "was," since pictures in the style of Figure 8.3 are unable to represent the use of a tensed identity-sign.

There are various ways to deal with this problem. One way would be to say that this sentence is not really an identity-sentence at all, but a predication. That is, to say that what the speaker of this sentence is doing is saying of a certain surgeon that he (the surgeon) is now such that as a boy he shined his (the speaker's) shoes and was, moreover, the only boy to do so. I shall not explore this avenue. I shall instead investigate a way of treating this sentence as a real identity-sentence. But what I am going to say is no more than a proposal for dealing with phase-sortal identity-sentences. The "predication" analysis, or some other analysis entirely, may turn out to be more fruitful.

A completely general treatment of phase-sortal identity sentences as real identities would involve a lot of detail. I will show how to treat a special class of phase-sortal identity-sentence, those in which phase-sortals occur only in descriptions of the form

"the" + PHASE-SORTAL + RELATIVE PRONOUN + PREDICATE.

(Our "surgeon" sentence is of this kind.) I do not think that a correct treatment of any phase-sortal identity-sentence will differ in any interesting way from the treatment I shall propose for sentences of this special kind. I propose that phrases of the form displayed above should be regarded as abbreviating phrases of the form

"the" + NON-PHASE-SORTAL + RELATIVE PRONOUN + "when a(n)" + PHASE-SORTAL + PREDICATE.

For example – assuming that "human being" is not a phase-sortal – our "surgeon" sentence can be regarded as an abbreviated version of

> The human being who, when a surgeon, removed a tumor from my brain is the human being who, when a boy, once shined my shoes.

If it is correct to regard our "surgeon" sentence as an abbreviation for this sentence, then the former sentence presents no difficulties for the "tag" model for understanding temporal identity-sentences, since there is no difficulty in picturing a man bearing two labels, each of them bearing one of the descriptions flanking the copula in this sentence; and there is no difficulty in supposing that the man so pictured is correctly labeled.


IV

I turn finally to a nest of interrelated problems about pictorial representation that are faced by anyone who holds that facts of temporal identity are best represented by pictures like Figure 8.3.

Let us begin with some problems about temporal identity-sentences whose subject no longer exists. For example:

> The dog I owned in 1957 was the dog I owned in 1955.

(A moment ago, I made an imaginary critic say, "pictures in the style of Figure 8.3 are unable to represent the use of a tensed identity sign." In the context in which I made him speak, he had a good point. But "was" in *this* sentence is not a tensed identity-sign in the sense that was there at issue. Its tense is not determined by the fact that 1955 was earlier than 1957. It merely reflects the fact that the dog I owned in 1955 and 1957 is now dead. If I had wished to state the same fact of temporal identity in 1958 – when the dog was still alive – I should have used the sentence "The dog I owned in 1957 is the dog I owned in 1955.") One question we might ask is this. What are the tags to be attached to, given that the thing they are supposed to be attached to no longer exists? But this question confuses the represented object with the representation. I am not saying that facts of temporal identity are facts of this form: there are currently existing objects that could be twice labeled with tags on which time-involving descriptions are inscribed. We are not talking about a possible practice of actually tagging objects we could put our hands on; we are talking about drawing pictures of tagged objects, the purpose of these pictures being to serve as graphic, intuitive representations of a certain sort of fact. The tags and the cords are merely diagrammatic representations of semantical reference. And it just is a fact that we can refer to objects that no longer exist: the fact that we can refer to Socrates is not a proof of the immortality of the soul. There may or may not be a philosophical problem about how it is that we can refer to objects that no longer exist, but it does not seem to have much to do with the problem of analyzing temporal-identity sentences. That is, this problem, if it exists, is equally a problem for the proponents of any theory of "identity across time." Therefore, the correct pictorial representation of the fact expressed by the sentence displayed above is simply a picture of a dog (a dog that no longer exists; but there can be pictures of dogs that no longer exist) labeled both "the dog I owned in 1957" and "the dog I owned in 1955."

But this answer suggests a second and much more interesting question. What exactly is the picture to show? Suppose my dog lost her tail in 1956. Will the picture show a tailed or a tailless dog? "Dog" is probably not a phase-sortal, but dogs, like most things, can fall under various phase-sortals (like "tailless dog") and a picture can avoid representing a dog as falling under a given phase-sortal only by eschewing detail; and a picture that eschews *all* detail is not a picture at all, but, like the Bellman's map, a perfect and absolute blank.

This problem, the problem of what exactly the picture is to show, is not a problem that the friends of Figure 8.3 face only when they are attempting to generalize the device exemplified by Figure 8.3 to enable it to depict those facts of temporal identity that involve objects that no longer exist. Figure 8.3 itself presents them with this problem. Suppose that Tooley's book had got a stain on its cover between $t$ and $t^\star$. Shall our diagrammatic representation of a book include a stain or not? We can, of course, depict the book so sketchily that we do not have to decide about that. But this tactic will not work in all cases: suppose we are concerned with a temporal identity-sentence about a human being who is at one time a frail four-year-old girl and at another time a grossly obese, bearded, six-foot-tall (surgical) male who has lost a leg? Even a stick-figure has to have a definite number of legs. (And, of course, someone who, like me, thinks that Danton was at one time a fetus and at another time a severed head will sometimes find it even more difficult to draw sufficiently sketchy pictures.) If we considered only cases like that of the stained book and the girl-man, we should probably be tempted to say that obviously, the picture should represent the book (or whatever) as it is at the time the picture is scheduled to be displayed. Thus, if the book was unstained at t, stained at $t^\star$, and now once again unstained, the picture, if it is to be shown now, should represent the book as unstained. But we have already seen why this will not work: there are temporal identity sentences whose terms denote objects that no longer exist; and, of course, an object that does not now exist cannot be depicted as it is now. (For that matter, there are identity-sentences that are not *temporal* identity-sentences and whose terms no longer exist. "The horse Caligula made a consul was the only horse to hold political office," for example.)

The solution to this problem is a simple one: it doesn't make any difference what the picture shows. Remember, the picture is only a picture. Showing one thing twice-tagged is simply a device for graphically representing the fact that the descriptions inscribed on the tags have the same referent. If we want to represent graphically the fact that "the most famous teacher of Aristotle" and "the most famous pupil of Socrates" denote the same man, we have only to draw a man labeled with tags bearing these phrases. We are no more constrained to draw him at some particular age or in some particular condition or circumstances, than the author of an illustrated history of philosophy is constrained to choose a picture of Plato that shows Plato as being of some particular age or as being in some particular circumstances. The author of the illustrated history of philosophy knows that he may print a picture (a detail from the *School of Athens*, say), that represents Plato as being – how else? – of a certain determinate age and in certain particular surroundings, and so on, and that it will be perfectly correct to label it simply "Plato." (This label, by the way, will not be a description of the picture; or not in the way "Raphael, 1509–12, *The Vatican*" is. It will be a description of the intentional content of the picture, like "the mechanism of a watch" or "the structure of RNA." We should think of the word "Plato" printed under a picture as applying to the figure in the picture and not to the picture.) That is, the label "Plato" is correct *tout court* and is not an abbreviation for "Plato in old age" or anything else. But if a detail from a picture showing a young man conversing with Socrates and a detail from a picture showing an old man conversing with Aristotle can both correctly be labeled "Plato," then they can both be correctly labeled "the philosopher who, in middle age, founded the Academy," because these two phrases denote the same object.

One minor point about the labeling of pictures. Suppose the author of an encyclopedia article on General MacArthur accompanied his article with a single photograph of MacArthur, one taken when its subject was an infant, and labeled "Douglas MacArthur"; suppose the article contained no word of explanation of the fact that it was accompanied by a picture of an infant. There would be a lot wrong with that, but the picture would not be mislabeled. David Lewis has reminded us that someone's use of a sentence can be faulted on lots of grounds other than falsity; similarly, someone's use of a captioned picture can be faulted on lots of grounds other than the incorrectness of the caption. When I say that it "makes no difference what the picture shows," I do not mean to deny the obvious truth that it would be a *queer* thing to do to represent the fact expressed by "The father of Charles II was the father of James II" by a picture of the infant Charles I twice-tagged. This would be queer (because it would be wholly unmotivated) even if both tags were inscribed in this style: "the human being who, as an adult, fathered the human being who, as an adult, became the second king of England to be named Charles." It would be a queer and unmotivated way to represent that fact, but it would be a perfectly *correct* way to represent that fact.

Figure 8.3, then, is the sort of picture I recommend that you use when you think about facts of temporal identity. If you use any picture at all, that is. I don't *like* pictures in philosophy, despite the fact that I constantly use them in my own thinking. Even the best attempts to picture essentially unpicturable things and states of affairs are bound to be misleading. Even so simple a fact as the fact that "the most famous pupil of Socrates" denotes Plato can be represented only very imperfectly in a picture. For example, as we have seen, if we represent this fact by a picture of an appropriately labeled man, our picture will show far too little (nothing about the mechanics of securing reference, for example) and far too much (the picture must represent Plato as having properties that do not figure in the fact that he is denoted by the phrase inscribed on the label). The mind is curiously unable to let the extraneous features of the picture alone. My mind is, at least. It is only with a real effort of will that I am able to keep myself from thinking that no picture can really *just* be a picture of Plato, that every picture must, at best, be a picture of Plato-at-some-particular-time. (To think this is to make the mistake made by those philosophers who held that a geometrical diagram can't *just* represent a triangle.) Most of our discussion of pictures in the style of Figure 8.3 has had only one object: to help us to see that such pictures have, of necessity, extraneous features, and to convince us not to attribute any significance to them.

There is another lesson that must be learned about these pictures. They do not, by themselves, teach us anything about facts of temporal identity. Their whole point is supplied by their rivals. If pictures in the style of Figure 8.3 are misleading, their rivals are just ruinously wrong. And these ruinous pictures underlie a lot of our thinking about time and identity. They do not contribute to our *arguments* for or against philosophical theories; they condition what premises we shall find plausible. Pictures come before argument, and, therefore, pictures cannot easily be dislodged from our minds by argument. I don't say this is *impossible*. After all, I have tried to dislodge Figures 8.1 and 8.2 from your minds by arguing that the temporal parts that figure essentially in these pictures do not exist. But if your view of "identity across time" is supplied by one or the other of these pictures, you will set out to find some premise or inference in my arguments that you do not accept (if you attend to these arguments at all). And, of course, you will succeed. No attempt to refute a view that rests on powerful and appealing pictures can hope to succeed unless it supplies a rival picture of its own. And that is my only reason for asking you to consider Figure 8.3.

v

I have called Figure 8.3 simple-minded, and I have said that it teaches us nothing about facts of temporal identity. I have said these things because, in my view, facts of temporal identity are (*per se*) rather simple-minded facts, and there is nothing to learn about them. There *are* facts of temporal identity that present us with grave metaphysical problems. There are, for example, facts about the persistence of objects through a complete change of parts. But such problems are not problems about facts of temporal identity, any more than problems about causal relations are problems about relations or problems about mental predicates are problems about predication. For all I have said, there may be metaphysical difficulties that infect every (alleged) fact of temporal identity; if so, these are metaphysical difficulties that are inherent in the very notion of time and which infect every (alleged) fact that involves the passage of time. In short, every one of the real problems about time and identity is either too special or too general to be correctly describable as "the problem of identity through time."

If this is so, why is there so very persistent a conviction among philosophers that there is such a problem? I am not enough of an historian of philosophy to answer this question. And I think that one would have to be an historian to answer it. One would have to find the most primitive, fumbling cases of wonder about the nature of "identity through time," cases that were clearly differentiated both from wonder about time itself and from wonder about special problems of identity like those presented by the Resurrection of the Dead or the Ship of Theseus. I would hazard a guess, however, that the root of the so-called problem of identity through time has something to do with what I have called "adverb pasting."

Here is a famous passage from Locke.

*Wherein identity consists.* – Another occasion the mind often takes of comparing, is the very being of things, when, considering anything as existing at any determined time and place, we compare it with itself existing at another time, and thereon form the ideas of *identity* and *diversity*. (*Essay*, Book I, Ch. 27)

I have a hard time resisting the impression that Locke thought that "itself existing at another time" was a name. Or perhaps, since the point I want to make has nothing to do with pronouns, I should say that I have a hard time resisting the impression that Locke thought that phrases like "Mary existing in 1689" and "Mary existing in 1690" are names, and, moreover, names for things that are in some sense two, even if they are also in some sense one. (If Locke did think this, however, it doesn't seem to have done his investigations of substantive problems about vegetable, animal, and personal identity any harm. My purpose is not to criticize Locke's whole treatment of his subject.) And it seems even clearer to me that, if Locke did not accept this thesis, neither did he reject it. Perhaps the most accurate thing to say is that the idea of "the two Marys" touched the fringes of his thought so delicately as to give him no occasion to ask himself what he thought about it. This judgment of mine is a matter of "feel" and is probably one I, who am no very experienced reader of seventeenth-century English prose, have no business making. But I am made uneasy by "itself existing at another time"; why not "itself as it had been at another time"? If someone repeatedly makes judgments like "Mary was sadder in 1690 than she was in 1689" and "Mary was wiser in 1685 than she was in 1680", there is nothing really wrong with saying of him, "He's always comparing Mary as she was at one time with Mary as she was at another." (But it would be better to say, ". . . comparing the way Mary was at one time with the way she was at another.") If, however, someone says, ". . . comparing Mary existing at one time with Mary existing at another," one begins to wonder if he isn't exhibiting at least some tendency to think of phrases like "Mary existing in 1690" as names. It is in this tendency, I believe, that the problem of identity through time is rooted. What was once only a faint tendency in the minds of a few people is now an established habit of thought, one that is very hard to break, and, indeed, very hard even to recognize as a mere habit. To the degree that this habit is persistent, the tendency to think that there is a problem of identity through time will be persistent, since a philosopher who thinks that "Mary existing in 1690" and "Mary existing in 1689" are names for objects that are in some sense one and in some sense two will very likely want to spell out the relevant senses of "one" and "two."

But this answer to the question "Why do philosophers persist in thinking that there is a problem of identity through time?", even if it is correct, leaves a much more interesting question unanswered. What is so special about time that philosophers should have a tendency towards temporal adverb-pasting and no tendency to paste other sorts of adverbs? Why is there no problem of cross-perspectival identity or cross-evaluational identity? Why is there no tendency to think that "Alice viewed full-face" and "Alice viewed in profile" (or "Hume according to A" and "Hume according to B") are names for objects that are in some sense one and in some sense two? To this more interesting question I have no answer.[10]

---

[10] Some of the early parts of this essay (and a bit towards the end) are taken from my essay "Plantinga on Trans-World Identity," in *Alvin Plantinga*, ed. J. E. Tomberlin and P. van Inwagen (Dordrecht, 1985) (Chapter 11 of the present volume).

# 9

# Materialism and the psychological-continuity account of personal identity

I am going to argue that a materialist should not accept a psychological-continuity theory of personal identity across time. I will begin by arguing that a materialist cannot consistently admit the possibility of a certain kind of case beloved of the proponents of psychological-continuity theories, so-called bodily transfer cases, and then attempt to generalize the essential point of the argument for this conclusion to show that a materialist should not accept a psychological-continuity account of personal identity.

Let us consider a representative philosopher who is a materialist and who believes that human persons really do exist and that they really do endure through time and that bodily transfer is possible. Sydney Shoemaker will do for my purposes. But I want to make it plain that it is not my purpose to attack Shoemaker or any other particular philosopher. My target is the combination of views that I have listed: materialism, realism about human persons and their endurance through time, and a belief in the possibility of bodily transfer. Here is a quotation from Shoemaker's well-known debate on the subjects of personal identity and dualism with Richard Swinburne:

A number of philosophers have envisaged the possibility of a device which records the state of one brain and imposes that state on a second brain so that it has exactly the same state the first brain had at the beginning of the operation. We will suppose that this process obliterates the first brain, or at any rate obliterates its current state . . . . Philosophers who have discussed this sort of case have differed in their intuitions as to whether the brain-state transfer would amount to a person's changing bodies – whether, as I shall put it, the procedure would be "person-preserving." Some think it would. Others think that it would amount to killing the original person and at the same time creating . . . a psychological duplicate of him.

Initially, I think, most people are inclined to take the latter view. But one can

First published in *Philosophical Perspectives* 11: *Mind, Causation, and World* (1997), pp. 305–319.

tell a story which enhances the plausibility of the former view. Imagine a society in which . . . periodically a person goes into the hospital for a "body-change." This consists in his total brain-state being transferred to the brain of [an artificial duplicate of his body]. At the end of the procedure the original body is incinerated . . . All of the social practices of the society presuppose that the procedure is person-preserving. The brain-state recipient is regarded as owning the property of the brain-state donor, [and] as being married to the donor's spouse . . . If it is found that the brain-state donor had committed a crime, everyone regards it as just that the brain-state recipient should be punished for it.

. . . If we confronted such a society, there would, I think, be a very strong case for saying that what *they* mean by "person" is such that the brain-state-transfer procedure *is* person-preserving . . . But there would also be a strong reason for saying that what they mean by "person" is what we mean by it; they call the same things persons, offer the same sorts of characterization of what sorts of things persons are, and attach the same kinds of social consequences to judgments of personal identity . . . But if they are right in thinking that the brain-state-transfer procedure is person-preserving, and if they mean the same thing by "person" as we do, then it seems that *we* ought to regard the brain-state-transfer procedure as person-preserving.[1]

There is a good deal more to what Shoemaker has to say about the possibility of bodily transfer than what is represented in this passage. But most of what Shoemaker thinks about bodily transfer that is not represented in this passage consists in epicycles designed to handle certain problem-cases, particularly those that arise when the brain-states of a particular person are imposed on the brains of two or more artificial bodies, and those that arise when the "original" brain continues to exist after its states have been imposed on some other brain or brains. Well, someone who holds this sort of view certainly does face problems when he or she confronts such cases, and Shoemaker is certainly right to devote a good deal of his time to attempting to solve these problems. But these problems will not be my concern. I will simply ignore the more elaborate cases and the epicycles they generate. I want to discuss only cases of the sort that Shoemaker discusses in the above passage, and I want to explain what I find incoherent about the sort of position he takes – roughly, the combination of materialism and an adherence to the possibility of bodily transfer.

Let us examine the story he tells. Many people would find it hard to accept the conclusion Shoemaker draws from it. As he says, "initially, most people are inclined to take the latter view" – that is, to the view

---

[1] Sydney Shoemaker and Richard Swinburne, *Personal Identity* (Oxford, 1984), pp. 108–110.

that the brain-state transfer operation is not person-preserving. But it is rather an understatement to say that most of us are "initially inclined" to suppose that a human being cannot go from one place to another simply in virtue of a transfer of information that could in principle be conveyed by fax or even by a letter carrier. This statement can be compared with the statement that most of us are initially inclined to suppose that you can't really bring a statue to life, or the statement that the majority of us have tentatively accepted, as a working hypothesis, the thesis that it is impossible to turn a woman into a laurel tree. In fact, it is in one way rather harder to believe that Shoemaker's story represents a real possibility than it is to believe that of the story of Pygmalion and Galatea or the story of the metamorphosis of Daphne – for in those two stories there is at least material continuity between the "before" and "after" states of the central characters.

Before I present my main line of argument, I want to make some remarks about Shoemaker's story that seem to me to be philosophically important. They are not so much a part of my argument as some things I want to get off my chest. Shoemaker is not much interested in the actual biology of human beings. He seems to suppose that it makes sense to talk about transferring the "state" of one brain to another, as if the living brain of an adult human being were a computer disk, a thing that had a well-defined "blank" state even when it was the size and shape of an adult brain (as opposed to the brain of a new-born infant) and which was capable of receiving the information stored in another brain in a way strongly analogous to the way in which a blank computer disk is capable of receiving the information stored on another disk. But suppose a living brain is more like, say, a city. A city stores plenty of information and, among lots of other things that a city does, it processes a flow of information – or at least there is no harm in talking that way. But a city does not have a well defined "blank" state into which just any information (provided there is not too much of it) can be programmed. To say, "Suppose the municipal state of New York were transferred to Beijing" is to say words that have no meaning whatever. How do we know that there is any way to have a living human brain that is a blank? What would happen if we were able to clone human cells and grow a human being or the brain of a human being in a tank (and were so wicked as actually to do so)? By genetic design, a human brain is supposed to grow to its adult size over a span of years during which it receives a certain sort of sensory input and produces all sorts of outputs that influence its environment. We know that certain parts of the brain atrophy or fail to develop normally if the persons whose brains they are don't engage in certain sorts of activities. That is why language acquisition is difficult if not impossible for those who are not allowed to participate interactively in a community of language-users while their brains are passing through certain developmental stages. If they grow to adulthood without being allowed to participate in such a community, their brains have missed the boat as far as the possibility of endowing their owners with full linguistic competence is concerned. Who knows how many boats would be missed by the brain of a human-adult-shaped thing grown from human DNA in a tank? Why suppose that there is any possible world in which the brain of anything grown from human DNA in a tank is capable of being the recipient of anything like the information stored in your or my brain? Maybe the brain of such a thing would be a brain only in terms of gross anatomy. Maybe it would not be at all analogous to a book with blank pages ready to be overwritten. Maybe it would be like a book with pages covered with random and indelible splotches or pages that came apart if you tried to write on them or pages where nothing at all would appear if you tried to write. How do we know that it is not a necessary truth that this is the way things are, that there is no possible world in which human beings enjoy the remarkable adventures that Shoemaker imagines?

Now that I have warmed up to this subject, I will take the opportunity to remark – even though the remark is even more tangential to my main line of argument – that I am similarly suspicious of all of the other imaginary technology that turns up in discussions of personal identity. The *Star Trek* transporter beam, for example, is suspect indeed. A one-second pulse of electromagnetic radiation that carried enough information to restructure a particular human organism – never mind whether the restructured organism would somehow be the same person as the original -- that arrived at a receiver a few meters across would simply vaporize the receiver and everything else in the vicinity and everything it had happened to encounter on the way there. Similar considerations from the theory of signals show that it would take months or years to transfer the amount of information from one brain to another that is required by the brain-state-transfer machine; try to speed up the process significantly and you will just melt all those little wires attached to the shiny cap on the recipient's head. Remember how long it took all the information that is stored in your brain actually to get there. And I

147

very much doubt whether this is a consequence of contingent features of the laws of nature. I am willing to bet that the statement "For any given level of efficiency of information transfer, the greater the amount of information passing through a channel per unit time, the greater the amount of energy passing through that channel per unit time" is a necessary truth, a principle that is a consequence of any coherent set of laws of nature. (Couldn't we simply imagine that the transfer takes a much longer time than Shoemaker has imagined – a year, say? But the recipient's brain would be alive and, presumably, changing throughout the whole procedure. Can a painting be copied on a shifting canvas?)

Well, these are no more than the grumbles of an annoyed enemy of the philosophical employment of fantastic thought experiments – an employment that is, I believe, the result of the widespread adherence of philosophers to the nonsensical idea of "logical possibility." I won't pursue the points that these grumbles raise. Let's assume that the brain-state-transfer machine is in some sense possible: it really is possible, in some coherent sense of possible, any coherent sense at all, to put shiny caps on the heads of two human organisms and, by the electrical transfer of information across wires connecting the caps, to turn one organism into a psychological duplicate of the other. Having made this assumption, let us return to Shoemaker's story.

If I understand Shoemaker correctly, he believes that each of us really exists and that we really persist through time. He is concerned to establish the thesis that, in the story, a certain human person would persist through time in the same sense of "persist" as that in which human persons normally persist through time. He has other things to say, epicycles to introduce, in cases involving "branching" and cases in which the brain-state donor continues to exist. But in the case he has described, he thinks that the brain-state recipient is identical with the brain-state donor. And that is the case I want to discuss. I am not satisfied that it makes any sense to talk of brain-state donation or reception, but it is clear that whatever an episode of donation-and-reception is supposed to be, it does not require that anything but information move across space from the donor to the recipient. I understand that *part* of his view, and that much understanding will suffice for my purposes.

Shoemaker believes that I – to take one example of a person – exist and that I can change my position from place $x$ to place $y$ even though nothing passes from $x$ to $y$ but information – that the person at place $y$ will, if the information transfer is done right, be literally I, literally the same person as the person who used to be at place *x*. Shoemaker is a sort of anti-realist about personal identity when he considers puzzle-cases like cases of "branching," cases in which the state of one's brain is transferred to two or more "blank" brains. In that case, it cannot be literally true that either of the brain-state-recipients *is* the donor – for it is obviously true that they can't *both* be the donor, and there could be no reason to say that one rather than the other was the donor. In such cases, Shoemaker argues, it could be rational even for an ideally perfect egoist to prefer having his or her brain-states transferred to two blank brains to simple annihilation; the rational egoist may even be willing to make a significant sacrifice today to replace threatened annihilation next week with a "double" brain-state transfer next week. (Explaining how this could be rational is one of the functions of the epicycles.) But Shoemaker is not an anti-realist about personal identity in normal, everyday cases or in the simplest and most straightforward brain-state-transfer cases. He regards the simplest and most straightforward brain-state-transfer cases as, to use his term, person-preserving.

And what is wrong with his position? Don't our intuitions tell us that we should survive a "simple" brain-state-transfer operation? If one had, in the normal course of events, six months to live, and if one's goal were to live (more exactly, to exist as a conscious being) as long as possible, wouldn't one accept the offer of a brain-state-transfer operation today – it's today or never – even though this meant the destruction of one's present brain today? The answer, of course, is Yes, and that shows how our intuitions run. And our intuitions are constitutive of our concept of a person, or at least display the features that belong to that concept.

This argument is deeply flawed. Our "intuitions" are simply our beliefs – or perhaps, in some cases, the tendencies that make certain beliefs attractive to us, that "move" us in the direction of accepting certain propositions without taking us all the way to acceptance. (Philosophers call their philosophical beliefs intuitions because "intuition" sounds more authoritative than "belief.") Our beliefs have all sorts of sources and can very easily be wrong. So even if it is true that most egoists would choose an immediate brain-state-transfer operation over a normal death that came significantly later, that fact (if it is a fact) does nothing whatever to establish the conclusion that the brain-state-transfer operation would be "person-preserving." It could be that these hypothetical egoists are simply confused or at least philosophically mistaken or metaphysically misinformed. I think that they are. I shall try to explain why I think so.

You believe that human persons really exist. And you are a materialist. So what do you think these human persons that you think really exist are? Well, material things, obviously. Perhaps whole human organisms, perhaps parts of human organisms like brains or cerebral cortices or cerebral hemispheres, but some sort of material thing. For the sake of having a concrete example, I'll suppose that you think, as I do, that human persons are whole human organisms; but the argument that I shall give would "go through" for any sort of material thing. So you are a certain living organism, $x$. And, if you hold views like Shoemaker's on the possibility of bodily transfer, you believe that there could be another, numerically distinct living organism $y$ such that, if the right sort of information flowed from $x$ to $y$, you would become $y$. (Perhaps you think that if you are to become $y$, the destruction of $x$ will also have to be accomplished. Perhaps you think that if you are to become $y$, the same sort of flow of information cannot occur between $x$ and any third organism.) But when the matter is put this way, it is evident that your belief is simply impossible, a violation of the very well established modal principle that a thing and another thing cannot become a thing and itself. Or, if you prefer symbols:

$$\forall x \forall y \, (x \neq y \rightarrow \, \sim \lozenge \, x = y).$$

And there are very good reasons why this principle is regarded as well established. Here is one that does not apply in all cases but does apply in the present case, which is a case in which an object is at one time not identical with another object and later becomes identical with it. In the present case, the objects under consideration have different histories. For example, you are here now and the physical object that you are going to become after the information has flowed from one brain to another is now over there – and each of them is in only one of these two places, not in both simultaneously. If you are this organism now at $t_1$ and will be that organism over there later at $t_2$, then, at $t_2$, (the person who is) that organism over there will, by a simple application of Leibniz's Law, be able to say, truly, "At $t_1$ I was right here and it is not the case that at $t_1$ I was right here." If you want to see the application worked out in detail, it goes like this. Let's look at what you believe at $t_2$. Being a materialist, you believe that you are material. That is, that you are identical with some material thing – call it "this human organism." You believe, as a factual matter, that at $t_1$ this human organism was right here. You believe, that, having become this human organism in virtue of a flow of information that came from a brain that was a part of a human organism that was *not* right here at $t_1$, at $t_1$ *you* were not right here. That is, you believe:

> You = this human organism;
> At $t_1$ this human organism was right here;
> It is not the case that at $t_1$ you were right here.

Here is Leibniz's Law:

$$x = y \rightarrow (\mathbf{F}. . .x. . . \leftrightarrow \mathbf{F}. . .y. . .).$$

And here is an instance:

$$x = y \rightarrow (\text{at } t_1 \, x \text{ was right here} \leftrightarrow \text{at } t_1 \, y \text{ was right here}).$$

It follows logically from what you believe and from this instance of Leibniz's Law that

> At $t_1$ you were right here and it is not the case that at $t_1$ you were right here.

(This consequence can be demonstrated very simply using Euclid's Law – the principle of the substitution of identicals – which is an immediate consequence of Leibniz's Law: substitute "you" for "this human organism" in "At $t_1$ this human organism was right here.") The lesson of this reductio is that you can't turn one thing into another thing simply by causing information to pass between them. You can't do that because you can't turn one thing into another thing at all. That is the lesson that one should draw from the reductio – *if* the reductio is really inescapable. Is there any way in which the friends of bodily transfer might avoid it?

As I have said, it is not my intention to try to refute Shoemaker. I have quoted him only to provide a concrete example of someone who holds a certain combination of views. Nevertheless, I should mention that Shoemaker is aware of a problem that is at least something like the problem I have posed and offers a solution to it, a solution that he admits is "prima facie counterintuitive." I think, however, that his proposed solution misses the real depth and difficulty of the problem he faces, and it is for that reason that I have used the words "a problem at least something like the problem I have posed." Shoemaker recognizes that, although his brain-state donor and brain-state recipient are (on his account) the same *person*, they are not the same animal or the same

151

human being.[2] His solution to this difficulty is to say that I am not and you are not and, in general, persons are not, animals or human beings. That is, persons are not *strictly* animals or human beings: no person is identical with any animal or any human being. Rather, persons ("human" persons, anyway) "share their matter with" and "occupy the same space as" and have "the same non-historical properties" as human beings. And, of course, he holds that it is in principle possible for one and the same person to bear these relations to different human beings at different times.

One can see why Shoemaker would concede that this position is prima facie counterintuitive. I would add that this position seems to be hard to reconcile with the mind–body identity theory. If the thought that it is nearly time for lunch occurs to one at a certain moment, then, according to the identity theory, the occurrence of this thought is identical with a certain physical event φ that takes place in one's brain. But if one – that is, the thinker of this thought – shares the matter and "momentary" properties of a certain human being $x$ (with which one is not, strictly speaking, identical), then φ is an event not only in one's own brain but in $x$'s brain as well. (One's brain and $x$'s brain may or may not be identical. We need not decide that issue.) But then why is it not true that the thought that it is nearly time for lunch occurs to $x$ at the moment φ occurs in $x$'s brain? A generalization of this consideration suggests that there must be something it is *like* to be $x$, and that what it is like to be $x$ must be just exactly what it is like to be *one* – the person, the first-mentioned thinker of the thought that it is nearly time for lunch. Why, then, is $x$ not a person too? And if there are these *two* persons simultaneously present – two distinct mereological sums of the very same atoms – which one would be preserved by the "person-preserving" brain-state-transfer device? And how does the device manage to preserve one of them rather than the other? If they have all of the same momentary properties, then the device would seem to be in a "Buridan's Ass" situation, for it is only the momentary properties of an object that confronts it that can differentially affect the operations of the device.

Let us leave this difficulty aside. It is a difficulty for Shoemaker's solution to a certain problem (the problem raised by the fact that operations of the brain-state-transfer device obviously do not preserve "animal identity"), but Shoemaker's solution is not a solution to the problem I

[2] See Section 11, "Personal Identity and Animal Identity," of Shoemaker's contribution to *Personal Identity*, pp. 112–114.

have posed. Let us grant for the sake of argument that one is not, that persons in general are not, strictly identical with any human being or any animal. Nevertheless, if one is a materialist and if one believes that persons really exist, then one must concede that every person is strictly identical with *some* material thing. Someone who holds views like Shoe-maker's is therefore committed to the proposition that there could be two simultaneously existing material things such that one of them could become strictly identical with the other simply in virtue of a flow of information between them. It is against this perfectly general proposition that my argument is directed. The argument does not essentially depend on the assumption (which was made only to supply two visualizable material objects to help us to focus our thoughts) that the two objects in the case considered are "human organisms." Substitute in the argument any material-object category you like for "human organism" and the point of the argument is unaffected.

One way out of the difficulty I have raised is provided by the idea that "identity is always relative to a sortal term," for if that notorious thesis were indeed correct, then it might be possible for x and y to be different *organisms* but nonetheless the same *person*. Shoemaker is aware of this possibility and rejects it. (That is, he rejects it as a solution to the problem that he considers, the problem of the relation between personal identity, on the one hand, and human or animal identity on the other.) Should he reconsider his rejection in the light of the fact that his solution is not a solution to the more general problem – and of the fact that his solution confronts all sorts of difficulties even as a solution to the special problem? I think not. It would be impossible for me to go into all the ramifications of the thesis that identity is always relative to a sortal term. I can only say that it has very radical logical and semantical consequences, and one might wonder whether any position in the philosophy of mind should be allowed to dictate radical consequences in logic and semantics. I will mention, without further comment, two of these consequences. First, if the classical conception of identity is abandoned, then the classical notion of reference or denotation (which essentially involves the idea that if a term denotes a certain object then it denotes those and only those things that are, in the classical sense, identical with that object) must be abandoned. Secondly, if the notion of "relative identity" is to do any work, the analogue of Leibniz's Law must fail for at least some of the relative-identity predicates: there must be an x and a y such that, despite the fact that x is the same *something* as y, x and y have different properties. Although I

153

believe that a logic of relative identity can be developed in way that is at
least formally coherent,[3] its consequences are so radical that one should be
deeply suspicious of any theory of personal identity that requires relative
identity as a part of the package; better – *much* better – to look elsewhere
for a solution to puzzles about personal identity. If our "intuitions"
present us with puzzles the only solution to which requires an appeal to
relative identity, then those intuitions should be regarded as suspect.

Another possible escape from the reductio that threatens the combination of views I am considering is provided by what I have elsewhere
called "four-dimensionalism."[4] This is the thesis that the things we normally regard as enduring through time are extended in time as well as in
space. Each physical thing, according to this way of looking at identity
across time, is extended in three spatial dimensions (or maybe nine, if
"superstring" theory is to be believed) and also in time.

This view of identity across time has been applied to the problems of
personal identity with great power and subtlety by David Lewis.[5] The
essential trick is this:

Any two spatiotemporal objects have a mereological sum that is itself a
spatiotemporal object. Certain spatiotemporal objects count as persons – this
word now being understood to apply to things extended in time as well as in
space. A spatiotemporal object is a person if it is a maximal aggregate of person-
stages. Leave aside the question of the meaning and purpose of the qualification
"maximal." A mereological sum of person-stages is an "aggregate" if the stages
are psychologically continuous with one another in the right sort of way.

It is consistent with this abstract account of the spatiotemporal unity of a
person that the operation of Shoemaker's brain-state-transfer machine
not represent a discontinuity in any sense that is incompatible with the
"before transfer" temporal part of the "donor organism" and the "after
transfer" temporal part of the "recipient organism" both being temporal
parts of a single temporally extended person. At any rate, abstract considerations of logic or semantics provide no reason for thinking that the
operation of the machine would have that effect. The question whether
the before-transfer temporal part of the donor organism and the after-
transfer part of the recipient organism are temporal parts of a single

---

[3] See Section 3 of my essay "And Yet They Are Not Three Gods But One God," in
*Philosophy And the Christian Faith*, ed. Thomas V. Morris (South Bend, Ind., 1988).

[4] See my essay "Four-Dimensional Objects," *Noûs* 24 (1990), pp. 245–255 (Chapter 7 of
the present volume).

[5] See, for example, David Lewis, "Survival and Identity," *Philosophical Papers, Volume I*
(New York, 1983).

person can be compared to the question whether North and South America are spatial parts of a single continent. In each case, the question reduces to the question whether a problematic patch "in the middle" displays an appropriate kind and degree of continuity.

To this approach to the problem of personal identity (considered as a proposal that would enable the friends of bodily transfer to avoid the threatened reductio I have laid out), I would say something similar to what I said about the previous proposal, the relative-identity proposal. There are many difficulties with the idea that time is sufficiently similar to space that it is appropriate to think of objects that endure through time as four-dimensional objects, extended in time as well as in space and composed of temporal parts. For example, I have argued elsewhere that this view of things commits its adherents to a counterpart-theoretical analysis of modal statements about individuals.[6] (Lewis, of course, being the inventor of counterpart theory, does not consider this a disadvantage of the four-dimensionalist theory of identity across time, but many will.) And isn't it just a strikingly queer idea that time is that much like space?

Writing a decade or so before the advent of special relativity and Minkowski spacetime diagrams, H. G. Wells presented (in the opening pages of *The Time Machine*) a powerful picture – perhaps partly inspired by Abbott's *Flatland* – of time as radically like space, as being "just another dimension." According to this picture, if two events occur in the same place at different times, there exists a line between them that is at right angles to the North–South, the East–West, and the up–down lines that pass through that place. I think that a lot of philosophers have got their picture of time, directly or indirectly, from Wells. But if you look at a real Minkowski diagram, you will find that what you see tends to undermine the "Wellsian" picture of time. For one thing, in the Wellsian picture, any spacetime coordinate system can be transformed into any other by simple displacement of the origin and rotation of the axes, whereas in Minkowski space this is not true. But let us waive that problem, and look at a coordinate system established by a particular observer of the spacetime world who is in a state of uniform motion – a so-called inertial frame of reference. In a Minkowski diagram – a drawing of Minkowski spacetime that is centered on the representation of a particular inertial frame of reference, so that the time axis and the spatial axes of that frame are drawn at right angles to one another – the temporal

---

[6] In van Inwagen, "Four-Dimensional Objects."

155

axis has properties radically unlike those of the spatial axes. In a Minkowski diagram, a timelike path does not represent anything like a spatial distance, but rather represents time as measured by a clock whose worldline is that path. The analogue of the Pythagorean Theorem for Minkowski spacetime has *minus* signs in front of the squared spatial variables, with the consequence that in many cases the longer a line representing a time-like path on the paper in front of you is, the *shorter* is the path through spacetime that it represents. (Any path traced out by a ray of light is of 0 length!) To my mind, these facts undermine the idea that the spacetime of the special theory of relativity is anything like the four-dimensional continuum through which Wells's time-traveler moved. If the Wellsian picture of spacetime were correct, it would make good sense to think of objects as being extended in time in the same sense as that in which they are extended in space. But I'm inclined to think that it isn't correct and that it doesn't make much sense to think of them that way. At least *I* don't understand that kind of thinking.

Even those who think that "four-dimensionalism" makes sense must agree that it is a controversial theory of persistence through time, one that makes very strong metaphysical claims. Shouldn't we regard any theory of *personal* identity across time that forced this general metaphysic of identity across time on us as suspect – at least if there were no independent reasons to accept it? (And I would argue that there are not, although that, of course, is a complex issue.)

I conclude that the only available escapes from the threatened reductio are too expensive. (I know of nothing else in the literature that offers an escape.) The combination of views that Shoemaker – along with many other philosophers – holds is not worth the price.[7] The materialist should, therefore, adopt either the extreme position that human persons do not really persist through time at all – that our talk of their persistence is some sort of fiction – or else the materialist should reject the possibility of bodily transfer.

But does it follow from the fact that a materialist should not believe in

---

[7] I will remark that it is not at all clear to me that, with the important exception of David Lewis, any of the materialists who adhere to a psychological continuity theory of personal identity is aware that there is a price to be paid. (Of course Lewis would not concede that his four-dimensionalism was appropriately described as a *price*.) It is at least uncommon for such philosophers to concede that the combination of views they hold requires allegiance to some logical or metaphysical thesis (some thesis about the nature of identity or about the nature of time) that has important ramifications outside the problem of *personal* identity across time.

the possibility of bodily transfer that a materialist should not accept a psychological-continuity account of personal identity across time? Well, it is not altogether clear that it does. Perhaps the psychological-continuity account is consistent with the impossibility of bodily transfer. Perhaps there is some version of the psychological-continuity theory that has the consequence that, if each psychological state is a state of a material object, then psychological continuity is possible only within a single material object — that is, psychological continuity must consist in a succession of psychological states that are realized in the same material object. If this were so, then the psychological-continuity theory — or this hypothetical version of it at any rate — would not imply the possibility of bodily transfer. It would go rather against the spirit of the psychological-continuity theory if the continuity theorist were simply to stipulate that psychological continuity was possible only within a single body, for one of the advantages of the psychological-continuity theory is supposed to be that it is neutral in respect of the ontology of persons; it is generally supposed to be a feature of the theory — and one of its attractive features — that it is consistent with dualism and materialism and any other theory of the metaphysical nature of the persons to which it applies. It might nevertheless be possible to give some abstract account of psychological continuity that, in conjunction with the thesis that each psychological state is a state of a material body, had the consequence that psychological continuity was possible only within a single body. I concede the possibility, but instead of exploring it, I want to proceed by generalizing the lesson of our examination of bodily-transfer cases.

If materialism and the psychological-continuity theory are both correct (and if there really are persons that strictly and literally persist through time), then it follows that there are cases of the following sort: $x$ is a material object that exists at one time and $y$ is a material object that exists at another time and whether $x$ and $y$ are identical is entirely a function of whether certain psychological states that are "tokened" in or realized in $x$ are continuously connected with certain psychological states that are tokened in $y$. This seems to me to be a very strange thesis. It could be compared with the thesis that whether a computer that exists at one time and a computer that exists at another time are identical is entirely a function of whether the information processing that is going on in the former computer at the one time is causally continuous with the information processing that is going on inside the latter computer at the other time. There may be all sorts of difficulties about the persistence of computers through time – cases of the Ship-of-Theseus sort are easy to imagine – but I doubt whether any continuity-of-information-processing criterion of the identity of computers across time could be even superficially plausible. A computer is a material object, and it certainly looks as if we know enough about how to follow the careers of material objects through time to see that there are perfectly clear cases of the causal continuity of information processing between distinct computers and perfectly clear cases of the causal discontinuity of information processing within a single computer. If human persons are material objects, the situation would seem to be perfectly analogous. Let us look at a few cases in which we make different assumptions about what kind of material objects human persons are.

Suppose that human persons are living human organisms. Can the answer to the question whether a living human organism that exists at one time and a living human organism that exists at another time are identical really be entirely a function of the continuity of the psychological states that are tokened within the former organism at the one time with the psychological states that are tokened within the latter organism at the other time? Surely we know enough about how to follow the careers of living organisms through time to see that questions about the continuity of such psychological states as may be tokened within a living organism are not relevant to questions about the continued existence of that organism? Even if the correct analysis of psychological continuity should have the consequence that a psychological state tokened in a given organism could be continuous only with psychological states tokened in that same organism, we do not need to know this or to examine the psychological states tokened in that organism to find out whether it continues to exist. I should think, in fact, that if the correct analysis of psychological continuity did have the consequence that a psychological state tokened in a given organism could be continuous only with psychological states tokened in that same organism, what we should conclude is that in order to find out whether a certain sequence of psychological states displayed "continuity," we should first have to find out whether they were all states of the same organism. And that would require us to have a way of following the career of an organism through time that did not depend on our first determining whether the psychological states that were tokened in that organism satisfied some definition of continuity.

Suppose that human persons are human brains. Can the answer to the question whether a human brain that exists at one time and a human brain that exists at another time are identical really be entirely a function of the continuity of the psychological states that are tokened within the former brain at the one time with the psychological states that are tokened within the latter brain at the other time? Surely we know enough about how to follow the careers of brains through time to see that questions about the continuity of the psychological states that are tokened within a brain are not relevant to questions about the continued existence of that brain? Even if the correct analysis of psychological continuity should have the consequence that a psychological state tokened in a given brain could be continuous only with psychological states tokened in that same brain, we do not need to know this or to examine the psychological states tokened in that brain to find out whether it continues to exist. I should think, in fact, that if the correct analysis of psychological continuity did have the consequence that a psychological state tokened in a given brain could be continuous only with psychological states tokened in that same brain, what we should conclude is that in order to find out whether a certain sequence of psychological states displayed "continuity," we should first have to find out whether they were all states of the same brain. And that would require us to have a way of following the career of a brain through time that did not depend on our first determining whether the psychological states that were tokened in that brain satisfied some definition of continuity.

Ask the corresponding question about the relevance of psychological continuity to identity across time for any sort of material object that is a plausible candidate for the sort of material object a human person is, and the answer seems in every case to be No. A material object is a material object, a thing that is at any given moment the mereological sum of certain quarks and electrons. The principles that govern identity across time for material objects, or for material objects in various categories, may be problematic, but whether a given material object will survive a given adventure does not seem to depend on any facts about the psychological states that may be tokened in it.

Suppose that a human brain is, after all, like a computer disk in that it has a well-defined blank state. Suppose that you are unfortunate enough to encounter some phenomenon that drives your brain into its blank state, an encounter that would presumably leave you alive but a drooling idiot. (Or, if I am begging the question by saying "you," I can at least say, ". . . would cause the matter that had composed you a moment ago now to compose a drooling idiot.") What material object ceases to exist when your brain is driven into its blank state? Not the whole organism; not the brain or either of the cerebral hemispheres or the cerebral cortex; not any cell; not any atom; not any electron. It seems to be impossible to find any material object that would cease to exist if your brain was driven into its blank state – just as it is impossible to find a material object that ceases to exist when the information on a computer disk is erased. But if no material object ceases to exist and if you are a material object, then you do not cease to exist, despite the fact that your brain's being driven into its blank state is a case of psychological discontinuity if anything is.

It is possible to argue that in this case you would cease to be a *person*. Well, perhaps that is so. I suppose it would depend on how one defined "person," a word notoriously productive of mutually incompatible definitions. Suppose it is so: suppose that in the case imagined you would exist without being a person. Still, *you* would exist. Still, you would *exist*. If there are possible cases in which you would exist without being a person, their possibility shows only that not all problems about whether and in what manner and under what conditions you would exist should be described as problems about *personal* identity.

I conclude that a materialist who believes that you and I and such other referents of the personal pronouns as there may be really exist should not accept a psychological-continuity account of what it is for things in this category to persist through time. In my view, the reason that there are materialists who accept a psychological-continuity account of our identity across time is that these materialists have supposed that they could philosophize about personal identity from a materialist perspective without troubling themselves with general, metaphysical questions concerning what kind of thesis materialism is and what its ramifications are. They have rather vaguely supposed that all they have to do to be materialists is to say that all psychological states (or at least all state-tokens) are states of material objects. But a materialist has to do more than that, for materialism is a metaphysic. A materialist, like any other metaphysician, has to be concerned not only with states, whatever exactly states may be, but with objects in all ontological categories. One of the tasks that confronts the materialists is this: they have to find a home for the referents of the terms of ordinary speech within a world that is entirely material – or else deny the existence of those referents altogether. A materialist, for example, must either be prepared to say just what material object a cow is, or else deny that there are cows. And the same goes for the referents of the personal pronouns. In my view, such initial plausibility as the combination of materialism and the psychological-continuity account of our identity across time may have cannot survive a careful attempt to answer the question, Just what material objects are we?[8]

[8] I am grateful to José Benardete and Sydney Shoemaker for comments on a draft of this paper. Versions of the paper have been read at a meeting of the Austrian Philosophical Society, and at departmental colloquia at the University of West Virginia, Arizona State University, the University of Arizona, the University of Florida, the University of Alabama (Tuscaloosa), and the University of Miami. I wish to thank the numerous people at these meetings whose comments and criticisms led me to think again about what I had said. Special thanks are due to Ned Markosian, David Cowles, and Dean Zimmerman. In all philosophical matters relating to personal identity and the ontology of the material world, I owe a great deal to Eric Olson.

# PART III

# *Modality*

# 10

# Indexicality and actuality

David Lewis has proposed the startling and ingenious thesis that "actual," as this term is used in philosophical discussions of modality, is an indexical term. He states this thesis in *Counterfactuals* in these words:

Our actual world is only one world among others. We call it alone actual not because it differs in kind from all the rest but because it is the world we inhabit. The inhabitants of other worlds may truly call their own worlds actual, if they mean by "actual" what we do; for the meaning we give to "actual" is such that it refers at any world *i* to that world *i* itself. "Actual" is indexical, like "I" or "here" or "now": it depends for its reference on the circumstances of utterance, to wit the world where the utterance is located.[1]

and in "Anselm and Actuality" in these:

I suggest that "actual" and its cognates should be analyzed as *indexical* terms: terms whose reference varies, depending on relevant features of the context of utterance. The relevant feature of context, for the term "actual," is the world at which a given utterance occurs. According to the indexical analysis I propose, "actual" . . . refers at any world w to the world w. "Actual" is analogous to "present," an indexical term whose reference varies depending on a different feature of context: "present" refers at any time t to the time t. "Actual" is analogous also to "here," "I," "you," "this," and "aforementioned" – indexical terms depending for their reference respectively on the place, the speaker, the intended audience, the speaker's acts of pointing, and the foregoing discourse.

I do not mean to say that "actual" has different meanings in the languages used in different worlds, so that for any world w, "the actual world" is a proper name of w in the native language of w. That is false. (Just as it would be false to say that "today" changes its meaning every midnight.) Rather, the *fixed* meaning we give to "actual" is such that, at any world w, "actual" refers in our language to w.[2]

The theory presented in these passages – I shall call it "the indexical theory of actuality" – is, if there is any reason to think it true, very

First published in *The Philosophical Review* 89 (1980), pp. 403–426.
[1] David Lewis, *Counterfactuals* (Oxford, 1973), pp. 85–86.
[2] David Lewis, "Anselm and Actuality," *Noûs* 4 (1970), pp. 184–185.

important. It is not a modification or refinement of some theory we learned about as undergraduates, but is entirely original. It offers us the possibility of a radical rethinking of many of the perennial questions of ontology, the possibility of looking at questions like "Is existence a property?" and "Why should anything at all exist?" from a wholly new angle. (Consider, for example, the latter question. I shall not attempt an adequate treatment of this question from the "indexical" point of view in this paper, for this would take us far afield. We may note, however, that the question "Why should anything at all exist?" is obviously closely connected with the question "Why is *this* world, *our* world – which is one of the worlds in which something exists – actual?", and *this* question is, according to the indexical theory, incoherent: it can be instructively compared with "Why is *this* century, *our* century, the present century? Why isn't it *now* 1738 or 2406?"[3])

Unfortunately, the indexical theory is not true. More precisely, the words Lewis has used to state "the indexical theory" are ambiguous. There are at least three theories that someone might, with some textual justification, claim to find in the passages I have quoted. Each of these theories is either not indexical or not true.

I

The body of this essay will consist of examinations of the several candidates for the office "indexical theory of actuality." Some groundwork is in order, however. Each of our candidates will be a theory about what it is we are doing when we apply the word "actual" to a possible world.

---

[3] The question "Why should anything at all exist *now*?" is not obviously incoherent, despite the fact that "the present time" is an indexical phrase. This fact might be thought to undermine the claim made in the text. But there is an important difference between times and worlds in virtue of which the two cases are not analogous. Every world has just the "inhabitants" it has *essentially*, while a moment or period of time has *its* "inhabitants" only accidentally. Thus it makes sense to ask why anything exists in, e.g., the twentieth century. (One might answer this question by citing the fact that something existed in the nineteenth century, together with certain conservation laws.) But the inhabitants of a given world are among its individuating conditions: one can no more ask concerning a particular world why it has the inhabitants it has than one can ask concerning a particular set of numbers why it has the members it has. (This much is true whether or not the indexical theory is correct.) Moreover, *if* the indexical theory is true, one cannot ask concerning a given world why it is actual. But surely (granting the intelligibility of the idea of a possible world) to ask why anything at all exists must be either to ask concerning a certain world (the actual one) *why* it is actual or else to ask why it has inhabitants.

But what is a possible world? If we are not clear about possible worlds, it is not likely that we shall get clear about what it is to call one of them actual. Our answer to the question "What is a possible world?" ought, I think, to satisfy two conditions. First, it ought to be Lewis's answer, or the sequel is liable to be an *ignoratio elenchi*. Secondly, it ought to be coherent. Unfortunately, these two reasonable conditions are inconsistent, for (as Stalnaker has pointed out) Lewis's account of what a possible world is is incoherent.[4] Let us see how this incoherency arises. Lewis has a pithy, one-sentence answer to the question "What is a possible world?": A possible world is a *way things could have been*. He argues for the existence of ways things could have been in a powerful and concise passage, part of which I shall quote:

> It is uncontroversially true that things might be otherwise than they are. I believe, and so do you, that things could have been different in countless ways. But what does this mean? Ordinary language permits the paraphrase: there are many ways things could have been besides the way they actually are. On the face of it, this sentence is an existential quantification. It says that there exist many entities of a certain description, to wit "ways things could have been." I believe that things could have been different in countless ways; I believe permissible paraphrases of what I believe; taking the paraphrase at its face value, I therefore believe in the existence of entities that might be called "ways things could have been." I prefer to call them "possible worlds."
>
> I do not make it an inviolable principle to take seeming existential quantifications in ordinary language at their face value. But I do recognize a presumption in favor of taking sentences at their face value, unless (1) taking them at face value is known to lead to trouble, and (2) taking them some other way is known not to. In this case, neither condition is met. I do not know any successful argument that my realism about possible worlds leads to trouble, unless you beg the question by saying that it already *is* trouble . . . All the alternatives I know, on the other hand, do lead to trouble.[5]

Like Lewis, I know of no successful argument for the conclusion that realism about "ways things could have been" leads to trouble. Moreover, I believe he adequately supports (in the paragraphs following the quoted passage) the contention that all known alternatives to such a realism do lead to trouble. If this is indeed the case, then the quoted passage and its supporting passages seem to me to demonstrate conclusively the existence of "ways things could have been." At any rate, the ontological method on display in this passage provides, I think, a paradigm of the

---

[4] See Robert C. Stalnaker, "Possible Worlds," *Noûs* 10 (1976), particularly p. 68.
[5] Lewis, *Counterfactuals*, p. 84.

167

right way to settle existence questions in philosophy, and I have never seen any argument against this sort of procedure that is at all convincing.

Now the incoherency. Lewis is not consistent about taking possible worlds to be ways things could have been. If we take "*x* is a way things could have been" seriously as an extensional open sentence, then surely those objects that satisfy it must be *abstract* objects. But Lewis very often says things about possible worlds that show clearly that he does not think of them as abstract. Consider, for example, the following passage, in which he argues against the view that a possible world is a set of sentences: "given that the actual world does not differ in kind from the rest, [this view] would lead to the conclusion that our actual world is a set of sentences. Since I cannot believe that I and all my surroundings are a set of sentences . . . I cannot believe that other worlds are sets of sentences either" (*Counterfactuals*, p. 86).

Yes. But neither can *I* believe that I and all my surroundings are a "way things could have been," not even that special one among them that is the way things in fact are. For one thing, it should seem that I and all my surroundings are many things, and thus not identical with *any* one thing, whether it be abstract or concrete. Of course, we might take "I and all my surroundings" to denote some single thing – say, the cosmos. Now if there is such a thing as the cosmos (and perhaps some philosophers would insist that "the cosmos" must be a disguised plural referring expression), then it must be a concrete object – this huge thing that astronomers investigate, and which we find ourselves within and parts of, as a gear is within and a part of a clock. Therefore, the cosmos, being concrete, is not a way things could have been. Indeed, it is difficult to see any important difference between "ways things could have been" and "ways the cosmos could have been." And surely the cosmos cannot itself be identical with any way the cosmos could have been: to say this would be like saying that Socrates is identical with the way Socrates is, which is plain bad grammar. (This was Stalnaker's point.) Moreover, there is only one cosmos (or, even if there are many cosmoi – many enormous closed causal systems – they are every one of them contingent objects and it should seem that there *might* have been just one – or none), but there are, and are necessarily, many ways things could have been. Even if there were no cosmos at all, but only an "enormous vacuum," that things were this way would not be a necessary truth, and thus there would exist, despite the absence of *concreta*, *many* ways things could have been.

Lewis's account of possible worlds, therefore, contains mutually incompatible elements, and if our own account is to be coherent it cannot be wholly faithful to Lewis. I think the best we can do is this. Let us retain the notion of a possible world as a way things could have been, and let us reject any suggestion that a possible world is a concrete object; in particular, let us reject any suggestion that "the actual *world*" – *whatever* "actual" may mean – is "all this." In other words, let us agree that the actual world is the way things are and carefully distinguish between the way things are and the things that are that way.

It may be that in so altering Lewis's account of possible worlds, I have altered it to the point at which he and I are no longer calling the same things "possible worlds." Moreover, it may be that the plausibility of thinking of "actual" as an indexical word in some way depends on regarding worlds as concrete objects; in that case, I shall be begging the question. But I can see no way to avoid excising *some* important feature of Lewis's account, for being a concrete object and being a way things might be simply do not seem to be compatible properties. It is conceivable that, though I am right about the mutual incompatibility of the several elements of Lewis's account of possible worlds, I have removed the patient from the tumor: perhaps the more reasonable way in which to have repaired Lewis's account would have been to have retained the thesis that possible worlds are concrete objects like the cosmos and to have rejected the thesis that possible worlds are ways things could have been. But this strategy would present us with a difficulty I do not know how to surmount: Lewis's only *argument* for the existence of more than one possible world depends upon his identifying worlds with ways things could have been. I conclude, therefore, that the alteration I have made is the one that permits us to remain as close to Lewis as possible without sacrificing internal coherence.

We can restate this "purified Ludovician" account of the nature of possible worlds in a way that is at once more precise, closer to ordinary language, and syntactically more convenient, if we replace talk of "ways things could have been" with talk of "possibilities." Such differences in sense as there may be between these two terms seem to me to be not very important, and "possibilities" has syntactical advantages over Lewis's phrase, in that terms that denote individual possibilities (phrases of the form, "the possibility that . . .") lie ready to hand.[6]

---

[6] The remainder of this section is a trivial modification of the account of possible worlds presented in Ch. 4 of Alvin Plantinga's wonderful book *The Nature of Necessity* (Oxford, 1974).

Possibilities are either *realized* or *unrealized*. For example, the possibility that Socrates die in the year 399 BC is realized, as is the possibility that some nineteenth-century president of the US who is not the father of any mayor of New York be impeached but not convicted. But the possibility that Plato die in 399 BC is unrealized, as is the possibility that every direct descendant of James II who is alive at some time or other during the eighteenth century rule England at some time or other during either the eighteenth or the nineteenth century. (Hereinafter, I shall use "$\pi$" to abbreviate "the possibility that.") Phrases like "$\pi\, 7 + 5 = 13$" are, of course, without a referent – there *is* no such possibility as $\pi\, 7 + 5 = 13$ – and may be treated in whatever way the reader thinks is the proper way to treat improper descriptions.

If A and B are possibilities, then we say A *includes* B just in the case that it is impossible for the former to be realized and the latter unrealized. A *precludes* B just in the case that it is impossible for these two possibilities to be jointly realized. Obviously, there are many pairs of possibilities such that neither one includes or precludes the other. If A includes B and B includes A, then A and B are *identical*, are one and the same possibility. Thus, $\pi\, 2 + 2 = 4 = \pi\, 2 + 6 = 8$, and each of these possibilities (strictly, this possibility) is identical with $\pi$ iron be malleable or not malleable. This is not to say that, e.g., "$\pi\, 2 + 2 = 4$" and "$\pi\, 2 + 6 = 8$" are synonymous, which they are not, but only that they denote the same object, to wit, the possibility that is necessarily realized.

If A is such that for every possibility $b$, either A includes $b$ or A precludes $b$, then we say that A is a *comprehensive* possibility, or (a stylistic variant) a *possible world*. To say of a given possible world that it is *actual* is to say of it that it is realized. (This definition of "actual" is not in competition with the indexical theory. Presumably the indexical theorist will insist on an indexical account of "realized.") I shall assume without argument that there is at least one such "possible world," and, moreover, that at least one of them is realized or actual. It follows that exactly one of them is actual. Possible worlds, then, make up a subclass of the class of possibilities, or possibilities as to how things might be, or, in Lewis's language, ways things could have been.

These definitions tell us what a possible world is. In order to complete our account of possible worlds, we must give meanings to the words that are customarily used to express the relations that hold between possible worlds and other objects. That is, we must explain what it is for an object to *exist in* or *at* a given world and we must explain what it is for a proposition to be *true in* or *at* a given world. I offer the following definitions:

> $o$ exists at $w =_{df} w$ includes the possibility that $o$ exist
> $p$ is true at $w =_{df} w$ includes the possibility that $p$ be true.

The definientia of these two definitions can easily be seen to be equivalent to

> if $w$ were actual, $o$ would exist
> if $w$ were actual, $p$ would be true,

and I shall generally treat "$o$ exists at $w$" and "$p$ is true at $w$" as stylistic variants on these two counterfactual sentences.[7] It may well be that Lewis would not accept these definitions of "exists at" and "is true at." There is certainly no evidence in his writings that he would. I can only say that I know of no other definitions, that these definitions seem eminently reasonable, and that I am not willing to take "exists at" and "is true at" to be clear enough to require no definitions.

We now have our account of possible worlds. I believe that this account is what one gets if one thinks carefully through the implications of the idea that a possible world is a way things could have been, and I think that it is therefore legitimate to investigate the indexical theory of actuality by trying to determine whether it is adequate to this account of possible worlds. Moreover, what I say in the remainder of this essay will be applicable to any serious account of possible worlds I know of. All accounts of possible worlds I know of are either incoherent, or so sketchy as to resist serious investigation, or else treat possible worlds as abstract objects. The theories that I know of that treat worlds as abstract objects other than special possibilities treat them as special *states of affairs* (the actual world being the one that *obtains*), as special *propositions* (the actual world being the one that is *true*), or as special *properties* (the actual world being the one that is *instantiated*). It would be easy to restate what I say in the sequel on the assumption that possible worlds are states of affairs, propositions, or properties.

---

[7] This equivalence holds because the realization of a comprehensive possibility determines the realization or nonrealization, as the case may be, of *every* possibility. Hence counterfactuals about what would be the case if a certain world were actual are equivalent to the corresponding strict conditionals. I prefer to employ the counterfactual definition of "exists at" and "is true at" in practice because it is easier than the official definition to grasp intuitively. But we had better let the official definition remain the official definition, in order not to rule out the possibility of a non-circular possible-worlds account of counterfactual conditionals.

I will now examine individually three theories that might be "the indexical theory of actuality."

II

I will call the following proposition the *Weak Theory*:

> At each world, "the actual world" refers to that world.

So far as I know, no one has said anything in print that commits him to the thesis that the Weak Theory *is* "the indexical theory of actuality," *is* the theory that Lewis means to be putting forth in the passages I have quoted above. But I have heard this thesis advanced sufficiently often in conversation that I think it deserves to be discussed. In any case, my discussion of it will be brief. I shall show, first, that the Weak Theory (charitably interpreted) is true, and, secondly, that it cannot properly be called an indexical theory. I think it is important to show this because I have heard people say that they accepted the indexical theory when what they really accepted (it eventually transpired) was merely the Weak Theory.

What does it mean to say that "the actual world" *refers to* a certain world *at* a certain world? More generally, what does it mean to say that a certain expression *e* refers to a certain object *x* at a certain world *w*? It might be thought that our definition of "*p* is true at *w*" provides an answer to this question. And so it does, but I do not think it is an answer that anyone would want to accept. The answer our definition provides, of course, is

> *e* refers to *x* at *w* = $_{df}$ If *w* were actual, *e* would refer to *x*.

But if this definition is accepted, then the Weak Theory is trivially false. There are certainly worlds in which "the actual world" has a different meaning from its actual meaning. That is to say, there are certainly worlds in which "the actual world" does not mean what it does in @, where "@" is a proper name for the world that is in fact actual. There is, for example, a world W in which "actual" means "present" (like *actuel* in French) and "world" means "age" (which it once meant in @). Then, I should think, if W were actual, "the actual world" would refer not to W but to the present age. Clearly, however, the words I used above to express the Weak Theory are not *supposed* to be interpreted in such a way that this undoubted fact about the meaning "the actual world" might have had is the *sort* of fact that could refute the Weak

172

Theory. We may solve this problem (rather programmatically) as follows. Let us relativize reference not only to worlds but to languages (cf. the suggestive but unclear thesis that "pain" refers-in-English to pain, but refers-in-French to bread), and think of a *language*, for present purposes, as a set-theoretical object of some sort, after the manner of formal logicians. Let "E" designate that "language" whose structure is instantiated in the actual usage of English speakers. Thus, in worlds where the natural language English is at all different, E is simply not "spoken," not instantiated in anyone's linguistic practice. Then we may define "*e* refers at *w* to *x*" to mean "If *w* were actual, *e* would refer-in-E to *x*." If this definition is acceptable, then, I think, we avoid the problem posed by our earlier definition, for if W were actual, then, though "the actual world" would refer *tout court* to the present age, it would *refer-in-E* to W. And, in general, for any world *w*, if *w* were actual, then "the actual world" would refer-in-E to *w*. Therefore the Weak Theory is true.

But is the Weak Theory in any interesting sense "indexical"? It is hard to see how this could be. Consider the following statement.

> There are many possible worlds. All of them *exist*, though, of course, only one of them is actual. Its actuality consists in its having a certain property – actuality – that the others all lack, though each of them *might have* had it. This is strictly comparable to the following assertion: "There are many people who entered the race. All of them exist, though only one of them is *the winner*. His being the winner consists in his having a certain property – having won – that the others all lack, though each of them *might have* had it."

Surely if any statement is incompatible with any theory that could properly be called an indexical theory, this one is. But this statement is compatible with the Weak Theory. In fact, I should think that anyone who accepted this statement would regard the Weak Theory as a trivial consequence of it: surely *everyone* will agree that if some nonactual world *had* been actual, it would have been denoted (-in-E) by "the actual world." Therefore, since the Weak Theory is compatible with a proposition that is incompatible with any theory that is the, or an, indexical theory, the Weak Theory is not the, or an, indexical theory.

III

If the Weak Theory is not an indexical theory, this is not because it is incompatible with the proposition that "the actual world" is an indexical phrase, but because it leaves out something essential to the idea of in-dexicality: it does not say the *wrong* things, but it does not say enough of the right ones. The most cursory inspection of the passages I have quoted in which Lewis expounds the indexical theory will show that *one* feature of Lewis's exposition that is unrepresented in the Weak Theory is this: a possible world (like a place or a time) is a *context* or *circumstance of utterance*. This suggests that Lewis's theory may be what I shall call the *Augmented Weak Theory* (AWT):

> At every world w, "the actual world" refers to w, and to specify the world in which an utterance is spoken is to specify a circumstance under which that utterance is spoken.

AWT, unlike the Weak Theory, does appear to be an indexical theory. For what is an indexical term but one whose reference depends upon the circumstances in which it is uttered? And obviously if AWT is true, then the reference of "the actual world" depends upon the circumstances in which it is spoken. ("The actual world," according to AWT, is what might be called a reflexive indexical, like "I," "here," and "now," and unlike "you," "there," and "then": its reference depends upon the cir-cumstances of its utterance because its reference is *to* those circumstances, or, at least, to some part or feature of those circumstances.)

But if AWT has the consequence that "the actual world" is an index-ical phrase, it has this consequence only at the expense of having a much more far-reaching consequence: that *every* definite description (with the possible exception of "rigid" definite descriptions like "the even prime") is an indexical phrase. Take, for example, "the originator of the Theory of Relativity." Though Einstein in fact enjoys the distinction of being the referent of this phrase, he might not have. There are worlds in which, e.g., Calvin Coolidge is the originator of the Theory of Rela-tivity. It is easy to see that it follows from this fact together with the second conjunct of AWT that the phrase "the originator of the Theory of Relativity" is an indexical phrase. Consider a world W in which Coolidge was the originator of the Theory of Relativity. Suppose someone in W utters the sentence, "The originator of the Theory of Re-lativity was a man of few words." Then that person refers to Coolidge by saying "the originator of the Theory of Relativity." And thus (a possible world being a circumstance of utterance), "the originator of the Theory of Relativity" depends for its reference upon the circumstances in which it is uttered, as does any other "nonrigid" description. It is true that, according to AWT, "the actual world" is a *reflexive* indexical and "the originator of the Theory of Relativity" is not, but I cannot see that this fact does anything to make the consequences of AWT any less counterintuitive. An irreflexive indexical is nevertheless an indexical, and "the originator of the Theory of Relativity" ought not to be any sort of indexical. Well, why not? Why *shouldn't* "the originator of the Theory of Relativity" be an indexical? Upon examining the intuitions that underlie this conviction, I find that they may be embodied in the following principle:

> (P)    If R is a referring phrase, and if it is not possible that there be distinct occasions of utterance A and B such that, on occasion A, R refers to some object O, and, on B, R does *not* refer to O, then R is not indexical.

It is easy to see that both "the originator of the Theory of Relativity" and "the actual world" are nonindexical according to (P). It is possible that there be an occasion of utterance on which "the originator of the Theory of Relativity" refers to Einstein and possible that there be an occasion on which it refers to Coolidge. It is possible that there be an occasion of utterance on which "the actual world" refers to @ and possible that there be an occasion on which "the actual world" refers to W. But we cannot infer from these conjunctions alone that either term is indexical, for the inference-rule:

$$\Diamond p \mathbin{\&} \Diamond q \vdash \Diamond(p \mathbin{\&} q)$$

is a notorious fallacy.

To this argument the defender of AWT has an obvious reply: "But you are simply begging the question. Your application of the principle (P) evidently depends on the assumption that an 'occasion of utterance' is something like a speaker-place-time triple. You are ignoring the fact that, according to AWT, a possible world is a circumstance of utterance. Therefore, according to AWT, an occasion of utterance must be thought of as something like a speaker-place-time-world quadruple. Hence it does not follow that there cannot be distinct occasions of utterance on which 'the actual world' refers to different objects. In fact, it follows that there *are* distinct occasions of utterance on which it refers to different objects. I must concede that it *also* follows that there are distinct occasions of utterance on which 'the originator of the Theory of Relativity' refers to different objects. But I will grasp the nettle with my fist: 'the originator of the Theory of Relativity' *is* an indexical phrase. I will admit that 'the originator of the Theory of Relativity' is not quite like 'I' or 'over there' or 'the first president of this country.' These are (as one might call them) *intramundane* indexicals, while 'the originator of the Theory of Relativity,' like 'the actual world,' is an *intermundane* indexical. That is, while the referent of, e.g., 'I' can differ from occasion to occasion of utterance *within* a given world, the referent of 'the originator of the Theory of Relativity' differs on two occasions only if these occasions are in different worlds. I'll grant that when philosophers have talked about indexicals in the past they have probably been thinking only of intramundane indexicals. But intermundane indexicals *are* indexicals, albeit their indexicality has hitherto escaped our attention."

Now it seems to me that if this defense of AWT is coherent at all, it requires us to understand "indexical" in a new and extended sense, comparable to the new and extended sense logicians gave to "predicate-letter" when they began to treat sentence-letters as "0–place predicate-letters." This new usage, of course, represented not a discovery by logicians (the discovery that closed sentences had all along been predicates), but a stipulation. If this is the case, then AWT begins to appear less exciting. It is exciting to suppose that "the actual world" is a description like "the present time"; less exciting to suppose it is a description like "the originator of the Theory of Relativity." In fact that seems to be what we believed in the first place: that a certain world, @, is distinguished from all other worlds by being the actual world in the same sense of *distinguished* as that in which a certain man, Einstein, is distinguished from all other men by being the originator of the Theory of Relativity.

One more point needs to be made about AWT. I have suggested that if AWT is coherent, its content is not very interesting, since that content seems to consist mainly of a device for applying the word "indexical" in a new and misleading way. But it is not at all clear that AWT is coherent because it is not at all clear that this device (that of interpreting "occasion of utterance" in such a way that possible worlds are among the ingredients that individuate occasions of utterance) is coherent.

According to AWT, there must be such a thing as *the* world in which an utterance containing "the actual world" is spoken. This is evident from the very wording of AWT, and it should be clear intuitively why this is so. (Consider, for example, "now." Each utterance of this word must take place at exactly one time. If there were many different times at which a given utterance of "now" took place, then it is very hard to see how this utterance could refer to *any* time.) But it does not seem to be the case that each utterance of "the actual world" takes place in a single world. Last week, talking to my class in the philosophy of religion, I said, "There is much evil in the actual world." This utterance of "the actual world" was, I suppose, a particular event, and, I would suppose, *this very event* took place in many distinct possible worlds. It seems evident, for example, that if any given electron in the Andromeda galaxy had failed to exist, this event (my utterance of "the actual world") would nevertheless have taken place. But if this is the case, if events in general, and utterances of "the actual world" in particular, are not what Plantinga has called "world-bound individuals," then AWT is incoherent (just as a theory that held that an utterance of "now" referred to the time at which it was spoken would be incoherent if every utterance of "now" *necessarily* was spoken at many different times).

I can think of no reason to suppose that concrete events like utterances are confined to single worlds that would not also be a reason for thinking that *all* particular objects are confined to single worlds. And no reason I know of for thinking *that* is a good reason. It is well known that Lewis has devised a theory called "Counterpart Theory" that embodies just this assumption.[8] (I doubt it is an accident that Lewis is the originator of both Counterpart Theory and the indexical theory.) Some philosophers, most notably Plantinga, have attempted to show that Counterpart Theory has absurd semantical and metaphysical consequences.[9] Other philosophers have denied this. This is not the place for me to enter that debate, and I will close this section with three observations that do not commit me to taking any particular position about the semantical or metaphysical adequacy of Counterpart Theory.

(i)   Counterpart Theory is *prima facie* wrong, which is not of course to say that it is wrong.

(ii)  There are no known good reasons for trying to see whether the *prima facie* objections to Counterpart Theory can be met. The only motivation that has ever been suggested for Counterpart Theory is this: it solves, or, perhaps, avoids, the "problem of identity across worlds." But, as Plantinga has shown, there are no intelligible statements of this "problem."[10]

(iii) Few philosophers other than Lewis are attracted to Counterpart Theory. Any theory of actuality that presupposes the truth of Counterpart Theory (as AWT would seem to) is too special and too partisan to be of much interest to the generality of philosophers.

---

[8] See David Lewis, "Counterpart Theory and Quantified Modal Logic," *The Journal of Philosophy* 65 (1968), pp. 113–126.

[9] See Plantinga, *The Nature of Necessity*, pp. 102–120.

[10] See ibid., pp. 88–101.

IV

If the principle (P) is true, and if "occasion of utterance" is interpreted in some way that does not lead to all nonrigid definite descriptions being indexical terms, then "the actual world" is not an indexical term. But I can claim no more for (P) than that I find it plausible. I must concede that there are certain phrases (phrases which, interestingly enough, purport to denote possible worlds) that may well be counterexamples to (P). One such is a particular favorite of Lewis's: "the world we inhabit." Another, "this world," is in common usage. If these phrases are indexical, then, clearly, (P) is false, since neither of them is such that it could refer to two different objects on two occasions of utterance. I am inclined not to regard these phrases as indexical, but I have no real reason for this other than my fondness for (P). There is certainly a not-too-bad *argument* for their indexicality: each contains a paradigmatically indexical word ("we" in the one case, "this" in the other). Moreover, while some phrases contain indexical words but only in an adventitious way (for example, "the man who is this man if this man is the tallest man and is the tallest man otherwise"), these two phrases do not seem to fall into this category.

In the sequel, I shall suppress my fondness for (P) and assume for the sake of argument that "the world we inhabit" and "this world" can properly be called indexical. If this is so, then it is evident that there are two propositions either of which could serve as a premise from which something that might reasonably be called an indexical theory of actuality could be derived:

(a) "The actual world" means "the world we inhabit"
(b) "The actual world" means "this world."

Lewis nowhere, so far as I know, explicitly endorses either (a) or (b). But the passage quoted above from *Counterfactuals* ("We call it alone actual . . . because it is the world we inhabit") suggests that he might very well accept (a). And perhaps some philosophers would accept (b). At any rate, many philosophers seem to use "the actual world" and "this world" more or less interchangeably.

However this may be, the important question is, is either (a) or (b) *true*? I think that both (a) and (b) are false, and I shall present brief arguments for this conclusion. These arguments, unfortunately, will depend on rather special features of (a) and (b), and will contain some controversial premises. I could argue at greater length for these controversial premises than I am in fact going to do, but I do not think the game is worth the candle. Instead of defending these arguments at length, I shall proceed to argue that no indexical theory of the *sort* that could be deduced from premises *like* (a) or (b) could possibly be right.

Let us first consider (a). What does "the world we inhabit" mean? This phrase can mean only "the world we exist in." And this latter phrase is a necessarily improper description (like "the volume of space we are within" or "the odd prime"). This is the case since each of us might have been at least a bit different and each of us, therefore, exists in more than one possible world.

According to Counterpart Theory, of course, it is (informally speaking) neither true that anyone exists in more than one possible world nor true that our existence in more than one world follows from the proposition that each of us might have been a bit different. But, as we saw in Section III, any theory of actuality that presupposes Counterpart Theory is objectionable. Therefore (a) is objectionable.

Premise (b) is more tricky. All of us who use the language of possible worlds occasionally speak of "this world," and no one seems to be much troubled by this phrase. But I am doubtful whether it has any very clear meaning. I am doubtful about this because I am doubtful about whether it is possible to make ostensive reference to the actual world (or to any world; but, presumably, if it is possible to make ostensive reference to any world, it is possible to make ostensive reference to the actual world). The problem is this: each of us exists in many worlds and, moreover, exists in many worlds epistemically indistinguishable from the actual world. (I shall not define "epistemically indistinguishable," but clearly there is some sense in which some worlds that contain just one more elementary particle than the actual world does are "epistemically indistinguishable" from it.) Now if it is possible to make ostensive reference to the actual world, then there must be some sense in which the actual world is salient for us, some way in which it stands out. But how could it stand out among all those worlds from which it is *indistinguishable*? (In considering this question, the reader should recall that the actual world, like the other worlds, is an abstract object; thus neither it nor any part of it – whatever precisely "part" might mean in this context – is present to our senses. The *causal* relations that obtain between us and the actual world are just those that obtain between us and any other world: none at all.)

179

One might be tempted to say that there is one property the actual world has that no other has: *actuality* (though it is not clear that the *indexical* theorist would be tempted to say this) and that actuality is sufficient for salience. I do not see this. Let us remember what a possible world is. A possible world is a possibility. The actual world is the comprehensive possibility that is realized. Let us note that a possibility's being realized does not in any obvious sense make it somehow more salient than "similar" possibilities that are not realized. Consider, for example, the possibility that there be an odd number of trees in Canada and the possibility that there be an even number of trees in Canada. One or the other of these possibilities is realized. But the one that is realized does not stand out, or the other fade into the background. Therefore, being realized is not *per se* a property that makes a possibility salient, any more than truth is a property that makes a *proposition* salient. Now this is not to say that there may not be a *certain class* of possibilities such that (i) exactly one member of that class must be realized and (ii) the member that is realized will be salient in comparison with the other members. Perhaps the class {π there be conscious beings, π there be no conscious beings} is such a class. And perhaps the class of all comprehensive possibilities is such a class. If it is, then my doubts about making ostensive reference to the actual world are unfounded. But I see no reason to think it is, since the class of possible worlds contains many members that are indistinguishable from the actual world, or are "distinguishable" only as the possibility that there be an odd number of trees in Canada and the possibility that there be an even number of trees in Canada: by the simple possession or non-possession of the property of being realized.[11]

If I am right about all this, then (b) is false, since "this world" does not mean anything in particular. An adequate defense of this thesis would have to be rather more extensive than this, however. If I were seriously to argue that "this world" is meaningless, I should at least have to

[11] The referee for *The Philosophical Review*, where this essay originally appeared, strenuously objects to this argument. The heart of his objection is contained in this example: "Why does something have to 'stand out' in some epistemically distinguishable way to be an object of ostensive reference? Suppose I am lying in bed at night, unable to sleep. Several times I say to myself, 'I wonder what time it is now?' It seems to me that I succeed in referring ostensively, or demonstratively, to particular times each time I say now, even if there is nothing distinctive about the times – even if I can't tell them from each other." But there *is* something distinctive about these times: each is *the* time at which certain thoughts and sensations of the insomniac occur, events which he in some sense experiences or is aware of. No world, however, is *the* world at which any event that anyone is aware of occurs.

explain, or explain away, our apparently perfectly meaningful use of sentences like, "This is the best of all possible worlds" and "No unicorns exist in this world." I think I could do this, but to do it would require a great deal of rather tedious argument by analogy. Fortunately this will not be necessary, since it is fairly easy to see that even if one could refer to the actual world as "this world," (b) must nevertheless be false. Moreover, a similar argument could be used to show that even if one could refer to the actual world as "the world we inhabit," (a) must nevertheless be false.

Plantinga has convincingly shown the falsity of (b) (on the assumption that one can refer to the actual world as "this world") in *The Nature of Necessity*. (See pp. 49–51.) I shall not repeat his argument here. Nor shall I adapt it to the task of showing that (a) is false (even assuming that "the world we inhabit" denotes the actual world), though this would be easy to do. I shall instead generalize the insights that underlie his argument to show that any indexical theory that could be deduced from premises like (a) and (b) must be wrong.

If "this world" designates anything, then it designates @ rigidly. And, presumably, if some other world had been actual, "this world" would have designated (-in-E) *that* world rigidly; that is to say, at each world, "this world" designates *that* world rigidly. Now if "this world" and "the actual world" mean the same, then it seems unavoidable to suppose that at each world, "the actual world" designates that world rigidly. And the same consequence seems to follow if "the world we inhabit" (supposing that phrase to be capable of designating anything) and "the actual world" mean the same, since "the world we inhabit" would *seem* to designate @ rigidly if – *per impossibile* – it designates anything at all.[12] Thus any indexical theory that could be deduced from (a) or (b) would have the consequence that, at any world, "the actual world" designated (-in-E) that world rigidly. Now even if I am right in thinking that "the world we inhabit" and "this world" are incoherent phrases, it might still be true that "the actual world" designates each world rigidly at that world. In fact, perhaps that just *is* the indexical theory. A referee for *The Philosophical Review* so interprets the indexical theory and, quite possibly, this

---

12 For example, if, *per impossibile*, there were only one possible world, "the world we exist in" would designate it rigidly; or if, *per impossibile*, Counterpart Theory were true on its intended interpretation, "the world we exist in" would designate the actual world rigidly.

interpretation is correct. Let us call the thesis that at each world "the actual world" designates that world rigidly, the *Strong Theory* (ST).

Section III of this essay consisted essentially of an argument for the conclusion that the second conjunct of AWT is false. But, since ST does not imply that a world is a context of utterance, the arguments of Section III do not refute ST. The arguments presented earlier in the present section refute or purport to refute two "special versions" of ST – or, more precisely, refute two propositions each of which entails ST – but do not refute ST itself. Let us, therefore, examine ST.

There are three questions we might ask about ST: Is it Lewis's theory? Is it properly called an indexical theory? Is it true? I shall say just a bit about the first two of these questions and discuss the third at some length.

I am not sure whether Lewis's theory is AWT or ST or some third thing. Because of the stress that Lewis lays on "contexts of utterance," I am inclined to think that he accepts AWT. On the other hand, the *examples* Lewis gives of indexical terms – "I," "you," "here," "now" – designate rigidly (in context), so there is something to be said for the "strong" interpretation of Lewis's words.[13] But perhaps the question is not terribly important, for ST is an interesting theory, whoever holds it.

Should ST be called an *indexical* theory? Not if (P) is true. But then perhaps (P) isn't true. Moreover, whether or not ST should be *called* indexical, it has a feature that will be attractive to those who are attracted to "indexical" theories: for any possible world, if someone applies to that world *at* that world a predicate meaning what "is actual" in fact means, then he says something true; not merely something true *at that world*, but something true at @. Thus ST, whether or not it is properly *the*, or even *an*, indexical theory of actuality, does the job an indexical theory is supposed to do: it militates against one's tendency to think of @ as in some important sense *unique*, as being the sole possessor of a property, actuality, that all worlds strive for but only one attains. Thus, ST, whether or not it *is* the indexical theory, has the same sort of importance I earlier claimed for the indexical theory. For example, let us consider again the question, "Why should there exist anything (contingent) at all?" This

---

[13] It may well be that Lewis's theory is what we might call the Augmented Strong Theory: the theory that (i) at each world "the actual world" designates that world rigidly and (ii) a world is a context of utterance. The Augmented Strong Theory is, of course, objectionable both for the reasons presented in the present section and for those presented in the previous section.

question would seem to be equivalent to the question, "Why did one of the worlds in which something contingent exists win the competition for the possession of actuality, rather than the world (or one of the worlds, if there is more than one) in which nothing contingent exists?" And this question is obviously incoherent if ST is true.

Is ST true? I think it can be shown that it is not. In order to see what is wrong with ST, let us state it more precisely and formally and examine its consequences:

> ST  For any world $w$ and any sentence-of-E S containing "the actual world," S expresses-in-E at $w$ a proposition necessarily equivalent to the proposition expressed-in-E at $w$ by the sentence obtained by replacing each occurrence in S of "the actual world" by a proper name of $w$.

Now consider the proposition

    (1)  In the actual world, Caesar was murdered.

According to ST, this proposition is equivalent to

    (2)  In @, Caesar was murdered,

which is necessarily true. But (1) is obviously *not* a necessary truth. Or perhaps I should not say this. Perhaps this thesis, perverse as it may seem, is just what the proponent of ST wishes to accept. At any rate, perhaps he will be *willing* to accept it.

What else must he be willing to accept? A great deal. Consider the proposition

    @ might not have been actual.

If ST is true, then this proposition is a necessary falsehood, being equivalent to

    @ might not have been @.

More generally, since

    $\forall w$, $w \neq$ @, $w$ could not possibly have been @,

ST has the consequence

    (3)  $\forall w$, $w \neq$ @, $w$ could not possibly have been actual.

Shall the proponent of ST simply *accept* this consequence? Well, perhaps so. But what, exactly, would he be accepting? I assume he thinks there are worlds other than @ – if there are not, of course, then it is trivially true that no world other than @ could have been actual – for if there are not, then the true and the necessarily true and the possible coincide. Now let W be one of these worlds that is not @. Is W a *possible* world? Note that, according to ST, we have

> W could not possibly have been actual.

But what could be meant by calling a world "possible" except that it is a world that might possibly be actual? Nothing that I can see, for that just *is* what "possible" means in the phrase "possible world": "possibly actual" (just as "possible" in "possible proposition" means "possibly true," and "possible" in "possible property" means "possibly instantiated").

So it would seem that ST is simply incoherent: either it leads to the consequence that there is only one possible world (and hence to the collapse of all modal distinctions), or else it leaves "possible world" without any graspable sense whatever.

The reader may be inclined to think that the weak step in this *reductio* of ST is the argument for (3). After all (the reader may want to protest), consider any world other than @ – say, W again. Though ST may have the consequence that W could not have been actual *from our point of view*, surely this theory also entails that W not only could be but *is* actual *from its own point of view*? Alas, no. This is not a consequence of ST. All that follows from ST is that the sentence-of-E "W is actual" expresses at W a proposition that is true at W. In fact, it expresses at W a proposition that is true at all worlds: the proposition that W = W, or, at least, a proposition necessarily equivalent to that proposition. And we agree with *that*. "Points of view," whatever they may be, have nothing to do with the matter, since the proposition expressed at W by "W is actual" is true from *everyone's* point of view. (That is, at every world. Of course, there is really no interesting sense in which a possible world is a "point of view," any more than there is an interesting sense in which a possible world is a context of utterance.) Moreover, what we express by "@ is actual" – that is, what these words *do* express, as opposed to what they *might* express – is, if ST is correct, something that is true "from the point of view of W." Thus, this objection comes to nothing, and our proof that no world save @ could possibly have been actual stands. It is true, of course, that in my statement of this result "actual" has the content its meaning assigns to it "for use in @." But that's all right, isn't it? What other content could, or should, it have?

Perhaps someone will suspect that this is *not* all right. Let him, then, consider the following line of reasoning. Suppose I want to find out what property actuality is. Someone tells me that the word "actuality" has (in the language in which I framed my metaphysical question) the following meaning: at each world it rigidly designates the property of being identical with that world (or a property necessarily coextensive with that property). Suppose I believe him. Then I can correctly infer that actuality is the property of being identical with @ (or a property necessarily coextensive with that property), and that no world that lacks actuality could possibly have had it; that is, that @ is the only possible world. But this result is absurd, and, therefore, ST is false.[14] And, therefore, the indexical theory of actuality is false unless it is some theory other than ST or AWT.[15] But if the indexical theory is neither ST nor AWT, then it is very hard to see what it might be.[16]

[14] Lewis and others who discuss the indexical theory are fond of drawing analogies between modal language and temporal language. While I do not generally find such analogies very convincing, I will mention in passing that I think that arguments like those used above could be constructed to show that the meaning of "the present moment" cannot be correctly explained by saying that at each moment it rigidly designates that moment.

[15] Lewis nowhere presents what is clearly intended to be an argument for the indexical theory, unless one counts as an argument his statement in "Anselm and Actuality" (p. 186) that the "strongest evidence" for the indexical theory is that it "explains why skepticism about our own actuality is absurd." But what does "our own actuality" mean? Or, to ask the same question in a rather more perspicuous form, what does "I am actual" mean? I can see nothing this phrase could mean but "I exist in the actual world" – that is, "I exist in whatever world is actual," not "I exist in @" – and this is equivalent to "I exist." And surely we do not need any recondite theory of actuality to explain why skepticism about one's own existence is absurd.

[16] I should like to thank a referee for *The Philosophical Review* for helpful comments on an earlier version of this essay, and, in particular, for calling to my attention the possibility that the indexical theory may be what I have called the Strong Theory.

I owe a great debt to Alvin Plantinga. Our discussions of the indexical theory have done so much to shape my thinking that I cannot say with any confidence that any of the ideas presented in this essay is original with me.

# 11

## *Plantinga on trans-world identity*

*The Nature of Necessity* is a treasure-trove. Among its treasures are Plantinga's treatments of the problem of evil and the ontological argument, his examination of the question whether there are nonexistent objects, and his discussion of the so-called problem of trans-world identity.

Plantinga's discussion of trans-world identity is a masterpiece of destructive philosophical analysis. Its virtues are a product of his virtues. He is a philosopher of exquisite clarity and a philosophical craftsman of the very highest order. *The Nature of Necessity* is founded upon a set of definitions of certain concepts that cluster round the concept of a "possible world." This set of definitions bears the unmistakable marks of Plantinga's clarity and craftsmanship. (If you think these definitions are obvious or trivial, you are the victim of an illusion: the mastery of an art consists in making the difficult look easy.) Anyone who brings Plantinga's definitions to an examination of the problem of trans-world identity will find his work half done for him. If he attends to the conceptual content of Plantinga's *definientia* rather than to the mental pictures (and other such distractions) that the *definienda* may have set drifting about in his mind, he will see that there is no problem of trans-world identity. He will find that all attempts he knows of to formulate the supposed problem are either incoherent or else have such obvious "solutions" that they do not deserve to be called problems. He will realize that it was all done with mirrors – that is, with empty words and confused pictures.

There is, therefore, no longer any excuse for talking as if there were a "problem of trans-world identity." And yet many philosophers persist in

First published in J. E. Tomberlin and P. van Inwagen (eds.), *Alvin Plantinga* (Dordrecht, 1985), pp. 101–120.

talking as if there were a problem that went by that name.[1] Some of them have even read the relevant parts of *The Nature of Necessity*. I can think of only one explanation for this: the empty words and confused pictures are capable of exerting a firmer grip on the philosophical imagination than Plantinga has supposed. What I mean to do in this essay is to examine what are, as I see it, the most important sources of the confusions that underlie the belief that there is a problem about trans-world identity, and to try, by bringing these sources into the open, to allow us to "command a clear view" of them. My hope is that one who commands a clear view of them will be no longer subject to the confusions of which they are the source and will, as a result, see that there is no problem of trans-world identity.

The present essay, therefore, is not a critical essay. It is not an attempt to correct Plantinga where he is wrong. It is rather an attempt to remove certain barriers to appreciating something he has to say that is right.

Before turning to this topic, however, I shall briefly outline the set of definitions I praised a moment ago – or those of them that are relevant to our purpose. Doubtless most of the readers of this book will be familiar with them. Anyone who is not in need of a review may skip the following section. But it must be constantly borne in mind that when I use the terms I shall define in Section II, I mean by them just what I say I mean by them and nothing more than or less than or different from what I say I mean by them. If I am charged with being unduly insistent on the point, I reply that, given the history of the reception of Plantinga's arguments, I am only being prudent. Several of Plantinga's critics have not only neglected to reproduce his definitions for the benefit of their readers, but have written as if these definitions did not exist – have written as if Plantinga had never explained what he meant by such terms as "possible world" and "exists in."[2] But one *cannot* discuss Plantinga's philosophy of modality with anyone who is unaware of Plantinga's definitions. This is not a matter of opinion: it is a simple statement of fact, the truth of which is evident to anyone who has read *The Nature of Necessity*. I cannot imagine what these critics supposed all those definitions were *for*.

---

[1] See, e.g., Baruch A. Brody, *Identity and Essence* (Princeton, 1980), and Michael Tooley, critical notice of *The Nature of Necessity* in *The Australasian Journal of Philosophy* 55 (1977), pp. 91–102.

[2] I have particularly in mind Tooley, critical notice, and Fabrizio Mondadori, review of *The Nature of Necessity*, *The Journal of Philosophy* 73/12 (24 June 1976).

## II

I shall assume that the reader is familiar with Plantinga's use of the terms "possible," "state of affairs," "obtains," and "proposition." These terms may be thought of as composing Plantinga's primitive vocabulary, or, at least, as much of it as we shall need to introduce to talk about trans-world identity, Having these terms (and the resources of ordinary English) at our disposal, we may proceed as follows. A state of affairs will be said to *include* a second state of affairs if it is impossible (i.e., not possible) for the former to obtain and the latter to fail to obtain. (Moreover, every state of affairs includes *itself*.) A state of affairs will be said to *preclude* a second state of affairs if it is impossible for them both to obtain. (Moreover, a state of affairs prelcudes *itself* only if it is impossible.) We call a state of affairs *maximal* if, for every other state of affairs, it either includes or precludes that other state of affairs. A *possible* maximal state of affairs is called a (*possible*) *world*. We shall assume that there are possible maximal states of affairs and that at least one of them obtains. Since any two maximal states of affairs are incompossible, exactly one maximal state of affairs obtains. We call it the "the actual world." (That is to say: when we are speaking of those special states of affairs that are worlds, we shall generally say "is actual" instead of "obtains"; this is a mere convention of style.)[3]

A proposition is said to be true *in* a given possible world if that world includes its being true. Or, what comes to the same thing, a proposition is true in a given world if it *would* be true if that world *were* actual. Similarly, an object exists *in* a given world if it *would* exist if that world *were* actual, and an object has a property *in* a given world if it *would* have that property if that world *were* actual.[4]

## III

What is the problem of trans-world identity according to those who say there is such a problem? According to Michael Tooley, it is a semantical problem, the problem of what it *means* to say that an object existing in

---

[3] "Possible worlds" are therefore abstract objects, and the actual world (roughly, the way things are) is to be distinguished from the universe or cosmos (the things that are that way).

[4] A given possible world thus exists in all possible worlds – at least given the "S-5 assumption," that what is possible in any world is possible in all, and given that a state of affairs can't have the property of possibly obtaining unless it exists – though, of course, a given world *is actual* or *obtains* in only one world: itself.

one world is the same as an object existing in another.[5] Let us accept this explanation.

The problem of trans-world identity, understood as Tooley proposes, is one of the simpler problems of philosophical semantics. It is comparable in difficulty with the problem of trans-encyclopedia identity. This latter problem, of course, is the problem of what it *means* to say that an object mentioned in one encyclopedia is identical with an object mentioned in another. I propose the following solution: to say this is to say that some object is mentioned in both encyclopedias. I propose a parallel solution to the problem of trans-world identity: to say that an object existing in one world is identical with an object existing in another is to say that some object exists in both worlds. And, given that there are worlds (possible maximal states of affairs), there is no problem about *that*. To say of, e.g., William P. Alston that he exists in both $W_1$ and $W_2$ is to . say that he would have existed if $W_1$ had been actual and would also have existed if $W_2$ had been actual. And there's no problem about *that*. Suppose the following English sentence expresses a truth: "It might have been the case that William P. Alston have got up ten minutes earlier this morning than he in fact did." And suppose that this sentence says what it appears to say: suppose it doesn't say merely that it might have been the case that someone *very like* Alston have got up ten minutes earlier than Alston in fact did; suppose it makes this modal claim on behalf of *Alston himself*. It follows from these two suppositions that Alston exists in more than one possible world. That is, it follows that more than one world has the following feature: if it had been actual, Alston would (still) have existed. The contention that Alston exists in more than one world, therefore, is no more in need of clarification than these two suppositions. And they are in need of no clarification at all.

"But all this is true only if you accept Plantinga's definitions of 'possible world' and 'exists in.'" This is doubtless correct. But what alternatives are there to these definitions?

If things are this simple, why did anyone ever suppose there was any problem about trans-world identity, and how can I regard Plantinga's treatment of it as masterly? People have come to think there was such a problem because, as I said in Section I, they are in the grip of confusions. Plantinga's treatment of it is masterly because it is a masterly analysis of these confusions.

---

[5] Tooley, critical notice, p. 99.

What confusions? They may be divided into two main groups: epistemological and metaphysical (or perhaps logical or semantical) confusions.

I shall have little to say about the epistemological confusions. They
are well known, and, I think, are nowadays pretty generally agreed to *be*
confusions. They are the confusions that are summed up in the questions,
"But how can we *tell* which of the objects in some non-actual world is
Socrates? What empirically manifest properties could be referred to in
the statement of a criterion that would enable us to decide whether an
object in some other world was Socrates?"[6]

The metaphysical (or logical or semantical) confusions are confusions
about identity. They will be the concern of the rest of this essay. These
confusions are on perspicuous display in two passages in the review of *The
Nature of Necessity* by Michael Tooley from which I have taken our statement of the problem of trans-world identity.[7] The second of these quotations concerns our stated problem, the problem of trans-world identity.
The first, however, is entirely about identity through time. It occurs in the
course of an attack on a rather tentative comparison of Plantinga's of the
problem of identity through time with the problem of trans-world identity. The point of Plantinga's comparison and the merits of Tooley's objection to it are matters that need not detain us; I am interested in the
picture of identity through time of which this passage is an articulation,
and not in the argument of the larger passage from which I have excerpted
it. I am interested in this picture of identity through time because I believe
that it is likely – in fact almost certain – to lead the philosopher whose
picture it is into analogous confusions about trans-world identity. (Indeed,
the route from confusions about identity through time to confusions
about trans-world identity is nicely laid out in the second quotation.)

IV

Here are the quotations:

[W]hat does it mean to say, for example, that the book on the table at time *t* is
identical with the book on the chair at time *t*★? One answer is that it means that

---

6 Saul Kripke's "Naming and Necessity," in *Semantics of Natural Language*, ed. Donald
Davidson and Gilbert Harman (Dordrecht, 1972), contains the classical diagnosis and
refutation of the epistemological confusions. See especially pp. 266–273.

7 Tooley's review displays the confusions I want to discuss in remarkably pure form. In
most writers who are confused about trans-world identity, one finds both the
metaphysical and the epistemological confusions. It is clear from Tooley's review,
however, that, whatever confusions about trans-world identity he may be subject to, he
has not been misled by questions like those mentioned in the preceding paragraph.

the object referred to by the expression "the book on the table at time *t*" is the same object as that referred to by the expression "the book on the chair at time *t★*". But one need not rest with this superficial account, since one can go on to ask what is meant by "the object referred to by the expression 'the book on the table at time *t★*.'" And one very natural answer is this. The expression "the book on the table at time *t*" picks out a certain spatially and temporally limited part of the world, and it does so either by picking out an instantaneous slice, of the book variety, which exists at time *t*, or else by picking out a relatively small non-instantaneous temporal part, of the book variety, which occupies a small interval containing time *t*, and then by linking this up with all other slices (or parts) of the relevant sort which stand in a certain causal relation to the slice (or part) existing at (or around) time *t*. (pp. 97–98)

Let us now turn to the question that lies at the heart of the problem of transworld identity. What does it mean to say that an individual in one possible world is identical with an individual in another possible world? The temporal analogy underlies the seriousness of this question, since it suggests that the predicate "is identical with" is not plausibly treated as semantically basic and unanalyzable in such contexts. To say that the book on this table at time $t_1$ is identical with the book on that chair at time $t_2$ is to say something that certainly appears to be analyzable in terms of some sort of relationship either between temporal slices existing at times $t_1$ and $t_2$, or between temporal parts occupying intervals containing times $t_1$ and $t_2$. The importance of this is that it will not do, apparently, to say that "identity" in the transworld case just has the meaning it has in the temporal case. For what could it mean to say that an object in one possible world is causally dependent upon an object in another possible world? (p. 101)

Let us examine these statements carefully. I begin with the first quotation. I shall write as if Tooley accepted his "one very natural answer," since this answer encapsulates the point of view I wish to examine, and it will be convenient to have someone to attribute it to; if Tooley is not fully committed to this answer, I apologize to him for taking this liberty.

There are two important theses on display in the first quotation. One is a thesis about the existence of certain objects and the other is a thesis about the relation of certain phrases in our language to those objects. The first thesis is that there are such things as "temporal parts" or "temporal slices." (The difference between very "thin" temporal parts and temporal slices does not matter much in the present context. I shall talk mainly about "slices" in the sequel, but what I shall say could be applied to "thin parts" easily enough.) The second thesis is that the way in which "time-involving" definite descriptions of physical objects like "the book on the table at *t*" relate to their *denotata* should be analyzed or explained in terms of slices.

There is one theory that fits this general description that Tooley clearly does *not* hold: that phrases like "the book on the table at time *t*" actually denote slices; that "the book on the table at time *t*" denotes the "*t*-slice" of the book. Philosophers who hold *this* view must either say that sentences like "The book on the table at time *t* is identical with the book on the chair at time *t*★" must always express propositions that are, strictly speaking, false, or else they must say that in such sentences "is identical with" does not intend numerical identity – two slices being *two* slices – but rather some relation of causal continuity.

Tooley's view of the matter is more artful and does not confront this awkward dilemma. As Tooley sees it, "the book on the table at *t*" is a name for a certain four-dimensional object,[8] one having slices "of the book variety" as parts, these parts being bound together into a whole by (again) some relation of causal continuity. As Tooley sees it, the phrase "the book on the table at *t*" means something like "the four-dimensional book the *t*-slice of which is on the *t*-slice of the table" and, similarly, "the book on the chair at *t*★" means "the four-dimensional book the *t*★-slice of which is on the *t*★-slice of the chair." And, of course, no particular problems are raised by the assertion that two such descriptions as these might be names for a single object.

Both these theories about the way in which time-involving definite descriptions relate to the world can be represented pictorially. The first theory can be represented as in Figure 11.1. The line drawn beneath this figure is a "time-axis": each point on it represents a point in time, the left-to-right arrangement of the points representing the past-to-future arrangement of points in time. The "books" drawn above the time-axis represent slices "of the book variety." I have, of course, been able to represent only a few slices: the viewer must somehow contrive to imagine that the sequence of book-drawings is continuous, just as the sequence of points on the line is. Each book-slice-representation is drawn directly above the point that represents the point in time it "occupies." Finally, the description-referent relation is represented by labels bearing the description and attached to the referent. (I don't mean this device in any sense to represent the "mechanics" of securing reference. It is meant to be neutral with respect to theories of what reference is and how it is

[8] Tooley does not use the words "four-dimensional object"; but I don't think that my use of them in my paraphrase of his view misrepresents him.

192

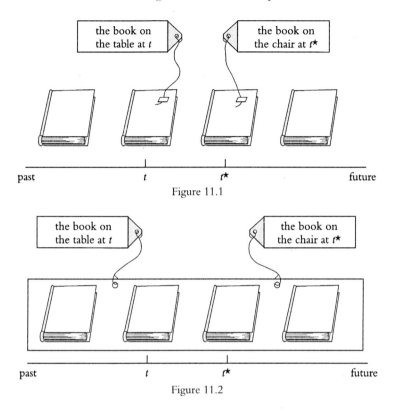

Figure 11.1

Figure 11.2

established. It is used merely to display the fact that certain phrases denote certain objects.)

The second theory, Tooley's theory, may be represented as in Figure 11.2. In this picture, the time-axis and the "books" mean what they meant in Figure 11.1. The rectangle represents the boundary of the four-dimensional object that is what the book really is. The description-referent relation is again represented by labels, but the labels are fixed to the "whole" book and not to slices of the book. (The points of attachment of the labels have no significance; I have to draw them as attached *somewhere*.)

In my view, these pictures embody grave illusions about the nature of time and about the way in which time-involving descriptions apply to their referents and about the kind of facts expressed by sentences formed by flanking the identity sign with time-involving descriptions. (Let us

Modality

call such sentences "temporal identity-sentences".) I believe it is a grave
illusion to suppose that there are four-dimensional objects or that things
are somehow composed of "temporal parts" or "slices" or that the facts
represented by temporal identity sentences even *look* as if they were facts
about such objects. I believe that people who suppose such things as
these are the victims of seductive but incoherent pictures – pictures like
Figure 11.1 and Figure 11.2, in fact. I believe these things, but I will not
argue for them. Instead I will draw another picture, for my present purposes will be served by pointing out that Figures 11.1 and 11.2 have at
least one rival, a rival that is far more different from them than they are
from each other. In this picture (Figure 11.3), as in the others, the
"book-drawing" represents a three-dimensional object. (But this is dangerously close to a pun. "Slices" are three-dimensional in the sense that
they have an extension of measure zero along one dimension and a non-
zero extension in three others. The book-drawing in Figure 11.3 represents not a slice "of the book variety" but a book: it has a non-zero extension in three dimensions, *tout court*. "Slices" do not *endure* through
time – this is what Wittgenstein would call a "grammatical proposition"
– but are *located* at a time; books endure.) As in Figure 11.1, each label is
attached to a three-dimensional object. As in Figure 11.2, each label is attached to the *same* object. (Thus temporal identity-sentences, according
to the theory represented by Figure 11.3, are straightforward expressions
of numerical identity.) Figure 11.3, unlike its two rivals, assimilates temporal identity-sentences to other identity-sentences. "The book that was
on the table at *t* is identical with the book that was on the chair at *t\**"
differs from "The book that Bill is reading is identical with the book that
Tom is looking for" in only one interesting respect: in the former sentence, "is identical with" is flanked by descriptions whose verbs are in
the past tense, and in the latter sentence it is flanked by descriptions
whose verbs are in the present tense.[9] (Both sentences, of course, are
equally well represented by pictures showing one book twice labeled,

[9] The acute reader will have noticed the transition in the present paragraph (and in Figure
11.3) from Tooley-style time-involving descriptions like "the book on the chair at *t*" –
verbless ones, that is – to the time-involving descriptions containing tensed verbs that are
the normal time-involving descriptions of everyday discourse. In some simple cases, the
verb in such descriptions can be dropped: "The book on the table at noon was red," is
good English, though, I would point out, a "that was" is present "in spirit" in this
sentence, even if it is unpronounced, for the adverbial phrase "at noon" modifies an
understood "was." (Philosophers who suppose that such phrases as "at noon" and "in
1950" are adjectives describing the location of temporal slices or whatnot are simply
mistaken.) In more complicated cases, there is no possibility of wholly eliminating tensed

194

the book that was
on the table at *t*

the book that was
on the chair at *t*★

Figure 11.3

which is what would intuitively seem right for a sentence that pivots
about "is identical with.")

This is how I see "identity through time" – though, of course,
someone who sees matters as I do is bound to find the word "through"
tendentious. "Through" is a word whose point is supplied by pictures
involving a time-axis. I should say that all the data that philosophers
might describe as belonging to the problem of "identity through (or
across) time" are the facts expressed by temporal identity-sentences, and
I perceive nothing in these sentences that should bring the words
"through" or "across" to mind. I have received strong hints from
various philosophers to the effect that I have blinded myself to a real
problem, but I have never heard a statement of this problem I can honestly say I understand.

I believe that the correct way to look at "identity across possible
worlds" is exactly analogous to the way I have contended is the correct
way to look at identity "across time." Let us now return to the topic of
trans-world identity, and I shall explain what I mean by this.

V

The second passage I have quoted from Tooley exhibits a view of what
it is for an object to exist in a given possible world that is in many re-

verbs from time-involving descriptions, as may be seen from, e.g., "the car that used to be
owned by the man who will marry the woman who had been the first woman President."

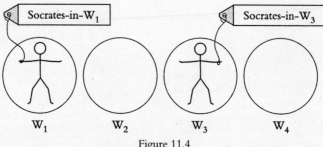

Figure 11.4

spects analogous to the view of what it is for an object to exist at a time that is embodied in Figure 11.1. Suppose there are just four possible worlds, $W_1$, $W_2$, $W_3$, and $W_4$. Suppose someone says that Socrates exists in both $W_1$ and $W_3$. According to Tooley's view of existence-in-a-world, this assertion about Socrates is of a sort that we might represent pictorially as in Figure 11.4. In this style of picture, we represent possible worlds by circles and the *exists-in* relation by drawing a picture of an object inside one of these circles. But, one might argue, Figure 11.4 shows graphically that statements of transworld identity cannot ever be *true*, and thus shows that the assertion that Socrates exists in both $W_1$ and $W_3$ cannot be true. For consider the sentence, "Socrates-in-$W_1$ is identical with Socrates-in-$W_3$." Figure 11.4 seems to make it plain that "Socrates-in-$W_1$" and "Socrates-in-$W_3$" denote *two* objects: just look at the picture and you'll see that the labels are attached to distinct things. Indeed it is probably not clear what we *mean* by the phrases "*Socrates*-in-$W_1$" and "*Socrates*-in-$W_3$." But it is clear that whatever these phrases may mean they cannot denote the same object.

The depiction of existence-in-a-world in Figure 11.4 is analogous to the depiction of existence-at-a-time in Figure 11.1. The philosopher who embraces Figure 11.1 must, as we have seen, either say that temporal identity-sentences never express truths or else say that the phrase "is identical with" that occurs in these sentences intends, contrary to all appearances, some causal relation. But the philosopher who is not willing to say that *trans-world* identity-sentences cannot express truths has no corresponding move open to him, since, obviously, objects existing in different worlds do not bear causal relations to one another: causal processes proceed from past to future *within* worlds; they can't, so to speak, jump the modal tracks. Thus, the problem of what it means to say

196

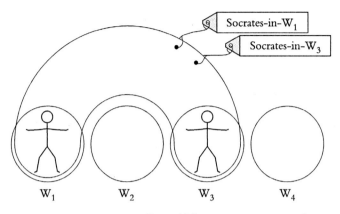

Socrates-in-$W_1$

Socrates-in-$W_3$

Figure 11.5

that an object existing in one world is identical with an object existing in another cannot be solved in the way that the philosopher who adheres to Figure 11.1 solves the problem of what it means to say that an object existing at one time is identical with an object existing at another time.

Can it be solved in a way that is analogous to the solution of the temporal problem that is represented by Figure 11.2? No, and for pretty much the same reason. Figure 11.5 is a picture of the (alleged) fact expressed by the sentence "Socrates-in-$W_1$ is identical with Socrates-in-$W_3$" that is analogous to the way Figure 11.2 depicts the fact that the book on the table at $t$ is identical with the book on the chair at $t^\star$.

In this picture, the objects that were labeled "Socrates-in-$W_1$" and "Socrates-in-$W_3$" in Figure 11.4 are represented as two parts of what David Lewis engagingly calls a "modal continuant."[10] The "horseshoe" represents the boundary of this modal continuant, in a way modeled on the way in which the rectangle in Figure 11.2 represented the boundary of a temporal continuant. The phrases "Socrates-in-$W_1$" and "Socrates-in-$W_3$" are now attached to the *same* object, a thing that exists in more than one world. The adherent of Figure 11.5 – so far as I know there are none – will argue that there is no reason to suppose than an object that can be correctly labeled "Socrates-in-$W_1$" need be entirely within $W_1$. He will, one would expect, support this thesis by a temporal analogy; he will point to the fact that an object that can be correctly

---

[10] See Postscript B to David Lewis, "Counterpart Theory and Quantified Modal Logic," in *Philosophical Papers I* (New York, 1983), pp. 40–42.

labeled "the book on the table at *t*" need not be temporally confined to the moment *t*.

What is wrong with Figure 11.5 as a picture of trans-world identity? Well, a lot is. Let me mention just one objection among many, an objection that Tooley and I would agree is decisive. First, the phrases "Socrates-in-$W_1$" and "Socrates-in-$W_3$" must simply be two names of *Socrates* – just as according to the adherent of Figure 11.2, "Socrates-in-400 BC" and "Socrates-in-450 BC" must be two names of Socrates.[11] (Otherwise we should not have *Socrates* existing in $W_1$ and $W_3$: there is no point in positing modal continuants if we are not willing to identify the referents of the terms of everyday discourse with these modal continuants.) But then Socrates has parts in more than one world, and we have said that causal relations cannot obtain between objects in different worlds. It follows that Socrates has parts between which no causal relations hold. But this seems plainly impossible. If one's ontology is liberal enough, one may allow the existence of, for example, an object made up of some of your temporal slices and some of mine and some taken from the book you are reading. Even if one believes in such objects, however, one must concede that they are not the ordinary objects of our reference and experience; they are not, e.g., people or books. If two objects – a hand and a temporal slice, say – are both parts of Socrates, then *some* sort of causal connection, however remote and involuted, must hold between them. Therefore the theory depicted in Figure 11.5 is incoherent if the object bounded by the "horseshoe" is Socrates and useless otherwise: the referent of "Socrates" cannot have causally unrelated parts.

The problem of trans-world identity would seem, therefore, to be a deep and intractable problem, owing to the fact that possible worlds are causally isolated from one another.[12]

As I have implied, however, this seeming is a mere seeming. It is an illusion one falls into as a consequence of doing one's thinking about possible worlds with the aid of pictures like Figures 11.4 and 11.5 – pictures, that is, drawn according to a convention that represents the *exists-in* relation by the placing of one symbol inside another symbol. This sort

[11] Of course the proponent of Figure 11.5 might use the phrase "Socrates-in-$W_1$" to denote the part of Socrates that, according to his theory, is wholly confined to $W_1$. How that particular hyphenated phrase is used is of no importance. The essential point of the theory represented by Figure 11.5 is that, whatever phrases we may use to refer to them in stating the theory, the objects of everyday reference and experience are objects that have parts that are distributed among various worlds.

[12] This would seem to be the central thesis of the second quotation from Tooley's review.

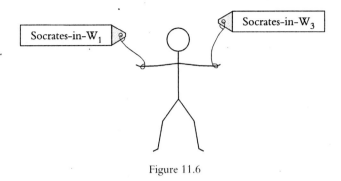

Figure 11.6

of convention encourages one to think of possible worlds as things that have insides, as enormous physical objects. (And if one thinks of possible worlds as enormous physical objects, then one will probably think that "exists in" means something like "is located within.") But possible worlds are not enormous physical objects. They are not concrete objects at all. They are, at least in Plantinga's book, abstract objects: states of affairs. There is really no reason to think of them and their relations to *concreta* pictorially at all, since Plantinga's definitions are simple and clear enough that the intellect can grasp and manipulate the concepts they define without the least need for diagrammatic aid. But if we must have a picture, the best picture is easy to draw (Figure 11.6). It is precisely analogous to Figure 11.3, our simple representation of (what is misleadingly called) identity through time. This picture, too, is simple. (Simpleminded, some would no doubt say.) But then *any* picture that perspicuously depicts the state of affairs represented by an identity-sentence should be a simple picture: it should show one thing twice tagged. Moreover the picture should not normally show a four-dimensional object or a modal continuant twice tagged; it should show objects of the sort that we encounter and have names for in the ordinary business of life as twice tagged, for it is just these sorts of thing that are referred to in the assertions we all make about time and identity and the assertions we philosophers should like to make about worlds and identity.

"But how is Figure 11.6 to be understood? What *world* is the person represented by the stick-figure supposed to be in?" What *worlds?*, you mean. The answer is obvious enough: if by "be in" you mean "exist in," $W_1$ and $W_3$. "Look, suppose Socrates has a hat on in $W_1$ and has no hat on in $W_3$. How would Figure 11.6 look if you elaborated it to represent

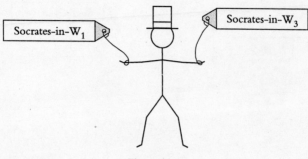

Figure 11.6a

*that* state of affairs?" That all depends on which, if either, of $W_1$ and $W_3$ is actual. Let's suppose neither is. Let's suppose that, in addition to existing in $W_1$ and $W_3$, Socrates also exists in $W_2$ and that $W_2$ is the actual world. Let's suppose that Socrates is wearing a top hat in the actual world, a bearskin busby in $W_1$, and a fool's cap in $W_3$. (Perhaps $W_3$ is the proverbial world in which Socrates is not wise.) Then we represent the fact that Socrates-in-$W_1$ is identical with Socrates-in-$W_3$ by Figure 11.6a. "But what happened to the busby and the fool's cap? How can you label something wearing a top hat 'Socrates-in-$W_1$' when Socrates is not wearing a top hat in $W_1$? Where did $W_2$, the actual world, get to?" You are confused. You are still thinking in ways that are infected by the figure-within-a-circle convention that is employed in Figures 11.4 and 11.5. And this convention is confused; or, at least, pictures drawn in conformity to it are liable to cause confusion in those to whom they are shown and are evidence of probable confusion in those who, in the course of presenting their arguments, use them as visual aids. Because you are thinking in terms of the conventions of Figure 11.4, you want to see something like Figure 11.4a. The best way to undermine the appeal of this picture is to ask what the phrases "Socrates-in-$W_1$" and "Socrates-in-$W_3$" mean. These phrases got into our discussion because they seemed to be natural things to write on the labels in Figure 11.4. But what do they *mean*? There seems to be only one thing that "Socrates-in-$W_1$" could mean: "the thing that in $W_1$ is Socrates," that is, "the thing that would be Socrates if, contrary to fact, the possible maximal state of affairs $W_1$ obtained." And, of course, it is Socrates who would be Socrates if that state of affairs obtained, just as it is William P. Alston who would be William P. Alston if Carter had been reelected in 1980. Let us

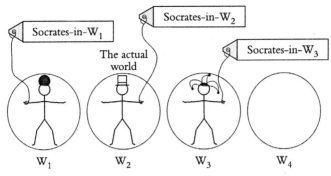

Figure 11.4a

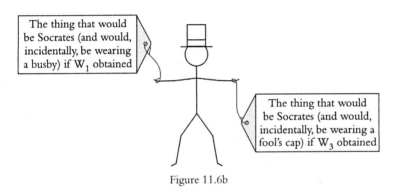

Figure 11.6b

remove the misleading phrases "Socrates-in-$W_1$" and "Socrates-in-$W_3$" from Figure 11.6a and replace them with their *definientia* (Figure 11.6b). (I have inserted into the *definientia* two parenthetical remarks for the benefit of those who have been worried about the busby and the fool's cap.) Getting oneself to think in terms of this sort of picture is – at least among those who think in terms of any sort of picture – the *pons asinorum* of the theory of possible worlds. If one does one's picture-thinking with pictures like these, one will not be troubled by questions about how, e.g. something wearing a top hat can be identical with something simultaneously wearing only a fool's cap. One will see that (in the case we have imagined) there is a single object that is being presented to one for one to make judgments about and that it is wearing a top hat and not a busby or a fool's cap. Having assimilated this point, one will be in a position

201

to generalize it: one will see that "trans-world identity" is just good, old-fashioned numerical identity,[13] the relation that Tully bears to Cicero, $2 + 2$ bears to 4, and heat (they say) bears to molecular motion. The proponent of "trans-world identity," one will come to see, does not say that Socrates must somehow be identical, in some novel and difficult sense of "identical" that philosophers are going to have to work hard to spell out, with something (else?) having a different set of properties. On the contrary, the proponent of trans-world identity – the philosopher who believes that objects can exist in more than one world – holds that there is only one Socrates, wise and snubnosed and all the rest, and that he is identical with himself (who else?) and has just the properties he has (what others?).[14]

It would be better not to think about identity and worlds in terms of pictures at all. No picture can be anything other than a (potentially) misleading representation of any abstract truth. Plantinga has shown us how to dissolve the so-called problem of trans-world identity without any appeal whatever to pictures. But if we must have pictures, let us at least not have utterly ruinous ones like Figure 11.4a. And let us be at least aware of relatively beneficent ones like Figure 11.6b.

VI

Is this really all there is to "the problem of trans-world identity"? Yes and no. *Yes* if that problem is the semantical problem posed by Tooley:

[13] Of course, I regard the phrase "trans-world identity" as tendentious: prepositions like "across" and prepositional prefixes like "trans-" and "cross-" get their point from pictures like Figure 11.4, pictures I regard as confused. I should say that all the data that philosophers might describe as belonging to the "problem of trans-world identity" or the "problem of identity across worlds" are the facts expressed by what we might call "counterfactual identity-sentences" (e.g., "Carter is identical with the man who would have been elected President in 1980 if Reagan had not been"), and I perceive nothing in these sentences that should bring "trans-" or "cross-" to mind: Carter and the man who would have been elected (etc.) both exist in the actual world (among others), and are equally accessible to us – naturally enough, since "Carter" and "the man (etc.)" are two names for one thing.

[14] I therefore see the "problem of trans-world identity" and the "problem of identity through time" as precisely analogous: as arising from precisely analogous confusions. But I am more confident in my diagnosis of the confusions that underlie the problem of trans-world identity. I am *right* about those. If I am wrong about time – and certain aspects of the General Theory of Relativity do *seem* to support a view contrary to my view of time; I think this seeming is mere seeming, but the question is a *very* subtle one – I am still right about worlds: if I am wrong about time, then I am also wrong in thinking that the two problems are analogous.

there is no problem whatever about what it means to say that an object exists in more than one possible world. Anyone who has grasped Plantinga's definitions and who is not held captive by a picture like Figure 11.4a can easily see this. On the other hand, I do not deny that real philosophical problems may arise when we ask ourselves certain questions that *could* be described as questions about trans-world identity. Might I exist in worlds in which there is nothing material? Is there a possible world in which Socrates is an alligator? Are there worlds in which horses – members of the very species we call "horse" – have wings? But the existence of such problems has no tendency to show that there is a general problem of trans-world identity, a problem that proceeds from the very notions of *possible world* and *identity*. Moreover, the three examples I have given of questions that "could be described as questions about trans-world identity" are not *best* described that way. They are better described as metaphysical questions *about* individuals and species that are *couched in terms of* trans-world identity. To call them questions *about* trans-world identity is like calling the question whether the truth of materialism commits one to the truth of determinism a question about truth; it is like calling the question whether the number of gods is zero a question about numbers; it is like calling the question whether the set of fetuses is a subset of the set of human beings a question about sets. Such examples could be multiplied indefinitely, but perhaps the point I want to make is sufficiently clear: it does not follow from the fact that there are real philosophical problems that can be stated – that can be *best* stated, for that matter – in terms of trans-world identity that there are real philosophical problems *about* trans-world identity.

The philosopher who says that objects exist in more possible worlds than one, therefore, faces no problems as a consequence of his holding this view. It is perhaps worth pointing out – I shall at any rate close by pointing it out – that the philosopher who *denies* that objects exist in more worlds than one faces a very grave philosophical problem indeed; in fact, the philosopher who says that there is even one object that exists in only one world had said something that seems to me to be hardly intelligible at all.[15]

[15] I except from this charge philosophers like David Lewis for whom "possible worlds" are concrete objects and for whom "exists in" means "is part of." Such philosophers do not mean what Plantinga and I (and Pollock and Stalnaker and Kripke and most others who have said anything about these matters) mean by "possible world." Therefore, these philosophers do not face the problem that will be raised in the text. They do, however, face the problem of finding any reason to believe in (more than one of) the

Let us call an object *counterfactually wholly unstable* if it would not have existed had anything whatever been different. More formally:

x is counterfactually wholly unstable = $_{df}$.
Every true proposition is such that if it were not true then x would not exist.

In one sense there is no difficulty about the words "wholly unstable object": they have been adequately defined. But, the same might be said about "propertyless object" or "two-dimensional cup"; at least we see immediately what the right way to define these phrases would be: they are not meaningless in the way "abracadabra" is meaningless. But there is a perfectly good sense – one I should not like to have to spell out – in which they express incoherent concepts. And I think that the words "wholly unstable object" are in pretty much the same boat. What would a wholly unstable object be *like*? Consider the cup on the table. What would it be like for the universe to be so arranged that this cup would never have existed if more cats had been born in Genoa last year? If Reagan had received six more votes in Utah? If I had used some other object as an example? If there were one more electron in the Andromeda galaxy? Now, doubtless, for any one of these conditions, we could cook up a story the truth of which would entail that if this condition held, the cup would never have existed. But can we tell a story that would have this consequence with respect to every condition? I very much doubt it. (Such a story would make of the world a tangled skein indeed.) I have a very hard time seeing how any object could have so weak a grip on existence, could be so ontologically fragile, as that. (A wholly unstable object would stand

things they call worlds and the problem of explaining what these things would have to do with modality if there were any of them.

I should note that the employment of pictures like Figures 11.4 and 11.4a is not "evidence of probable confusion" if the employer means what Lewis means by "possible world." In that case, such pictures are perfectly appropriate. What is a cause of and evidence of confusion is this: the employment of pictures like Figures 11.4 and 11.4a in a context in which "possible worlds" are possible maximal states of affairs.

In a recent paper ("Individuation by Acquaintance and by Stipulation," *The Philosophical Review* 92/1 [Jan. 1983]) Lewis discusses at length "the famous problem of identity across possible worlds." The problem that Lewis designates by these words is not the problem called "the problem of trans-world identity" herein, and the arguments of the present paper are quite irrelevant to the question whether Lewis is guilty of any confusion. I do not think that "the problem of trans-world identity" is a good *name* for the problem that Lewis discusses. In fact, one of the data of Lewis's discussion is the thesis that no possible concrete object is in (in his sense of "in") more than one world (in his sense of "world"). But I concede that there is some historical justification for his choice of this name for it.

at the opposite end of the spectrum of existent objects from a necessary being: it would be the next thing to an inconsistent object.) I have an even harder time seeing how *every* object could be wholly unstable. Of course I may be wrong. Perhaps the idea of a wholly unstable object is a coherent one. Perhaps the proposition that (there are objects and) every object is wholly unstable is at least possibly true. I am willing to concede that I know little about what is and isn't possible. But my confession of modal ignorance does not mean that I am in the slightest degree sympathetic with the philosopher who announces the existence of "the problem of stable objects," the problem of explaining how there can be objects other than wholly unstable objects, or the problem of what it means to say that there are objects other than wholly unstable ones. So far as I can see, if a philosopher wants to talk of wholly unstable objects, it's up to him to show that the notion of a wholly unstable object makes any sense and that there is some reason to believe that there might be such objects. An unqualified announcement of "the problem of stable objects" could only be called brazen impudence. If a philosopher wishes to discuss "the problem of stable objects" and if he wishes to be taken seriously, he will have to produce an argument that militates against our ordinary convictions about counterfactual stability and which is at least as worthy of serious philosophical consideration as the classical arguments for skepticism or McTaggart's arguments against the reality of time. And, of course, no one has yet devised any such argument.

It should be clear why I have said this. It is evident that the proposition that every object exists in exactly one world entails the proposition that every object is wholly unstable. Therefore, if there is some problem about what it could mean to say that there are wholly unstable objects, there is a problem about what it could mean to say that there are objects that exist in only one world. And there is indeed a semantical problem about "wholly unstable object": as with "propertyless object" or "two-dimensional cup," it is very hard to see what the denotatum of such a phrase would be *like*. Therefore, if any philosopher says that objects exist in just one world, it is *he* who has the problem and not the philosopher who says that objects exist in many worlds.

Almost everything I have said in this paper is an elaboration or a paraphrase of something Plantinga has said in Chapter 6 of *The Nature of Necessity*. No one who has understood that chapter can take seriously the notion of a "problem of trans-world identity." I hope I have removed certain barriers to understanding it.

# 12

## *Two concepts of possible worlds*

As recently as ten years ago, it was not uncommon to hear philosophers sneer at the newfangled notion of a possible world. Today the sneers have died away, and possible worlds are recognized as a respectable philosophical tool. But what *are* they?

I

Let us approach this question by considering a famous – or notorious – passage from David Lewis's book *Counterfactuals*.

I believe that there are possible worlds other than the one we happen to inhabit. If an argument is wanted, it is this. It is uncontroversially true that things might have been otherwise than they are. I believe, and so do you, that things could have been different in countless ways. But what does this mean? Ordinary language permits the paraphrase: there are many ways things could have been besides the way they actually are. On the face of it, this sentence is an existential quantification. It says that there exist many entities of a certain description, to wit "ways things could have been." I believe that things could have been different in countless ways; I believe permissible paraphrases of what I believe; taking the paraphrase at its face value, I therefore believe in the existence of entities that might be called "ways things could have been." I prefer to call them "possible worlds."[1]

The notoriety of this passage derives not so much from its content – which I think is pretty unexceptionable – as from its setting. For Lewis did not content himself with saying that there were entities properly called "ways things could have been"; nor did he content himself with implying that "possible world" was a heuristically useful stylistic variant on "way things could have been." He went on to say that what most of us would call "the universe," the mereological sum of all the furniture of earth and all the choir of heaven, is one among others of these "possible

First published in *Midwest Studies in Philosophy* 9 (1986).
[1] David Lewis, *Counterfactuals* (Cambridge, Mass., 1973), p. 84.

worlds" or "ways things could have been," and that the others differ from it "not in kind but only in what goes on in them" (p. 85). And to suppose that the existence of a plurality of universes or cosmoi could be established by so casual an application of Quine's criterion of ontological commitment has been regarded by most of Lewis's readers as very exceptionable indeed.

Whether or not the existence of a plurality of universes can be so easily established, the thesis that possible worlds are universes is one of the two "concepts of possible worlds" that I mean to discuss. Peter Unger employs a similar concept of possible worlds.[2] The other concept I shall discuss is that employed by various philosophers who would probably regard themselves as constituting the Sensible Party: Saul Kripke, Robert Stalnaker, Robert Adams, R. M. Chisholm, John Pollock, and Alvin Plantinga.[3] These philosophers regard possible worlds as abstract

---

[2] Lewis's current views can be found in his book *On the Plurality of Worlds* (Oxford, 1986). See also Peter Unger, "Minimizing Arbitrariness: Toward a Metaphysics of Infinitely Many Isolated Concrete Worlds," *Midwest Studies in Philosophy* 9 (1984), pp. 29–51.

In the sequel, I am going to treat a "universe" or "cosmos" as a thing spread out in space and time – as a thing all of whose parts are related to one another in space *or* time *or* in space-time. (Thus, even if a Cartesian ego has no position in *space*, it is still a part of the same universe as the one its body inhabits if the events occurring within it belong to the same temporal series as the events occurring within its body. "Spacetime" is used in its relativistic sense. We may note that even if the products of the Big Bang soon became separated into isolated domains – as one theory holds – the contents of one domain are parts of the same "universe" as the contents of another, since they are connected by a spacetime path that skirts the Big Bang.) For short: all the parts of a "universe" are spatiotemporally related. In so treating a "universe," I follow Lewis – but with one simplification. Lewis wants to leave open the question whether there are relations that are not spatiotemporal but which are somehow *analogous* to spatiotemporal relations and which play the role in some possible universes that spatiotemporal relations play in ours (Lewis, *On the Plurality of Worlds*, pp. 75–78). I will ignore this question, which is irrelevant to the problems I wish to discuss.

It might occur to someone to protest that *causally* related objects ought to count as parts of the same universe, even if they are spatiotemporally unrelated. Lewis would reply that spatiotemporally unrelated objects cannot be causally related (ibid., pp. 78–81). I am doubtful about this, but I will concede it for present purposes.

[3] See Saul Kripke, *Naming and Necessity* (Cambridge, Mass., 1980), pp. 15–20, 43–53; Robert C. Stalnaker, "Possible Worlds," *Noûs* 10 (1976), pp. 65–75; Robert Merrihew Adams, "Theories of Actuality," *Noûs* 8 (1974), pp. 211–231; Roderick M. Chisholm, *The First Person* (Minneapolis, 1981), appendix; John Pollock, *The Foundations of Philosophical Semantics* (Princeton, 1984), Ch. 3; Alvin Plantinga, "Actualism and Possible Worlds," *Theoria* 42 (1976), pp. 139–160. This concept has its roots in the Carnapian notion of a "state description," but its earliest indisputable appearance in print was probably in Pollock's "The Logic of Logical Necessity," *Logique et Analyse* 10 (1976), pp. 307–323.

objects of some sort: possible histories of *the* world, for example, or perhaps properties, propositions, or states of affairs.

I shall call these two groups of philosophers Concretists and Abstractionists, respectively.

There are only a few points of agreement between the two parties. Each would accept the words of the passage I have quoted from Lewis: except that it bears the unmistakable stamp of Lewis's prose style, it might have been written by any of the philosophers I have named. And each party would agree that "worlds" are objects that are in some sense "maximal." For example, those Abstractionists who hold that worlds are states of affairs would identify worlds with (possible) states of affairs that are maximal with respect to the inclusion (or entailment) of other possible states of affairs: A world is a possible state of affairs $W$ such that the conjunction of $W$ and any state of affairs not entailed by $W$ is *not* a possible state of affairs. And Lewis, who holds that worlds are objects spread out in space and time, identifies worlds with spatiotemporal objects that are maximal with respect to spatiotemporal interrelatedness: A world is a spatiotemporal object $W$ such that the mereological sum of $W$ and any object not a part of $W$ is *not* a spatiotemporal object. Both Abstractionists and Concretists evidently regard the word "world" as appropriate to the extension they give it. (It could be argued that each party is availing itself of one of the two main historical semantic branches of this word.[4]) This

---

[4] There is a remarkable passage in the chapter on the word "world" in C. S. Lewis's book *Studies in Words* (Cambridge, 1960). In the pages immediately preceding the passage I have in mind, Lewis has made a distinction between two senses, or families of senses, associated with the word "world"; he calls them *"World A"* and *"World B."* (The similarity between Lewis's term *"World A"* and my *"A-world"* in the text is an accident.) The passage is a description of one of the senses in the *A* family:

Another way of putting it would be that, just as *"World B"* is the Region that includes all other regions, so *"World A"* in the sense we are now considering is the State of Affairs which includes all other states of affairs; the over-all human situation, hence the common lot, the way things go. *Things* or *life* would often translate it. (p. 222)

We may remark in connection with this passage that "world" in most of its senses is used with varying degrees of inclusiveness. (The metaphysician, naturally enough, uses the word in the most inclusive way possible.) Thus, for *"World B"* we have the series: the *oikoumene*, the inhabited parts of the surface of the earth, the surface of the earth, the earth, the universe. The metaphysician who calls a possible state of affairs that is maximal with respect to the inclusion of states of affairs a "world" is simply using "world" in its *A* sense with a degree of inclusiveness that stands to that of "the overall human situation" as that of "the universe" stands to that of "the inhabited parts of the surface of the earth."

is no doubt at least partly because, whatever else a "world" may be, it is certainly something maximal.

Let us introduce the term "*A*-world" as a term whose meaning or intension is just that description that Abstractionists give of the objects they say are "what possible worlds are"; and let us do the same, *mutatis mutandis*, for "*C*-world" and the Concretists. (Note that it does not follow that Abstractionists *mean* "*A*-world" by "world," or that Concretists *mean* "*C*-world" by "world" – any more than it follows from the fact that dualists and materialists give different descriptions of the items in the extensions of "person" or "sensation" that these two groups of philosophers therefore differ about the *meaning* of "person" or "sensation." We shall return to this point presently.)

It will be useful to define these two terms formally. Let us begin with "*A*-world." We take as undefined "state of affairs" (e.g., Reagan's having been elected president in 1984), "obtains" (Mondale's having been elected in 1984 does not obtain; Reagan's having been elected in 1984 does obtain), and "conjunction" (the conjunction of two states of affairs is the state of affairs that consists in their both obtaining). A state of affairs $x$ is said to *include* a state of affairs $y$ if it is impossible "in the broadly logical sense" for $x$ to obtain without $y$'s also obtaining. Then:

> $x$ is an *A*-world $=_{df}$    $x$ is a possible state of affairs (one that possibly obtains), and the conjunction of $x$ and any state of affairs that $x$ does not include is not a possible state of affairs.

Now "*C*-world." We take as primitive – more for convenience than anything else, since it would be possible to make this notion more precise – the notion of two objects being spatiotemporally related. (Cf. fn. 2.) An object will be said to be *spatiotemporal* if, for any $x$ and $y$, if $x$ and $y$ are parts of that object, then $x$ and $y$ are spatiotemporally related. Then:

> $x$ is a *C*-world $=_{df}$    $x$ is a spatiotemporal object, and the mereological sum of $x$ and any object that is not a part of $x$ is not a spatiotemporal object.

We may note that although "*A*-world" is obviously a modal concept, "*C*-world" is a nonmodal concept – at least in the sense that it can be defined using only paradigmatically nonmodal concepts.

I have given the definitions in these forms in order to stress their structural similarity, a similarity that is rooted in the fact that they are both "maximality" definitions. But I might have given (equivalent) definientia that reproduce more closely the forms of Plantinga's and Lewis's official accounts of what a "possible world" is:

> $x$ is a possible state of affairs, and, for any state of affairs, $x$ includes either that state of affairs or its negation (the negation of a state of affairs $y$ being the state of affairs that consists in $y$'s not obtaining)

> Each of $x$'s parts is spatiotemporally related to all of $x$'s parts, and anything spatiotemporally related to any of $x$'s parts is one of $x$'s parts.[5]

This second way of defining "$C$-world" makes it clear that there are two ways in which an object that is a sum of spatiotemporal parts could fail to be a $C$-world: (i) it could be spatiotemporally related to something not one of its parts, as, e.g., the Eiffel Tower is, or (ii) it could have spatio-temporally unrelated parts; this second possibility is realized by the mereological sum of the Eiffel Tower and any spatiotemporal object – assuming that there are such – that is spatiotemporally unrelated to that structure.

Perhaps this is as good a time as any at which to call attention to a puzzling – and to the Abstractionist rather annoying – asymmetry between Abstractionism and Concretism: The difference between Abstractionism and Concretism is thought to be much clearer and more important by Abstractionists than by Concretists. Let the Concretist speak. "You Abstractionists say that a 'world' is a possible state of affairs that is maximal with respect to the inclusion of states of affairs. But *I* say that a 'state of affairs' is a set of worlds and that a state of affairs $x$ 'includes' a state of affairs $y$ if and only if $x$ is a subset of $y$. Hence, such a 'maximal' state of affairs is just a set whose sole member is an object that is maximal with respect to spatiotemporal interrelatedness. If we ignore the distinction between a set whose sole member is an individual (non-set) and that individual (and Quine has shown us how to dispense with that distinction altogether, if we want to), then $A$-worlds *are* $C$-worlds and *vice versa* – even if you Abstractionists don't realize it."

The Abstractionist will find this fantastic. He will protest that he is *called* an Abstractionist because he holds that possible worlds are abstract objects; he will protest that it is incredible to suppose that any state of

---

[5] See Plantinga, "Actualism and Possible Worlds," p. 144, and Lewis, *On the Plurality of Worlds*, pp. 2, 69, 70, 71. See the chapter from Pollock's *The Foundations of Philosophical Semantics* cited in fn. 3 for an important refinement of Abstractionism involving a distinction between "transient" and "nontransient" states of affairs.

affairs, even a "maximal" one, is a concrete object. The Concretist will reply (at least he will if he is David Lewis) that *he* did not choose the name "Concretism" for his position, and that, in fact, he is far from being clear about the (alleged) distinction between abstract and concrete objects. This reply raises large issues.[6] For the moment, let us simply stipulate that it is a part of the Abstractionist's position that states of affairs, whatever they may be, are neither spatiotemporal objects nor mereological sums of spatiotemporal objects nor set-theoretical constructs on mereological sums of spatiotemporal objects.

Those who use the term "possible world," whether they are Abstractionists or Concretists, use this term in conjunction with certain other closely related terms that, taken together, may be said to constitute "possible-worlds talk." Possible-worlds talk comprises, at a minimum, besides "possible world" itself, the terms "actual" and "in" (or sometimes "at"). (Various other terms like "accessible from" and "closer to" may count as items in possible-worlds talk, but I shall not consider them.)

Abstractionists and Concretists, owing to the fact that they assign very different objects to the extension of "possible world," see "actual" and "in" as marking out very different attributes and relations. Let us do for "actual" and "in" what we did for "world." We begin with "actual." Let us give to the terms "$A$-actual" and "$C$-actual" senses derived, respectively, from the Abstractionists' and the Concretists' accounts of "actuality."

For the Abstractionist (if he thinks of worlds as states of affairs), actuality is just obtaining: the actual world is the one world – the one among possible states of affairs maximal with respect to the inclusion of other states of affairs – that obtains. (Or if the Abstractionist thinks of worlds as propositions – possible propositions maximal with respect to entailment – he will say that actuality is just truth.) Let us, therefore, define "$A$-actual" to mean "obtaining." The Concretist, on the other hand, will say that "actual" is an indexical term. For the Concretist, to call a world actual is to say that one is a part of it. Let us, therefore, define "$x$ is $C$-actual" to mean "I am a part of $x$" (or, in manifestos and such, "we are parts of $x$"). In this connection, some rather delicate ontological points need to be made.

This characterization of "$C$-actual" accurately reflects David Lewis's account of actuality. But Lewis is a Quinean as regards existence: he believes that everything exists, that existence is what is expressed by the existential quantifier, that the idea of a non-existent object is self-contradictory.[7] Suppose there were a Concretist who was not a Quinean but a Meinongian (or, better, a Parsonian), that is, someone who believed that there were objects that did not exist. Such a philosopher might well want to say that actuality is just existence; that just as a nonactual horse is a nonexistent horse, a nonactual *C*-world is just a nonexistent *C*-world. I do not know of any philosopher who has explicitly endorsed this sort of Concretism in print, but I believe it to be widespread.[8]

Meinongian Concretism is an interesting view. I think that it faces no very grave problems beyond those that it inherits from Meinongianism *simpliciter* (but those are considerable). I will not, however, discuss it in this essay. I mention it only to distinguish it from Lewis's version of Concretism.[9] (I pointed out above that "*C*-world," which is based on Lewis's account of worlds, is not a modal concept. We should note that a Meinongian account of concrete worlds would have the consequence that "concrete world" *was* a modal concept, owing to the fact that Meinongians believe that some objects are impossible, and, therefore, would have to define "concrete world" in some such way as this: "object that is maximal with respect to spatiotemporal interrelatedness and is also possibly existent."[10])

Abstractionists apply the words "actual" and "nonactual" only to

---

[7] See ibid., p. 98.

[8] Kit Fine once described to me, and endorsed, an ontology of possible worlds that I would describe as Meinongian Concretism. But this endorsement would appear to be contradicted by his published work. (See, for example, his postscript to *Worlds, Times and Selves* [London, 1977], and "Plantinga on the Reduction of Possibilist Discourse," in *Alvin Plantinga* [Dordrecht, 1985], ed. James E. Tomberlin and Peter van Inwagen.) Perhaps the explanation is that Fine believes that, *strictly speaking*, there are no merely possible worlds (or other "nonactual" objects) and that talk that is apparently about such things should be paraphrasable as talk about proposition-like entities – that is, as talk about the things that Abstractionists say *are* possible worlds. But (if I have Fine right) when we are talking as if there *were* possible worlds – a heuristically useful practice – we should talk about them as the Meinongian Concretist does.

Sometimes Jaakko Hintikka talks rather like a Meinongian Concretist. See, for example, Section VIII of "Semantics for Propositional Attitudes," in *Reference and Modality*, ed. Leonard Linsky (Oxford, 1971), pp. 145–167.

[9] In "The Trouble with Possible Worlds," in *The Possible and the Actual*, ed. Michael J. Loux (Ithaca, 1979), William G. Lycan mistakenly supposes that Lewis is a Meinongian. See especially n 7 p. 277. That such an acute philosopher as Lycan could make this mistake is a tribute to the power of the slippery word "actual" to confuse people.

[10] Lewis's ontology includes things he calls "impossible objects," although none of them is a world. But his notion of an impossible object can be spelled out in nonmodal terms: an object is impossible if it overlaps two or more worlds. Such objects are called

certain abstract objects. That is, they do *not* apply them to concrete objects. If you asked an Abstractionist to defend this practice, he would reply along these lines: "It is reasonably clear what it means to say of a state of affairs, which is an abstract object, that it is 'actual': that it obtains. Possible states of affairs are, or represent, ways things could be and are, therefore, the sort of thing that can fail to 'come off.' In a way somewhat analogous to pictures and declarative sentences, they represent things as being arranged in a certain way, and they may represent incorrectly. If they do, we call them 'nonactual.' But what could it mean to say of a concrete object like a horse that it was 'actual'? Horses and other concrete objects do not represent things as being a certain way; they cannot 'fail to come off' – they're just *there*. If we examine the way in which, e.g., 'nonactual horse' has in fact been used, we see that this phrase almost always means, in the mouths of its habitual employers, 'nonexistent horse.' (We must, of course, except David Lewis from this generalization.) And, indeed, it is difficult to see what else it might mean. But we Abstractionists are Quineans (about existence). In this sense of 'actual,' we say that there are not, and could not possibly be, nonactual horses. Like 'round square,' 'nonactual horse' is a contradiction in terms. Some of us Abstractionists have described themselves as 'actualists,' or have said that they were unwilling to countenance nonactual objects. This is what they meant. (Note that even David Lewis is an 'actualist' in *this* sense. Note also that when Abstractionists call a state of affairs 'nonactual,' they don't mean that it does not exist, only that it does not obtain. 'Nonexistent state of affairs' is as much a contradiction in terms as 'nonexistent horse.')"

Now, as is well known, the standard formal semantics for quantified modal logic (in conjunction with plausible assumptions about what is possible) strongly suggests a metaphysic of modality according to which there are "objects that exist only in other possible worlds." Sometimes the words "actual" and "nonactual" have been introduced this way: an actual object is one that exists in the actual world, and a nonactual object is one that exists only in nonactual worlds.[11] But this way of introducing "actual" (as an adjective that applies to objects in general, and not only

---

impossible because (as will be evident from our discussion of the Concretist's use of "exists in"), they exist in no world. See Lewis, *On the Plurality of Worlds*, 211.

[11] This procedure is the reverse of the procedure adopted by David Lewis in "Counterpart Theory and Quantified Modal Logic" (*The Journal of Philosophy* 65 [1968], pp. 113–126), in which "actual" as a predicate of objects-in-general is taken as primitive, and an actual *world* is defined as one that contains the actual objects.

to worlds) depends on the remaining item in the vocabulary of possible-worlds talk, "in," to which we must turn before we can evaluate this way of introducing "actual."

I shall continue with the policy I have followed above and define two terms, one modeled on the Abstractionists' explanation of "in," and the other modeled on the Concretists' explanation. Since "*A*-in" and "*C*-in" are awkward, I shall use "at" for the "Abstractionist sense" and "in" for the "Concretist sense" of "in."

The Abstractionist uses "at" or "in" in two contexts: in ascribing truth or falsity to propositions, and in ascribing existence, or the possession of a property, to objects. Our definitions are:

$p$ is true [false] at the $A$-world $w =_{df}$ $w$ is an $A$-world, and if $w$ were $A$-actual, $p$ would be true [false];

$x$ exists [has P] at the $A$-world $w =_{df}$ $w$ is an $A$-world, and if $w$ were $A$-actual, $x$ would exist [have P].[12]

No such neat definitions of "in" are possible. The Concretist, in fact, will probably claim to be using "in" in more or less its ordinary English sense, the sense exemplified in such adverbial phrases as "in Australia" or "in Chicago." In some sentences, this sense would seem to be closely connected with parthood. If we think of Chicago as a large physical object, the mereological sum of certain people and buildings and so on, we can say that "In Chicago there is an $F$" means "An $F$ is a part of Chicago." And it might seem that, by analogy, we could write the following definition:

$x$ exists in the $C$-world $w =_{df}$     $w$ is a $C$-world, and $x$ is a part of $w$.

And, if $p$ is a sentence (rather than a proposition):

$p$ is true in the $C$-world $w =_{df}$     $w$ is a $C$-world and $p$ true if the range of the variables of $p$ is restricted to parts of $w$.

---

[12] See the works of Plantinga and Pollock cited in footnote 3. These definitions need not take a subjunctive form; we might have written, e.g., "$w$ includes the state of affairs: $p$'s being true." "If $w$ were actual, $p$ would be true" is equivalent to "necessarily, if $w$ is actual, then $p$ is true," since there is only one word, $w$ itself, at which the antecedent of the subjunctive conditional holds. The second way of writing the definitions is theoretically preferable, since it allows a noncircular possible-worlds account of subjunctive conditionals. But the definitions in the text are more intuitive. We may also note that the definition of a proposition's having a truth-value at a world is redundant, since this is a special case of an object's having a property at a world.

But this account of truth-in-a-world runs into trouble with certain existential quantifications that would normally be taken to express necessary truths – and, therefore, presumably, to be true in all worlds – such as "$\exists x\, 2 + x = 4$" and "$\exists x\, x$ is a possible world in which all men are blind." No part of the C-actual C-world (i.e., the universe) is such that when added to 2 it yields 4; nor is any part of the C-actual C-world a C-world having no sighted men as parts. Moreover, there are apparently necessary truths, such as "$2 + 2 = 4$," that contain no variables. These problems can be solved if we assume that although "in $w$" *usually* acts so as to restrict our domain of quantification to the parts of $w$, it sometimes means something we might express by the words "from the point of view afforded by $w$." And these words mean something like, "people in $w$ who believe that . . . are right"; but, of course, *that* isn't quite right because (at least if C-worlds are as numerous and diverse as the Concretist presumably thinks) some C-worlds are unpopulated.[13] Let us take "from the point of view afforded by $w$" as requiring no further explanation. It seems reasonable to read the occurrences of "in $w$" in "in $w$, $\exists x\, 2 + x = 4$" and "in $w$, $\exists x\, x$ is a world in which all men are blind" as meaning "from the point of view afforded by $w$." It could be argued that we are here following the natural semantic bent of the English word "in." If I say (perhaps making a point about the economic policies of Mongolia) "Even in Mongolia, $2 + 2 = 4$," presumably I mean that the principles of arithmetic are valid from the point of view afforded by Mongolia, and not just that these principles apply to all the objects in Mongolia: I mean that people doing arithmetic in Mongolia must apply these principles to whatever they reason about arithmetically – even nonspatial objects and spatial objects outside Mongolia. (But one would not say, "In Mongolia, some European countries are democracies,"[14] despite the fact that anyone in Mongolia who believes that some European countries are democracies is right.)

Having defined the Abstractionist "at" and the Concretist "in," we may now return to the proposal to introduce "actual" (as a predicate, applying to horses and such) as "exists in (at) the actual world." The proposal bifurcates. The Abstractionist will point out that "$x$ exists at the A-actual A-world" is easily seen to be equivalent to "$x$ exists," reducing

---

[13] And, of course, unless we call on divine aid, we must assume that in *no* world does anyone believe *all* necessary truths.

[14] Or, at least, if one did, one would be describing the Mongolian official "line," or something like that.

the proposal to one already considered and rejected. The Concretist, however, will find the proposal useful and acceptable: he will point out that "*x* exists in the *C*-actual *C*-world" is satisfied by many objects that are not worlds. Moreover, he will tell us, there are objects that *fail* to satisfy this open sentence. Or at least he will tell us this if he believes, as he presumably does, that there are any *C*-worlds besides the one that is *C*-actual. Furthermore, if he believes, as he presumably does, that there are *C*-nonactual *C*-worlds that have proper parts, he will tell us that there are objects that fail to satisfy this sentence and which are not themselves *C*-worlds. Suppose we use "*OC*-actual" as an actuality-predicate that is applicable to concrete objects in general, and not to *C*-worlds alone:

$x$ is $OC$-actual $=_{df}$ $\qquad\qquad$ $x$ exists in the $C$-actual $C$-world.

Inspection of the definitions of "*C*-actual" and "*C*-world" shows that "*x* exists in the *C*-actual *C*-world" is equivalent to

Every part of $x$ is spatiotemporally related to me.

We may note that this open sentence is equivalent to the definiens of "*C*-actual" in the domain of *C*-worlds: a *C*-world is *C*-actual if and only if it is *OC*-actual. There is no point, therefore, in our retaining both terms. Let us drop the term "*OC*-actual" and redefine "*C*-actual":

$x$ is $C$-actual $=_{df}$ $\qquad\qquad$ Every part of $x$ is spatiotemporally related to me.

And, of course, a *C*-nonactual object will be one that has at least some parts that are spatiotemporally unrelated to me. Thus, if the Concretist believes, as presumably he does, that there might have been other horses than those that there are, he will believe that there are *C*-nonactual horses. Nevertheless, he remains a good Quinean, for he believes that all these *C*-nonactual horses *exist*. For a Quinean, to say, "*F*s exist" is simply to say, "The number of *F*s is greater than 0"; and Concretists believe that the number of *C*-nonactual horses is greater than 0.

But, someone may object, suppose that there are no hairless horses, although there might have been some, and that the Concretist believes that there might have been hairless horses. In possible-worlds talk, his modal belief reads thus: hairless horses exist in some possible world. Or, in explicitly Concretist possible-worlds talk: hairless horses exist in some *C*-world. And if he accepts this, then, by the argument of the preceding paragraph, he should agree that hairless horses exist – which is false. The

Concretist will reply that, *strictly speaking*, hairless horses do exist. But if we say, "Hairless horses exist" in any ordinary context, that context will enforce a tacit domain of quantification on us, the domain of C-actual objects, and what we say will be false. In our present extraordinary context, however – a discussion of the metaphysics of modality – this restricted domain is not forced upon us, and we may say truly that there are hairless horses, or that hairless horses exist. In this context, our quantifiers are, as it were, wide open. Restricted quantification is, of course, common in everyday life, as may be seen by reflecting on everyday utterances like "There's no beer" or "Everyone was at the party."

II

If Abstractionists and Concretists are talking about such very different things when they talk about possible worlds, how can they be talking about the *same* thing? How can an Abstractionist and a Concretist who are ·discussing a philosophical problem couched in possible-worlds talk be doing anything but equivocating? Well, it would certainly seem that Abstractionists and Concretists *do* have fruitful discussions that are couched in possible-worlds talk. For example, in an autobiographical essay in *Alvin Plantinga*,[15] Plantinga reproduces an elegant simplification of an argument (couched in possible-worlds talk) that he had presented in *The Nature of Necessity*, a simplification communicated to him by David Lewis. But how is such communication possible? What is going on when this happens?

I think that this problem is difficult but not serious. I believe that its solution lies in recognizing that "possible world" is, in some sense, a functional concept: The concept "possible world" is the concept of a thing that plays a certain role. An analogy may give some content to this rather vague thesis. It is widely believed that many of the central concepts studied in philosophical psychology and cognitive science are functional concepts; and this (apparently) means that they are concepts of this form: "thing that fills the following role . . ." (For example, some say that the concept of a person is the concept of a thing that mediates in a certain way between sensation and action.) Functional concepts may be distinguished from *ontological* concepts, such as "physical body" or "immaterial substance," which are concepts of the form: "thing of the

---

[15] The book is cited in footnote 8; p. 212.

following *kind . . .*". It is, therefore, possible for dualists and materialists to talk to each other without equivocation about persons in the ordinary business of life; it is even possible for the two groups to dispute about what ontological concepts are coextensive with "person" (that is, to dispute about what persons *are*). In philosophical psychology, the "roles" that figure in functional concepts are generally causal roles. But disputes in the more abstract areas of philosophy, disputes about what (say) numbers or propositions or universals are, have the same sort of "feel" as disputes in philosophical psychology about persons. This suggests that "number," "proposition," and "universal" are functional concepts, though, of course, the appropriate roles in these cases cannot be causal roles. Perhaps the concept of a proposition is the concept "bearer of truth-value," for example, and philosophers who argue about "what propositions are" are arguing about what sorts of object (sentence tokens; sentence types; purely abstract objects directly graspable by the mind . . .) fill this role. (This is all very crude, of course. A more sophisticated approach to the idea of a functional concept might be based on the notion that the functional/ontological opposition is context- or level-relative: perhaps "sentence-token" is an ontological concept relative to "proposition"; but perhaps it is a functional concept on another level of analysis, the concept of an object that plays a certain role in linguistic behavior. In the philosophy of mind, "person" may be a functional concept and "physical body" an ontological concept, while in the philosophy of physics, "physical body" may be a functional concept.)

I would suggest that the concept of a possible world is the concept of an object that can fill a certain role in philosophical discourse about modality, essence, counterfactuality, truth-theories for natural languages, and so on, and that a dispute between Plantinga and Lewis about what possible worlds are should be understood on the model of a dispute between Plantinga (a dualist) and Lewis (a materialist) about what persons are. I am not under the illusion that I have said enough to give this idea much content; to do so in any adequate way would be impossible without a fundamental discussion of roles and functional concepts. But perhaps I have said enough to make the question raised at the beginning of this section a bit less worrisome. In terms of the functional/ontological distinction introduced above, we can describe the dispute between the Abstractionists and the Concretists in this way: It is a dispute about which of two ontological concepts ("*A*-world" or "*C*-world") is coextensive with the functional concept "possible world," and about what ontological concepts are coextensive with the functional concepts "actual" and "in/at." This explains in what sense the present essay is about "two concepts of possible worlds" and explains the reservations expressed in the previous section about saying that Abstractionists *mean* "*A*-world" by "world" and that Concretists *mean* "*C*-world" by "world." As to the question, "How can they be talking about the same thing when they are talking about such different things?", the answer is that they are not talking about different things at all. Unless the Abstractionist and the Concretist are somehow *both* wrong, they are both talking about *A*-worlds or both talking about *C*-worlds; one of them, of course, is profoundly mistaken about the nature of the things he is talking about (as is either the dualist or the materialist).

### III

What can be said for and against Abstractionism and Concretism? It is not surprising that opinions differ about this. What the Abstractionist says is an awkward or unfortunate feature of Concretism, the Concretist will very likely say is not a feature of Concretism at all – or is a positively desirable one. And of course the same goes for the defects the Concretist claims to find in Abstractionism. We may outline the principal claims made on behalf of, and charges brought against, the two theories of possible worlds in the following table.[16]

### Concretism

#### pro

- Provides a reductive analysis of modality [Lewis].
- Can actually do the work for which it is designed [Lewis].

#### contra

- Has the consequence that modal statements are equivalent to nonmodal statements, ones having (in general) different truth-values from the modal statements they are supposedly equivalent to [some Abstractionists].
- Evokes incredulous stares [Lewis].
- Is incredible [all Abstractionists].

[16] Here I draw upon Lewis, *On the Plurality of Worlds*. See Section 2.8 and Ch. 3.

- Requires a counterpart-theoretical analysis of modal statements about individuals, thus misrepresenting the modal facts [most, if not all, Abstractionists].

## Abstractionism

### pro

- Is credible; presupposes the existence of nothing beyond what is already needed for other philosophical purposes, such as states of affairs or propositions [all Abstractionists].

### contra

- Cannot provide a reductive analysis of modality [Lewis].
- Cannot do the work for which it is designed [Lewis].

In the remainder of this essay, I shall attempt to evaluate these pros and cons. With one exception: I shall say nothing about counterpart theory and the analysis of modal statements *de re*. This is an important issue, but it has been extensively discussed elsewhere, and I have nothing new to say about it. The reader may have been surprised that I said nothing about counterpart theory in my exposition of Concretism. This is the explanation: we shall simply ignore the whole topic of *de re* modality, and an exposition of counterpart theory will, therefore, be unnecessary for our purposes. (One example – not of my own devising – will involve a particular individual, and the word "counterpart" will appear two or three times in connection with this example; your program contains biographies of the principal players only, and not of the walk-ons.)

Up to this point, I have tried to preserve a strict neutrality between Abstractionism and Concretism. From now on, however, I shall write as an Abstractionist. My evaluations of the pros and cons listed above will be frankly partisan and, indeed, are intended to add up to an argument for Abstractionism and against Concretism.

I begin with an examination of Lewis's claim that Concretism provides a reductive analysis of modality,[17] and of the related charge of the Abstractionists that it is a consequence of Concretism that modal statements are equivalent to nonmodal statements – ones that they are, in fact, *not* equivalent to.

[17] Ibid., Section 1.2; see also ibid., pp. 150–157, 167–170, 176.

An example will make clear what is at issue. Consider the modal statement

(1) There is no million-carat diamond, but there could have been one.

In possible-worlds talk, this becomes

(2) No million-carat diamond exists in the actual world, but a million-carat diamond exists in some possible world.

According to Concretism, (2) is equivalent[18] to

(3) No million-carat diamond exists in the C-actual C-world, but a million-carat diamond exists in some C-world.

If we assume, and this seems obviously true, that a diamond could not possibly have spatiotemporally unrelated parts, (3) can be reduced by elementary logical manipulations to

(4) No million-carat diamond is spatiotemporally related to me, and there is a million-carat diamond.

Obviously, (4) contains only paradigmatically nonmodal terms. Since Concretism allows us in a similar way to reduce any modal statement to one containing only paradigmatically nonmodal terms, we can see what David Lewis means when he boasts that Concretism provides a reductive analysis of modality. But let us not be hasty. That Owl can spell "Tuesday" is no proof of his erudition – not unless he can spell it right; that Owen Glendower can call spirits from the vasty deep is no proof of his sorcerous powers – not unless the spirits do come when he calls for them. And it is no argument for Concretism that it provides a reductive analysis of modality – not unless that analysis is right.

Is it? Specifically, is (4) equivalent to (1)?

One obvious objection to the thesis that (4) and (1) are equivalent is that (4) is a first-person sentence, and (1) is not – or, at any rate, it certainly doesn't seem to be. (That (4) is a first-person sentence is, of course, a consequence of the Concretist's indexical theory of actuality.) This is an interesting point, but I shall not pursue it, since I wish to concentrate on features of (4) unrelated to this one.[19]

A second obvious objection takes as its point of departure the fact that

---

[18] Not equivalent in meaning, perhaps; but it follows from Concretism that (2) and (3) must have the same truth-value.

[19] It is interesting to compare Concretism on this point with Intuitionism in the philosophy of mathematics, according to which seemingly impersonal theorems of mathematics are really of the form "I have effected a construction, according to which . . ."

"There is no million-carat diamond" is a conjunct of (1) and that, more-over, "There is a million-carat diamond" is a conjunct of (4). This might be thought to be a bad omen for those who hope that (1) and (4) will turn out to be equivalent. I will not develop this objection in detail, since there is a satisfactory reply to it, and this reply does not turn on any matters of detail. The essentials of the reply are found in the closing para-graph of Section I. If someone were to utter (1) in any very normal context, that context would restrict his domain of quantification to actual objects. (In general, this will be true of any sentence that employs modal operators – as opposed to quantification over possible but nonac-tual objects – to convey modal information.) In sentence (4), however, the quantifiers are meant to be unrestricted. In sum, the Concretist's thesis is that the proposition expressed by (4), if the quantifiers in that sentence are unrestricted, is equivalent to the proposition expressed by (1) when its quantifier is restricted to *C*-actual objects. (Might someone protest that if there are mere *possibilia*, then an unrestricted quantifier is a modal term? Not, I think, unless he was willing to say that an unres-tricted quantifier was an astronomical, a geographical, and every other sort of term.)

Keeping the Concretist's point about restricted and unrestricted quan-tification in mind, let us return to the question whether (4) is equivalent to (1). *I* certainly don't think so. The following two theses seem to me to be true.

- Though there indeed could have been a million-carat diamond, there simply *is* [absolutely unrestricted quantifier] none. (At any rate, there is an *n* such that there could have been an *n*-carat diamond and there is none.) At least, this may well be true. I believe it, and I see no reason to feel uneasy about believing it, though I can't prove it.
- Nothing [absolutely unrestricted quantifier] is spatiotemporally unrelated to me (unless, like a number or a proposition, it is not spatiotemporally related to anything). At least, this may well be true. I believe it, and I see no reason to feel uneasy about believing it, though I can't prove it.

The former thesis is, by itself, sufficient for the truth of (1) and the falsity of (4). The latter thesis is sufficient for the falsity of (4).

Abstractionists find these two theses pretty obvious, and that, I think, is the reason, or a part of the reason, for those incredulous stares with which, on Lewis's testimony, he finds himself continually transfixed. Another part of the explanation, of course, is the fact that not only do Concretists believe in million-carat diamonds spatiotemporally unrelated to us, but they believe that fairly mundane modal facts (at least most of us would take them to be facts), expressible in ordinary English by the use of modal operators, are the very same facts as certain facts about objects spatiotemporally unrelated to us. For example, the Concretist must accept the proposition expressed by his utterance of the sentence

> The fact that there is no million-carat diamond but could have been one is the same fact as the fact that although no million-carat diamond is spatiotemporally related to me, some million-carat diamond is spatiotemporally unrelated to me.

This thesis seems to the Abstractionist to be not only incredible in itself, but to entail a further incredible thesis: that if the set of "modal facts" is as rich as even the most conservative estimate makes it, then there is an enormous number and an inconceivable variety of concrete objects. (Well, perhaps the *most* conservative "estimate" is Spinozism, the thesis that if there are no objects of a given kind, it follows that it is a necessary truth that there are no objects of that kind. Few philosophers these days, I would suppose, are Spinozists. Let us say, "the most conservative estimate after Spinozism.") The reason is simply the inconceivable profusion of sorts of thing that might be but are not. There might have been not only million-carat diamonds but elves and trolls and unicorns (or, at any rate, creatures that looked and acted the way these creatures are supposed to look and act), and French colonies in Australia, and two-hundred-year-old cats, and a falling asteroid that destroyed the Roman Empire . . . And, if Concretism is true, there are possible worlds that contain all these things. In fact, if Concretism is true, then every possible configuration of matter and radiation in spacetime ("physical configuration" for short) must be realized in some *C*-world. For if a possible physical configuration ϕ were realized in no *C*-world, then, according to the Concretist, "It is possible that ϕ occurs" would express a falsehood; but, *ex hypothesi*, this sentence expresses a truth, since ϕ is a *possible* configuration.

It is mildly embarrassing to the Concretist that the requirement that every possible physical configuration be realized in some *C*-world is, according to *his* view, a trivial requirement, one that is, by definition, automatically satisfied. The triviality of this requirement is a consequence of the fact that, for the Concretist, a possible physical configuration just *is* a *C*-world (or a part of one). This requirement would be satisfied, in Lewis's words, "if there were only seventeen worlds, or one, or none" (*On the Plurality of Worlds*, p. 86). If it happens that there is no *C*-world

223

having a million-carat diamond as a part, it is a consequence of this fact and Concretism that (whatever one might have *thought*) the idea of a million-carat diamond is *not* an idea of a possible configuration of matter.

So a problem is posed for the Concretist by the fact that the seemingly substantive requirement that every possible configuration of matter be realized in some *C*-world is, if Concretism is true, automatically satisfied no matter how small and miscellaneous a collection of *C*-worlds there is. Lewis calls this problem "the problem of expressing the plenitude." He solves it by stipulating, in essence, that the set of possible physical configurations (the set of *C*-worlds) is not miscellaneous but, in a certain sense, "complete." One way to give content to such a stipulation would be to match "possible physical configurations" one-to-one with some large class of mathematical objects, a class that is in no way arbitrarily restricted. For example, consider the "*Ersatz* worlds" invented by Quine, so named by Lewis, and described in *Counterfactuals*.[20] One might "express the plenitude" of *C*-worlds by saying that to every Ersatz world, there corresponds at least one *C*-world. (Call this the plenitude principle.) In *On the Plurality of Worlds*, Lewis employs a more sophisticated device for the same purpose,[21] but the device of matching *C*-worlds to Ersatz worlds at least shows what a solution (even if it is not the best one) to the plenitude problem would look like. And it allows us to put a lower limit on the number of *C*-worlds: There are at least 2-to-the-*c* of them. A moment's reflection will show us that if Lewis is right, there must also be at least 2-to-the-*c* million-carat diamonds.

Lewis apparently thinks that the enormous number of concrete (albeit *C*-nonactual) objects whose existence is entailed by Concretism is the main source of the incredulous stares he meets when he expounds Concretism. He says:

[Concretism] *does* disagree, to an extreme extent, with firm common sense opinion about what there is. (Or, in the case of some among the incredulous, it disagrees rather with firmly held agnosticism about what there is.) When [Concretism] tells you – as it does – that there are uncountable infinities of donkeys and protons and puddles and stars, and of planets very like Earth, and of people very like yourself . . . small wonder if you are reluctant to believe it.[22]

This is not an accurate report of the sources of *my* incredulity. (I don't know about "common sense opinion," by the way. It seems to me that

---

20  Lewis, *Counterfactuals*, pp. 89–91.
21  Lewis, *On the Plurality of Worlds*, pp. 87–92.
22  Ibid., p. 133 (suspension points in original).

the office of common sense is to keep us from playing cards for high stakes with people we meet on trains, and not to endorse metaphysical opinions.) Most people think that the number of donkeys is finite. If Aristotle is right, the number of donkeys (past, present, and future) is aleph-zero. There are no doubt good reasons to reject the cosmological and biological theories on which this numbering is based, but the number itself doesn't seem to be any reason to reject these theories. And I don't see that the fact that Lewis's theory has the consequence that there are 2-to-the-$c$ or more donkeys is a particularly good reason to reject it.

The good reasons have already been laid out: the theory asks us to believe that there are, e.g., naturally hairless donkeys. And there are none. It asks us to believe that there are donkeys spatiotemporally unrelated to us. And there are none. It's not so much that I object to the thesis that the number of donkeys is uncountably infinite; it's more that I object to the thesis that the number of donkeys spatiotemporally unrelated to us is other than 0 – and there are no hairless ones either! (I must, however, concede that if there were uncountable infinities of donkeys, most of them would have to be spatiotemporally unrelated to us; otherwise, there'd be no room for them all. Therefore, I do find an uncountable infinity of donkeys objectionable – but only because of its consequences for the distribution of objects in space and time.)

I find one difficulty in Concretism that could be described as a difficulty about cardinality (one that is not a consequence of the difficulties I have with spatiotemporally unrelated objects). Suppose that there are some C-worlds other than the one we are all parts of. Why should I suppose that there are all the C-worlds that the plenitude principle generates? Now this difficulty is not best described as a difficulty about *cardinality*. The plenitude principle is designed to ensure a *variety* of C-worlds, to make logical space a plenum: it forces a minimum cardinality on the set of worlds only because the variety of worlds it ensures requires that there be at least a certain number of them. Nevertheless, let us consider only the question of cardinality. Suppose I have somehow discovered that the number of C-worlds other than this one is, contrary to my very strong expectations, greater than 0. But suppose that my source of information is absolutely silent about how many of these things there are. How many should I *think* there are? Suppose that I must guess, and you must guess, and lots of people must guess and that the one whose guess is furthest from the truth will suffer an eternity of torment.

How shall I guess? No guess, it seems to me, would be much more rational than any other. I note in introspection some slight preference for a finite answer, and, among finite answers, a slight preference for those numbers commonly called "small." I like some infinite numbers a bit better as answers than others. I like aleph-zero best, and 2-to-the-$c$ next best, whatever aleph it may be. Numbers beyond the reach of iterative set-theory are right out, though I am attracted to some small degree by the idea that the $C$-worlds form a proper class. Lewis doesn't see matters this way. He thinks that 2-to-the-$c$ is a much better guess than six. One does see his point if $C$-worlds are the same as ways $C$-worlds could be. I would say that because 2-to-the-$c$ is *not* a better guess than six, $C$-worlds are *not* the same as ways $C$-worlds could be.

And, really, how *could* they be? If we think of the universe, we may see some sense in saying that it is (i.e., is identical with) a way a universe could be. Some sense, but not enough. Stalnaker and I have independently contended that this assertion is not even grammatical.[23] What one should say, surely, is that the universe *represents* or *realizes* or *instantiates* a way a universe could be. But the case is worse if we think of unrealized possibilities. How *could* one suppose that the (unrealized) possibility that the universe be thus-and-so is a thing that has a mass of $3.4 \times 10^{57}$ grams and is rapidly expanding? Or turn the point round: suppose there *is* an object (maximal with respect to spatiotemporal interrelatedness) that has these two features and which is spatiotemporally unrelated to us. What makes it an "unrealized possibility"? What is it besides an enormous physical object that has the feature, cosmologically fascinating but modally irrelevant, of being spatiotemporally unrelated to us? What would such things and their parts have to do with modality? Why should I call a horse that is a part of one of these things a "merely possible horse"? Why is that a good thing to call it? (In José A. Benardete's book *Infinity*,[24] Benardete considers the concept of a "pluriverse" consisting of spatiotemporally unrelated universes in order to show that one can imagine a case in which the higher infinite cardinals would be needed to count physical objects. It never occurred to him that it would be appropriate to describe parts of other universes in the pluriverse as mere *possibilia*, and he still doesn't see it.)

I conclude that Concretism is incredible and, therefore, that the "re-

---

[23] Stalnaker, "Possible Worlds," p. 68; Peter van Inwagen, "Indexicality and Actuality," *The Philosophical Review* 84 (1980), pp. 403–426, especially 406–407 (Chapter 10 in the present volume; see p. 168).

[24] José A. Benardete, *Infinity* (Oxford, 1964), pp. 143–154.

ductive analysis of modality" that it provides is a *correct* analysis only on the assumption that the incredible is true. The charges against Concretism are thus vindicated, and one of the charges against Abstractionism, that it cannot provide a reductive analysis of modality, is disarmed: better no analysis than an incorrect one. The score in the reductive-analysis game is thus 0 to − 1, in favor of the Abstractionist.

But what of the remaining charge against Abstractionism: that it just doesn't work, that it cannot do the job for which it was designed? If this charge is correct (and if Concretism *can* do the job), the tables are turned. It seems to be the practice of scientists (one we philosophers should adopt) not to reject the only workable theory simply because that theory is (or seems to be) incredible. It is incredible to suppose that something could be both a wave and a particle; it is incredible to suppose that the Galilean Law of the Addition of Velocities should fail; it is incredible to suppose that the geometry of physical space should be non-Euclidean; it is incredible to suppose that there should be a well-defined condition to which no set corresponds. But we have accepted all these incredible things. And if the remaining charge against Abstractionism is correct (and if there is nothing against Concretism other than its being incredible), then we shall have to accept Concretism after all. To that charge, which has been made by David Lewis, I now turn.

IV

What I call Concretism, Lewis calls Genuine Modal Realism. What I call Abstractionism, he calls Ersatz Modal Realism. I shall retain my own terms in my exposition of his argument.[25]

Lewis recognizes three varieties of Abstractionism: Linguistic, Pictorial, and Magical Abstractionism. He believes (i) that each of these varieties of Abstractionism can be refuted, (ii) that any very explicit version of Abstractionism must be of exactly one of these three types, and (iii) that the available writings of Abstractionists (other than those who explicitly espouse Linguistic Abstractionism) are insufficiently informative about the nature of states of affairs (or propositions or whatever

---

[25] In the sequel, I shall sometimes attribute to Lewis long speeches that are by no means quotations. I believe that these speeches are fairly accurate representations of what Lewis would say in certain circumstances, though I do not, of course, claim that he would have chosen the words I have chosen to express these points. Lewis's own words on these topics can be found in *On the Plurality of Worlds*, Ch. 3.

*A*-worlds are supposed to be) to enable one to discover which variety of Abstractionism their authors adhere to. I believe that (ii) and (iii) are correct and that Lewis's refutations of Linguistic and Pictorial Abstractionism are valid. I shall, accordingly, briefly describe these two varieties and outline his objections to them. I shall devote the remainder of this paper to a defense of "Magical" Abstractionism.

Remember that we said earlier (in our explanation in Section I of why Abstractionists refuse to apply the word "actual" to concrete objects) that *A*-worlds belong to the class of things that can represent concrete objects as being a certain way. (Thus, an *A*-nonactual *A*-world is one that *misrepresents* the way concrete things are.) There are three varieties of Abstractionism, in Lewis's view, because there are three kinds of answer to the question "How does that thing represent?" They are, roughly, "It represents the way a sentence does"; "It represents the way a picture does"; "It just represents, and there's nothing more to be said."

According to Linguistic Abstractionism, possible worlds represent the way sentences do. Sentences are structures built from a stock of basic elements – characters, we may call them. A sentence represents by convention: By convention, "The cat is on the mat" represents the cat as being on the mat. Suppose an Abstractionist identified "worlds" with possible distributions of matter and radiation in spacetime, and identified possible distributions in their turn with the Quine–Lewis "Ersatz worlds" mentioned in Section III in connection with the problem of expressing the plenitude.[26] This philosopher would be a Linguistic Abstractionist, for it is a matter of convention how an Erstaz world represents physical stuff as being distributed – indeed, *whether* it does.

Lewis argues that Linguistic Abstractionism is defective because it cannot coherently formulate the thesis that the actual world is impoverished in a way in which it probably *is* impoverished. If Linguistic Abstractionism is right, then all *possible* uninstantiated properties are ones that would be instantiated if objects of types that actually exist were sufficiently numerous and properly arranged. (For example, if the Ersatz-world variety of Linguistic Abstractionism is adopted, then any possible property – any property that is instantiated in some possible world – is

---

[26] In *On the Plurality of Worlds*, Lewis uses "Ersatz world" in a broader sense than in *Counterfactuals*. (In the more recent book, "Ersatz world" is used in more or less the sense of "*A*-world.") In the present paragraph, "Ersatz world" is used in the narrow sense of *Counterfactuals*.

one that would be instantiated if there were enough filled spacetime points and these filled points were arranged in the right way.) We can imagine simple worlds having the following feature: Suppose their inhabitants adopted the view that any possible property would be instantiated if objects of existent types were sufficiently numerous and properly arranged; then their inhabitants would be wrong. Consider, for example, a world in which protons, or the objects that play the role of protons in the physical economy of that world, are not composed of more fundamental particles. Consider some property possessed in our world only by quarks: "having an R-G color-charge of $-\frac{1}{2}$," say. This is a possible property, since it is instantiated in some world: the actual one. But it is not instantiated in *any* world that contains only things composed of things of kinds that exist in the simple world we have imagined.

Now if we can imagine a simple world in which Linguistic Abstractionism thus gives the wrong result, is there any reason to suppose that Linguistic Abstractionism gives the right result in the actual world? What warrant have we to suppose that there is in actuality such a rich variety of kinds that every possibility could be realized by some numerical augmentation or diminution and clever arrangement of the things there are? Even if one believed this, surely, one should regard it as a substantive metaphysical thesis (something having to do with God's bounty, perhaps, or with some other causally effective principle that is supposed to make actuality coincide with ontological richness), and not as something that could properly be forced on us by the most general and abstract features of our modal ontology. Is it even evident that there is *any* possible world that is not, in the sense described above, "impoverished"? Or even if there is a nonimpoverished world and it is the actual world, shouldn't we want our modal ontology to "work" in any world? Should we want to say that our modal ontology works only because of the lucky accident that a very rich world happens to be actual? These considerations seem to me to be cogent. Linguistic Abstractionism is defective.

Pictorial Abstractionism, a theory that no one in fact holds, asserts that worlds represent the way pictures or statues or models or maps do: by some sort of (relatively) nonconventional spatiotemporal isomorphism with the things represented and their spatiotemporal arrangement. But this seems impossible. The map is normally simpler than the territory. If something adequately represented (in the pictorial sense) the universe, it would have to be as detailed in its spatiotemporal structure as the universe. The point is tautological: if it left something out it would leave something out. And this point about pictures of the way things are applies to pictures of ways things might be but aren't. They would, of course, be different from, but some at least would have to be as detailed as, a fully accurate picture of the way things are. Suppose there were such detailed pictures of ways things might be. Wouldn't they just be C-worlds? Or would they be like C-worlds in being spread out in space and time, but, nevertheless, somehow "abstract"? There is no clear sense in this suggestion. Pictorial Abstractionism, like Linguistic Abstractionism, is defective.

The last refuge of the Abstractionist is Magical Abstractionism. (But I will not accept this dyslogistic name for the position I propose to defend. I will call it *Unsound* Abstractionism, which is an acronym for Unscientific Naive Superstitious Obscurantist Unenlightened Neanderthal Dogmatic Abstractionism.)

According to Abstractionists of all three factions, *A*-worlds are proposition-like entities. (The three factions may be said to differ just on the point of what, exactly, a "proposition-like entity" is.) In the previous sections, I have treated *A*-worlds as states of affairs, out of deference to Plantinga, who has done the most to make Abstractionism precise. In the sequel, however, it will simplify matters if we think of *A*-worlds as propositions pure and simple: An *A*-world is a possible proposition that, for any proposition $p$, entails either $p$ or the denial of $p$; and actuality is simply truth. Moreover, these "propositions" are not what David Lewis calls "propositions"; they are not sets of *C*-worlds. More generally, as I said of states of affairs in Section I, a proposition is not, for the Abstractionist, a spatiotemporally extended object, or a sum of extended objects, or a set-theoretical construct on sums of extended objects.[27] (In my view, there are only two of the things Lewis calls propositions – the false one, which is the empty set, and the true one, the set whose only member is the universe.)

A proposition is, of course, either true or false. A contingent proposition – and every *A*-world is a contingent proposition[28] – is *made true* or

---

[27] This stipulation does not rule out Linguistic Abstractionism, since the Linguistic Abstractionist's "worlds" could be (and may as well be) pure sets – which is what the Ersatz worlds of *Counterfactuals* are. It is hard to see whether it rules out Pictorial Abstractionism, since it is hard to see what kinds of things the "worlds" of that theory are supposed to be.

[28] Provided there are any contingent propositions at all: an *A*-world is a contingent proposition unless all truths are necessary truths (in which case, it would be *the A-world*).

*made false* by the way things happen to be arranged. If we allow ourselves the distinction between intrinsic and relational (or extrinsic or "mere-Cambridge") properties, we may say that truth and falsity are relational properties of propositions. The proposition that there are cats is true (because there *are* cats); if things had been arranged differently, if cats had never come to be, it would have been false. But its intrinsic properties would have been just as they are. Thus, truth is like accuracy (said of a map). (This simile, however, is dangerous because an inaccurate map can be altered and can thereby become accurate without any change in the territory. But all of a proposition's intrinsic properties are essential to it; it cannot be "altered.") We might say that a contingent proposition is indifferent to its own truth-value: remove the cats and you change the truth-values of many propositions, but the propositions remain unchanged – just as a map becomes inaccurate, and yet is unchanged, when the territory changes.

There is, therefore, for the Abstractionist, only one C-world.[29] There is a certain relation borne by this C-world to propositions, which we may call the *makes-true* relation. It bears this relation to the proposition that there are cats because it (the C-world) has feline parts. It fails to bear this relation to the proposition that there are elves because it has no elvish parts. If it, the only C-world, had been at all different in its intrinsic properties, it would have borne the *makes-true* relation to a different set of propositions. Of necessity, it bears the *makes-true* relation to exactly one proposition that is maximal with respect to entailment (to exactly one A-world): if the one C-world bears *makes-true* to both $p$ and $q$, then $p$ and $q$ are not both A-worlds. The one C-world, in virtue of the way its components are arranged, makes one and only one of the vast array of A-worlds actual. Any Abstractionist will say this much. The Unsound Abstractionist will add that a proposition's "truth-value dispositions" – dispositions like the one embodied in the conditional "$p$ would be made true by a C-world having elvish parts" – have nothing to do with human convention (or with divine decree, for that matter). For the Unsound Abstractionist, propositions are necessarily existent objects[30] that have their truth-value dispositions essentially. And, of

---

[29] Or *maybe* there are more. But if there were, they would (according to the Abstractionist) be parts of the one universe. If there are two C-worlds, and the other one contains dragons, then (according to the Abstractionist) there *are* dragons, in the same sense as that in which there are donkeys.

[30] Or, at any rate, "purely qualitative" propositions are. Some philosophers believe (*a*) that sentences containing proper names express propositions that are not purely qualitative,

course, the Unsound Abstractionist will deny that the truth-value dispositions of a proposition are in any way like the "accuracy dispositions" of a map: they are not grounded in the spatial or spatiotemporal structure of propositions – a kind of structure wholly alien to their nature.

Lewis's criticism of Unsound Abstractionism is, in a nutshell, that if things were as the Unsound Abstractionist claims, that philosopher could not understand or grasp the *makes-true* relation. Or put the matter this way: the Unsound Abstractionist, in claiming to grasp the *makes-true* relation, is claiming a magical power (hence the epithet "magical"[31]). Better still: (i) the Unsound Abstractionist has not really said what relation the *makes-true* relation is; (ii) he has made certain negative statements about the relation (it does not hold in virtue of convention or in virtue of spatiotemporal isomorphism between its *relata*), and he has made certain negative statements about the things it is borne to (they are neither spatiotemporal objects nor constructs on spatiotemporal objects), and he has made certain formal statements about it (it is borne by one thing to *some but not all* of the objects to which something might bear it); (iii) although there are doubtless uncountable infinities of relations satisfying the conditions laid down in (ii) – at least there are if there are nonspatiotemporal objects other than pure sets – no one could possibly grasp, or even refer to, any *one* relation satisfying these conditions.

Lewis's argument for this conclusion turns on a distinction between *internal* and *external* relations. Only dyadic relations figure in the argument, and I shall use "relation" to mean "dyadic relation." An internal relation is one grounded in the intrinsic properties of its *relata*: A relation *R* is internal if, given two objects *x* and *y* that stand in *R*, any two objects having the same intrinsic properties as *x* and *y* must stand in *R*. A relation *R* is external if there could be a pair of objects that stand in *R* and could also be a pair of objects that have the same intrinsic properties but do not stand in *R*. Thus, *being the same shape as* is internal, and *being ten feet from* is external.

Now: *makes-true* is either internal or external.

Suppose it is external. We note that it is not an ordinary external relation, like *being ten feet from*, which a given pair of objects (you and I, say)

---

owing to the fact that these propositions somehow "involve" the individuals to which these names refer, and (*b*) that a proposition of this type would not have existed if one of the individuals it involved had not existed. We shall not consider this thesis.

[31] The epithet "magical" may also partly derive from the fact that the Unsound Abstractionist can give no answer to the question "How do propositions represent?" beyond "They just do."

might or might not stand in. *Makes-true* has modal implications: if the one C-world bears *makes-true* to *p*, that is no accident. Given the properties of the C-world, it could not have failed to bear *makes-true* to *p*. But if we suppose that *makes-true* is external, then, since the intrinsic properties of the C-world are obviously relevant to whether it bears *makes-true* to *p*, we must conclude that the intrinsic properties of *p* are *irrelevant* to whether it bears *makes-true* to *p*. In fact, we may as well assume for the sake of convenience that propositions all have the same intrinsic nature: they are individuated by those intrinsic properties of the C-world in virtue of which it bears or fails to bear *makes-true* to them. Thus, the proposition that some donkeys walk and the proposition that some donkeys talk have the same intrinsic properties; the identity of each resides in the fact that (in the former case) the C-world bears *makes-true* to it just in virtue of the fact that the C-world has walking donkeys as parts and (in the latter case) fails to bear *makes-true* to it just in virtue of the fact that the C-world has no talking donkeys as parts. But the modal implications of *makes-true* noted above would appear to be inconsistent with this thesis about the individuation of propositions. I quote Lewis (but where I write "makes true," he wrote "selects," and where I write "proposition," he wrote "element" or "abstract simple"; *makes-true* is a special case of what he calls selection, and propositions are a special case of what he calls elements or abstract simples):

> The concrete world makes various propositions true. We are now supposing that this making true has nothing to do with the distinctive natures of the propositions – they haven't any – but it still has to do with what goes on in the concrete world. Necessarily, if a donkey talks, then the concrete world makes these propositions true; if a cat philosophizes, it makes those true; and so on. I ask: how can these connections be necessary? It seems to be one fact that somewhere within the concrete world, a donkey talks; and an entirely independent fact that the concrete world enters into a certain external relation with this proposition and not with that. What stops it from going the other way? Why can't anything coexist with anything here: any pattern of goings-on within the concrete world, and any pattern of external relations of the concrete world to the propositions?[32]

The implication is that if *makes-true* were really an external relation, and if the intrinsic properties of all propositions were the same, then the following could be the case: though the C-world in fact bears *makes-true* to the proposition that there are cats, the C-world might have had the very

---

[32] Lewis, *On the Plurality of Worlds*, p. 180.

same intrinsic properties and yet have failed to bear *makes-true* to that proposition; it might, in fact, have been just as it is and yet have borne *makes-true* to any set of propositions whatever. But this is clearly absurd, and we must conclude that *makes-true* is an internal relation: whether it holds between the *C*-world and *p* is determined partly by the intrinsic features of the *C*-world and partly by the intrinsic features of *p* and by nothing else. As a consequence, distinct propositions must have distinct intrinsic properties.

Suppose, therefore, that *makes-true* is internal and that propositions have distinct intrinsic natures in which *makes-true* is partly grounded. But how (Lewis asks the Unsound Abstractionist) did you ever manage to single out or grasp that relation? For a configuration of spatiotemporal objects (such as a *C*-world) to bear a graspable internal relation to a proposition must be for the structure of the proposition somehow to match the structure of the configuration of objects. But you say that propositions have neither spatiotemporal nor mereological nor set-theoretical structure. What other sort is there? If you reply that propositions have a *nature* even if they have no structure, I'll ask how you could ever learn the nature of any proposition when you can't observe or examine objects that are nonspatiotemporal and are, therefore, incapable of entering into causal relations. This *a priori* argument for your being unable to learn the intrinsic nature of propositions is underwritten by the observation that you can't individuate them without employing descriptions like "the proposition that there are cats." In other words, you can individuate them only by specifying what makes them true: "the proposition that there are cats" is just a way of saying "the proposition that is made true just by there being cats." Note that *I* don't have this limitation. I can refer to the proposition containing all and only those *C*-worlds that have cats as parts. And I can then go on to say what makes it true: I am a part of one of its members. But if you can't discover the intrinsic nature of any proposition, how can you grasp the supposedly internal relation *makes-true*? To grasp an *internal* relation, surely, is to know when *x* bears it to *y*, given the intrinsic properties of *x* and *y*. (To grasp *is the same color as* is to understand what is meant by the color of a thing and to know that this relation is the one that *x* bears to *y* just in virtue of the color of *x* being the color of *y*.)

I will call the problem that Lewis has posed "the Lewis–Heidegger problem." Heidegger has pointed out certain difficulties that face the traditional correspondence theory of truth:

We speak of corresponding [*übereinstimmen*] in various senses. For example, we say when considering two five-mark coins before us on the table: They are in correspondence with each other. The two coins agree [*übereinkommen*] in appearance. Hence, they have this appearance in common and are in that respect the same. But we also speak of correspondence if we say, for example: The coin is round. Here the statement [*Aussage*] corresponds with the thing. The relation now holds not between thing and thing, but between statement and thing. But in what is the agreement of the thing and the statement supposed to consist, given that they present themselves to us in such manifestly different ways? The coin is made of metal. The statement is not material at all. The coin is round. The statement has no spatial features whatever. One can buy something with the coin. The statement about it is never legal tender. But, for all their dissimilarity, the statement, being true, corresponds with the coin. And this correspondence, according to the common concept of truth, is supposed to be a matching. How can the statement match the coin, to which it is completely dissimilar? It would have to become the coin and so wholly cease to be itself. The statement never succeeds in doing that. The moment it did succeed, it could no longer correspond with the thing in the way a statement does. In the act of matching, the statement must remain . . . what it is. In what does its essence, so completely different from that of a thing, consist? How does the statement have the power, just precisely by retaining its essence, to match something other than itself, the thing?[33]

Heidegger asks how a proposition could match or correspond structurally with a configuration of matter. Lewis asks this and goes on to ask how, if the supposed internal relation between matter and proposition, the *makes-true* relation, held in virtue of some nonstructural feature of the proposition, we could even *grasp* this relation, owing to the inaccessibility of any nonstructural features that noncausal, and hence imperceptible, objects like propositions might have.

It is evident that the Lewis–Heidegger problem can arise quite independently of any questions about the ontology of possible worlds. It is a problem for anyone who believes that the bearers of truth-value are anything other than constructions out of individuals and the empty set. (If you believe that sentences are the bearers of truth-value, you believe that the bearers of truth-value are such constructions.) It is equally evident that anyone who can solve the Lewis–Heidegger problem can be an Unsound Abstractionist with impunity – or at least he will have nothing to fear from Lewis's argument for the thesis that if *makes-true* is an internal relation, then it cannot be grasped. Let us look carefully at this argument. How does it work? I believe that its most important premise is a

[33] Martin Heidegger, "Vom Wesen der Wahrheit," in *Wegmarken* (Frankfurt am Main, 1967), pp. 78–79.

principle about language – a principle about terms that purport to name internal relations. Since I wish to have a careful statement of this principle, I will present it in the form of a rather lengthy speech.

> Suppose someone makes a claim of the following general form:

>> There is a certain internal relation I call "*R*." I cannot define the term "*R*"; it is one of my primitives. I know that each member of a certain set *A* bears *R* to some but not all members of a certain set *B*, that only members of *A* bear *R* to anything, and that *R* is borne by things only to members of *B*. I am absolutely unable to make distinctions within *B* – except by using the term "*R*." I can sometimes refer to members or nonempty proper subsets of *B* by calling them things like "the object that both $a_1$ and $a_2$ bear *R* to" or "the set of all things $a_3$ bears *R* to"; but unless I use "*R*," I can single out neither any member nor any nonempty proper subset of *B*.

> This person, in claiming to understand his own relation-name, "*R*," is claiming magical powers.

The defense of this principle, I think, is as follows. "*R*" is supposed to be a name for an internal relation, a relation that holds between its *relata* wholly in virtue of their intrinsic features. But if *R* is borne only to members of *B*, and if I can distinguish among members of *B* only by considering which objects bear *R* to them, then I know of no intrinsic features of the members of *B* that differentiate them one from the other – that fit any of them for the office of having *R* borne to it by a given object. And to understand or grasp an *internal* relation borne by each of the *a*s to some but not all of the *b*s is to know how the intrinsic properties of an *a* must correspond with the intrinsic properties of a *b* if that relation is to hold between that *a* and that *b*.

This is a profoundly tricky argument. Let us try to orientate ourselves within its mazes by considering an example. Suppose I make the following claim.

> There are exactly ten cherubim. There is a certain internal relation I call "typosynthesis." I cannot define the word "typosynthesis"; it is one of my primitives. I know that each human being bears typosynthesis to some but not all cherubim, that only human beings bear typosynthesis to anything, and that typosynthesis is borne by things only to cherubim. I am absolutely unable to make distinctions among cherubim – except by using the term "typosynthesis." I can sometimes refer to individual cherubim or to nonempty proper subsets of the set of all cherubim by calling them things like "the one cherub that all Greeks and all Tasmanians bear typosynthesis to" or "the set of all cherubim that any Cartesian dualist bears typosynthesis to"; but unless I use the term "typosynthesis," I can single out neither

any one of the ten cherubim nor any one of the 1022 one-to-nine-membered sets of cherubim.

Then, according to Lewis, in claiming to understand the term "typosynthesis," I am claiming a magical power. If typosynthesis is really an internal relation borne by human beings to cherubim, then to understand the word "typosynthesis" must be to know when to apply this word, given the intrinsic properties of human beings, on the one hand, and the intrinsic properties of cherubim on the other. And, in the example, I know none of the intrinsic properties of cherubim; or, at least, I know of none that are properties of some but not all cherubim. Therefore, Lewis says, in the example I am claiming the magical power of being able to understand a name for an internal relation without knowing any relevant intrinsic features of the things it is borne to.

"And," Lewis will tell us Unsound Abstractionists, "you are claiming magical powers when you claim to understand the relational term '*makes-true*.' You say that the one C-world bears the internal relation *makes-true* to some but not all members of a certain class of things. And yet you cannot differentiate among the things this supposedly internal relation is borne to, except by reference to that relation itself. You tell me that one of those things is the proposition that there are cats, but that's just another way of saying 'the object that a C-world bears *makes-true* to just in virtue of having feline parts.' (And don't tell me that you can differentiate among propositions by means of the English sentences that express them. Expression is an internal relation, and you will have the same problems with this relation that you have with *makes-true*.) It is instructive to compare what you call propositions with what I call propositions. For me, a proposition is a set of possible worlds – of what you call C-worlds. For example, the proposition that Heidegger's coin is round is just the set of all worlds that have round counterparts of that coin as parts. (Note that I picked this proposition out without saying anything about what makes it true.) A proposition is true if and only if it contains the actual world. For example, Heidegger's coin is round; it is a counterpart of itself; it is a worldmate of ours; and, hence, the set of worlds in which it has a round counterpart contains the actual world. Therefore, it is a *true* proposition. According to *my* theory, then, '*makes-true*' can be defined in terms of the relations *is spatiotemporally related to* (which is needed to define 'world'), *is a part of*, and *is a member of*, which we certainly understand."

This is Lewis's argument against Abstractionism. Let us briefly recapitulate its structure. Abstractionism must be of either the Linguistic, the

Pictorial, or the Unsound variety. Linguistic and Pictorial Abstractionism are defective. If Unsound Abstractionism is correct, then the one *C*-world, in virtue of its intrinsic features, makes one among all the abstract, structureless *A*-worlds true. This *makes-true* relation is either external or internal. If it is external, then the *C*-world might have borne *makes-true* to a different set of propositions, even if that world had had exactly the same intrinsic properties; and this is absurd. If it is internal, on the other hand, then it cannot be grasped, and the Unsound Abstractionist does not understand his own theory.

I am convinced that Lewis's argument is defective, if only because, if it weren't, either Concretism or Linguistic Abstractionism or something even worse would have to be right. I will present an argument for the conclusion that there is something wrong with his argument. But I confess I am unable to say what is wrong with it. (I am inclined to think that the defect has something to do with the distinction between intrinsic and relational properties, a distinction that we may not understand as well as we think we do.) What is even more shameful to confess, I am unable to say what is right about it. And there is *something* right about it; the "cherubim" case is very convincing, and so is the argument for the thesis that *makes-true* is an internal relation. My argument is a *tu quoque*: by reasoning parallel to Lewis's, we can show that one could grasp set-theoretical membership only by magic; and Lewis's ontology requires at least some set-theoretical constructions.[34]

Suppose we have three individuals, $X$, $Y$, and $Z$. Assume we have no problem in picking out or identifying these individuals. Consider the objects we call "$\{X,Y\}$", "$\{X,Z\}$", and "$\{Y,Z\}$". Do we understand what it is to bear *is a member of* to one of these objects? We should note that we are unable to individuate these objects except *via* the membership relation: $\{X,Y\}$ is the object to which $X$ and $Y$ bear that relation and to which nothing else bears it, and so on. There is no way to pick out *any* set except by somehow specifying the things that bear membership to it. (Or, at least, this is true in the long run. We can refer to a set as "Tom's favorite set," but we could not do this unless we – or Tom, or *someone* – could specify the membership of this set.[35]) Does it follow from this fact and

---

[34] This strategy was suggested to me by Alvin Plantinga, who is, of course, not responsible for the quality of its execution.

[35] "Specifying the membership" is a vague enough notion. "The set that contains just 0 if Jack the Ripper was born in London, and just 1 otherwise" counts; "the set having just the membership of Tom's favorite set" does not.

from Lewis's principle about terms that purport to name internal relations that in claiming to understand "is a member of," we are claiming magical powers? Not unless membership is an internal relation.

And it would seem that it is not. Suppose that $X$, $Y$, and $Z$ are three distinct individuals, and that $X$ and $Y$ have the same intrinsic properties. Then, although $X$ is a member of $\{X,Z\}$, $Y$ is not. (I owe this point to David Lewis, who attaches no importance to it.) But there is more to be said. Call the objects to which a (dyadic) relation is borne by something its *range*. (I realize that the distinction between "the objects that bear $R$ to something" and "the objects to which $R$ is borne by something" is, at best, rough and intuitive and, at worst, confuses features of two-place predicates with features of dyadic relations. But this is of no import. As long as our practice is consistent, it will make no difference to our argument whether we take, e.g., the fathers or the children to constitute the "range". of fatherhood.) Call a relation *range-internal* if, necessarily, whatever bears it to $x$ bears it also to anything having the same intrinsic properties as $x$. Thus, the relation expressed by "$x$ is ten feet from something the same color as $y$" is range-internal, but not internal *simpliciter*.

Now if Lewis's principle about names for internal relations is right, it would seem that the corresponding principle about names for range-internal relations is right.

Consider "archetyposynthesis," a relation that human beings bear to seraphim. Its specification is similar to our earlier specification of typosynthesis; but two human beings with the same intrinsic properties may bear it to different seraphim. Nevertheless, if a human being bears it to a given seraph, he bears it to all seraphim having the same intrinsic properties as that seraph: it is range-internal.. And let us suppose that we can individuate seraphim only *via* archetyposynthesis. It is clear that if a magical power is required to understand typosynthesis, a magical power would also be required to understand archetyposynthesis – if anything, archetyposynthesis would require even more impressive magical powers.

Well, is membership range-internal? If $x$ bears it to $y$, must $x$ also bear it to anything having the same intrinsic properties as $y$? That's hard to say. What, after all, *are* the intrinsic properties of a set? What (to focus our attention) are the intrinsic properties of $\{$the earth, the moon$\}$? It is not at all clear what the intrinsic properties of this object are – other than "being a set," which is of no use to one who wishes to individuate sets. There would seem to be only two further types of properties that are even superficially plausible candidates for the office "intrinsic properties of a set": containing a given object or objects (type *A*), and containing various numbers of objects having certain intrinsic properties (type *B*). For example:

Type *A*   having the earth as a member[36]

Type *B*   having at least one spherical member; having exactly two spherical members; having no nonspherical members.

We may contrast these properties with such *clearly* extrinsic properties of sets as "having been used as an example by van Inwagen" or "having a member that has passed through the tail of a comet" or "being equinumerous with the set of Martian moons."

If any property of type *A* is extrinsic, all are; if some property of type *A* is not extrinsic, none are. And the same goes for type *B*. There are, accordingly, four possibilities:

(1) All properties of types A and B that a set has are intrinsic properties of that set, and it has no intrinsic properties other than those entailed by a complete specification of its type-A and type-B properties.

(2) All properties of type A that a set has are intrinsic to it, and it has no intrinsic properties other than those entailed by a complete specification of its type-A properties.

(3) All properties of type B that a set has are intrinsic to it, and it has no intrinsic properties other than those entailed by a complete specification of its type-B properties.

(4) Neither properties of type A nor properties of type B are intrinsic; accordingly a set has no intrinsic properties, other than those it shares with all sets: those entailed by *being a set*.

We may distinguish two cases:

### Case One

Either possibility (1) or possibility (2) is realized. In this case, membership is range-internal, since the only object that has all the same intrinsic properties as a given set is that set itself. And if membership is range-internal, then by reasoning parallel to Lewis's, and (apparently) valid if his reasoning is valid, we do not understand membership.

### Case Two

Either possibility (3) or possibility (4) is realized. In this case, membership is not range-internal. It is, in fact, *purely external*: it is possible that *x* belong

[36] Let us classify *having no members* as belonging to type *A*: its possession by a set does, after all, determine with respect to each individual whether that individual is a member of that set.

to $y$ and $z$ not belong to $w$ and, at the same time, possible for either or both of the following conditions to hold: $x$ and $z$ have the same intrinsic properties; $y$ and $w$ have the same intrinsic properties. Suppose, for example, that three individuals, Tom, Tim, and Tam have the same intrinsic properties. Then {Tom, Tim} and {Tom, Tam} have the same intrinsic properties. And Tom is a member of {Tom, Tim}, while Tim is not a member of {Tom, Tam}.

Is it possible that membership is an external relation? Let us adopt the reasoning Lewis used to show that it is absurd to suppose that *makes-true* is external. We recall that in that piece of reasoning, Lewis stipulated that propositions were without distinctive intrinsic properties, justifying this convenient assumption with the observation that such distinctive in-trinsic properties as propositions may have play no role in determining whether the *C*-world bears the external relation *makes-true* to them. Let us, with the same justification, assume that sets have no distinctive in-trinsic properties: $x$ is a different set from $y$ because and only because different objects bear the external relation of membership to them. Here is an adaptation of Lewis's argument against the externality of *makes-true* to the case of membership:

> Tom and Tim belong to various sets. We are now supposing that this belonging has nothing to do with the distinctive natures of the sets – they haven't any – but does have to do with Tom's and Tim's existence. Necessarily, if Tom and Tim exist, they belong to {Tom, Tim}. I ask: how can these connections be necessary? It seems to be one fact that Tom exists and another that he enters into a certain external relation with this set and not with that. What stops it from going the other way? Why can't anything coexist with anything here: any population of individuals and any pattern of external relations of these individuals to sets?

To take an example, if the intrinsic properties of {Tom, Tim} and {Tom, Tam} really are the same, and if membership really is an external relation, why *couldn't* Tim bear membership to {Tom, Tam} as easily as to {Tom, Tim}? What would prevent it? (Of course, if Tim were a member of {Tom, Tam}, it would presumably be incorrect to *call* that set "{Tom, Tam}"; but why couldn't Tim be a member of *it*?) But this is an absurd result: Tim *could not have* been a member of {Tom, Tam}, and there's an end on't.

Therefore, membership is not a purely external relation, or even a "range-external" relation. And, therefore, we do not understand member-ship – or we don't if Lewis has made no false step in his argument for the conclusion that the Unsound Abstractionist does not understand *makes-true*.

That we do not understand set-membership entails that we do not understand much of classical mathematics, a hard conclusion to accept. Moreover, as I have remarked, Lewis's own ontology seems to be committed to sets: A proposition is a set of *C*-worlds, and truth is having the *C*-actual *C*-world as a member; a property is a set of objects (*C*-actual or *C*-nonactual), and exemplification is membership.[37]

Propositions, perhaps, do not have to be sets of *C*-worlds. Lewis could as easily have said that a proposition was a mereological sum of *C*-worlds and that a proposition was true if the *C*-actual *C*-world was a part of it. Properties, however, could not survive the demise of set theory so handily. One cannot say that a property is a sum of objects and that an object exemplifies a property if it is a part of that property. If sphericality were the sum of all spheres (including the *C*-nonactual ones) and if exemplification were parthood, then the sum of two spheres would be spherical, as would a cubical part of a sphere. The problem of representing properties and exemplification in mereological terms has no obvious solution.

I conclude that Lewis's argument against Unsound Abstractionism is as damaging to his own ontology (and to classical mathematics, to boot) as it is to Unsound Abstractionism and that, given the strong *prima facie* case against Concretism, Abstractionism is to be preferred to Concretism.[38]

[37] See Lewis, *On the Plurality of Worlds*, Section 1.5.
[38] Parts of this essay were read as comments on a paper by David Lewis called "Possibilities: Concrete Worlds or Abstract Simples?" at the 1984 Chapel Hill Philosophy Colloquium. I have benefited from discussion and correspondence with Allen Hazen, David Lewis, Alvin Plantinga, and Peter Unger.

# 13

# *Modal epistemology*

Philosophy abounds in modal arguments. A surprisingly high proportion of these arguments have the following features: they are formally valid; one of their premises is far more controversial (doubtful, disputable, problematic) than any of the others; it is a modal premise.[1]

In all the most interesting arguments of this sort, the "crucial" modal premise is an assertion of possibility, a statement of the form "it is possible that *p*."[2] I would suppose that we find arguments that proceed from assertions of possibility more interesting than arguments that proceed from assertions of necessity for two reasons. First, we are inclined (at least initially) to regard assertions of possibility as easier to establish than assertions of necessity. Secondly, we are inclined (at least initially) to find it surprising that anything about how things are or must be can be deduced from a premise about how things might be; but it is hardly surprising that conclusions about how things are or must be can be deduced from premises about how things must be.

Here are three examples of interesting arguments whose crucial premises are assertions of possibility:

- It is possible for there to be a perfect being (that is, a being that has all perfections essentially)

  Necessary existence is a perfection

*hence,*

First published in *Philosophical Studies* 92 (1998), pp. 67–84.

[1] But philosophers have employed many formally valid modal arguments that cannot be so described. Here is a trivial example: it is possible for there to be cases of justified true belief that are not cases of knowledge; hence, knowledge is not justified true belief. Kripke's arguments for the essentiality of origins or the impossibility of unicorns might provide non-trivial examples – at least for those who were willing to say that these arguments were formally valid or could easily be made so.

[2] Or, of course, an assertion of non-necessity – since "it is possible that *p*" is equivalent to "it is not necessary that not-*p*."

> There is a perfect being;
>
> - It is possible that I exist and nothing material exist
>
>   Whatever is material is essentially material

*hence,*

> I am not a material thing;
>
> - It is possible that there exist vast amounts of suffering for which there is no explanation
>
>   If there exists an omniscient, omnipotent, and morally perfect being, there cannot also exist vast amounts of suffering for which there is no explanation.

*hence,*

> It is impossible for there to be a necessarily existent being that is essentially omniscient, omnipotent, and morally perfect.

Let us call such arguments "possibility arguments." (This is no more than a handy tag. Many arguments that are not of this type – see footnote 1 – involve assertions of possibility.) Each of the three arguments I have laid out has had its advocates. But I know of no case in which a possibility argument has turned an atheist into a theist, a materialist into a dualist, or a theist into an atheist; I know of no case in which a possibility argument has changed any philosopher's mind about anything. No one (I think) would now dispute the logical validity of the three possibility arguments I have laid out; but a philosopher who rejects the conclusion of any of them will simply – I know of no exceptions to this generalization – reject (or at least refuse to accept) the crucial modal premise of the argument that has the unwelcome conclusion. One important defense of this cavalier approach proceeds by pointing out that possibility arguments can often be "inverted" to produce an argument for the denial of the conclusion of the original argument. For example:

> It is possible that I exist and nothing immaterial exist
>
> Whatever is immaterial is essentially immaterial

*hence,*

> I am not an immaterial thing.

Having presented this "inversion" of our second argument, a materialist can proceed to argue as follows.

Whatever merit the crucial modal premise of your argument may have, you can't expect the philosophical world to accept it unless you can show why it is somehow better or more reasonable than the crucial modal premise of the argument for the opposite conclusion that I have presented. And I don't see how you can do that. At any rate, until you have done it, the two arguments, so to speak, cancel each other out – and are therefore both without any force.

It is not always possible to "invert" a possibility argument. But it is always possible to replace the crucial modal premise of a possibility argument with the denial of its conclusion and to replace its conclusion with the denial of its crucial modal premise. The resulting argument will, of · course, be valid if the original argument was valid, and those who reject the conclusion of the original argument will invariably claim to find the resulting "contrapositive" argument at least as plausible as the original argument.

The apparent inevitability of this sort of exchange when a possibility argument is put forward has naturally led philosophers to begin to think systematically about the status of our beliefs about modal matters. How do we know (or *do* we ever know?) the truth-values of assertions of possibility – or of any modal assertions? What kind of justifications can be given for theses of the form "Such-and-such is a possible [impossible, contingent, necessary] state of affairs [proposition, property]"? If we ever do know theses of this form to be true (or to be false), what is the source – or what are the sources – of this knowledge?

My own view is that we often do know modal propositions, ones that are of use to us in everyday life and in science and even in philosophy,[3] but do not and cannot know (at least by the exercise of our own unaided powers[4]) modal propositions like the crucial modal premises of our three possibility arguments. I have called this position "modal skepticism."[5] This name was perhaps ill-chosen, since, as I have said, I think that we do know a lot of modal propositions, and in these post-Cartesian days,

---

[3] For example: we know that there could be a full-scale papier-mâché mock-up of a barn that looked like a real barn from a distance, or that the legs and top of this table might never have been joined to one another.

[4] It is plausible to suppose that one can learn from the testimony of others what one could not learn by the exercise of one's own unaided powers. It would be therefore consistent with my thesis for me to affirm, say, that I knew that a perfect being was possible because God existed and had informed me that He was a perfect being – or (to anticipate an example that I shall later discuss) that I knew that transparent iron was possible because the Wise Old Beings from the Center of the Galaxy had assured me that their physics (which surpasses human understanding) had demonstrated this possibility.

[5] Peter van Inwagen, *God, Knowledge, and Mystery: Essays in Philosophical Theology* (Ithaca and London, 1995), pp. 11–14.

"skeptic" suggests someone who contends that we know nothing or almost nothing. It should be remembered, however, that there has been another sort of skeptic: someone who contends that the world contains a great deal of institutionalized pretense to knowledge of remote matters concerning which knowledge is in fact not possible. (Montaigne was a skeptic in this sense, as were, perhaps, Sextus and Cicero.) It is in this sense of the word that I am a modal "skeptic."

One way to get an intuitive grasp of what I mean when I speak of "modal skepticism" is to consider the analogy of distance. In my view, many of our modal judgments are analogous to judgments of distance made by eye. That is, they are analogous to judgments of the sort that we make when – just on the basis of how things look to us – we say things like, "That mountain is about thirty miles away" or "It's about three hundred yards from that tall pine to the foot of the cliff." Such judgments are not, of course, infallible, but in a wide range of circumstances they can be pretty accurate. There are, however, circumstances – circumstances remote from the practical business of everyday life – in which they are not accurate at all. People had no idea about how far away the sun and the moon and the stars were till they gave up trying to judge celestial distances by eye and began to reason. ("You can see a significant portion of the shadow of the whole earth on the moon when the moon is entering or leaving the earth's shadow, so the moon must be a lot farther away than anyone would have guessed . . .") Analogously, I should say, we are able to discern the modal status of some propositions in a way that, like our intuitive judgment of distance, is "noninferential." I know that it is possible that – that there is no intrinsic impossibility in its being the case that – the table that was in a certain position at noon have then been two feet to the left of where it in fact was. I know that it is possible (in this sense) that John F. Kennedy have died of natural causes, that it is impossible for there to be liquid wine bottles, and that it is necessary that there be a valley between any two mountains that touch at their bases. And, no doubt, reason – operating on a combination of "basic" modal knowledge like that displayed in the previous sentence and facts about the way the world is put together – can expand the range of our modal knowledge considerably.[6] And

---

[6] Suppose, for example, that we know that it is not possible for water to be a different physical stuff from the physical stuff it is – that no *other* physical stuff would be water (an example, perhaps, of "basic" modal knowledge); and suppose we know that water is the physical stuff composed of molecules formed by joining a hydrogen atom to a hydroxyl

where reason cannot, strictly speaking, extend the range of our modal knowledge, it can perhaps extend the range of our reasonable belief about modal matters. I myself have argued for the impossibility of the "bodily transfer" cases that figure so prominently in discussions of personal identity, and for the impossibility of the moon's being made of green cheese;[7] like most philosophers who offer arguments, I'd like to think that my arguments lend reasonable support to their conclusions.

All these things we can do. All these capacities we have. But I should say that we have no sort of capacity that would enable us to know whether the crucial premises of our three possibility arguments are true – or whether it is possible for there to be a pure, phenomenal color in addition to red, yellow, green, and blue, whether it is impossible for there to be a three-inch-thick sheet of solid iron that is transparent to visible light, or whether it is necessary that the laws of physics have the same structure as the actual laws. To my mind, philosophers who are convinced that they can hold, say, the concept of transparent iron before their minds and determine whether transparent iron is possible by some sort of intellectual insight are fooling themselves. (They could be compared to an inhabitant of the ancient world who was convinced that he could just *see* that the moon was about thirty miles away.)

The illusory character of their conviction is sometimes disguised by talk of "logical possibility," for it is often supposed that there is a species of possibility that goes by this name and that one can determine *a priori* whether a concept or state of affairs is logically possible. But there is no such thing as logical possibility – not, at least, if it is really supposed to be a species of possibility. Belief in the reality of "logical possibility" may be based, at least in part, on a faulty inference from the reality of logical *impossibility*, which is real enough. Logical impossibility is an epistemological category: the logically impossible is that which can be seen to be impossible on the basis of logical considerations alone – or, to be liberal, logical and semantical considerations alone.[8] A round square is logically

radical (a "fact about how the world is put together"); then – or so at least many have argued – we can validly conclude that water is *essentially* hydrogen hydroxide.

    For an interesting discussion of the ways in which reason, starting with a stock of "basic" modal knowledge, can extend our modal knowledge, see Phillip Bricker, "Plenitude of Possible Structures," *The Journal of Philosophy* 88 (1991), pp. 607–619.

7  "Materialism and the Psychological Continuity Account of Personal Identity," *Philosophical Perspectives* 11: *Mind, Causation, and World* (1997), pp. 305–319 (Chapter 9 in the present volume); review of Richard Swinburne, *The Coherence of Theism*, *The Philosophical Review* 88 (1979), pp. 668–672.

8  If there is logical impossibility, there is also logical necessity, for a state of affairs is

impossible because a square must, by definition, have vertices or corners and a round thing must, by definition, have no corners, and a round square would therefore both have and not have corners. I do not want to dispute the cogency of arguments like this one. What I dispute is the contention that if a concept or state of affairs is not logically impossible, then it is "logically possible." It hardly follows that, because a certain thing cannot be proved to be impossible by a certain method, it is therefore possible in any sense of "possible" whatever. Suppose that the infallible Standard Atlas marks many islands as uninhabitable, none as inhabitable, and makes no claim to completeness in this matter. We could, if we liked, say that the islands marked "uninhabitable" in the Standard Atlas were "cartographically uninhabitable." In doing this, we should be calling attention to the fact that our knowledge that these islands were uninhabitable had a certain source. But would there then be any sense in saying that an island was "cartographically inhabitable" just in the case that it was *not* cartographically *un*inhabitable? Very little, I should think. We *could* use words this way, but if we did we should have to recognize that "cartographical inhabitability" was not a species of inhabitability. (Similar points could be made about mathematical impossibility and "mathematical possibility.")

Perhaps at this point some readers will protest that they are puzzled about what the object of my skepticism is. "You say you believe we have no knowledge of whether certain concepts or states of affairs are possible – but what is this "possibility" knowledge of which you are skeptical *about*? It is not epistemic possibility, and (you say) it is not logical possibility, and it is obviously not supposed to be physical possibility or biological possibility or technological possibility or any of the other kinds of possibility with which we are familiar. What is it, then?" It is what ties all these "qualified possibilities" together and makes them all species of a genus – the genus "possibility." Take physical possibility, possibility given the laws of nature. A proposition is physically possible if its conjunction with the laws of nature is . . . well, *possible*. Possible *tout court*. Possible *simpliciter*. Possible *period*. Explanations come to an end somewhere. I can say only that by possibility I mean possibility without qualification. If there were no such thing as modality without qualification, there could be no qualified modalities like physical and biological

logically necessary if and only if its negation is logically impossible. The logically necessary is that which can be seen to be necessary on the basis of logical (or semantical) considerations alone.

possibility and necessity. If we understand "qualified" modal statements (of any sort), we must understand "unqualified" modal statements.[9] Let us return to the topic of our capacity for making (warranted) modal judgments. Many philosophers have a far more sanguine view of this capacity than I. They are very confident that they can make philosophically interesting modal judgments about concerns remote from everyday life, and they are impatient with anyone who challenges their claim to have this ability. Richard Gale is an excellent example of such a philosopher.[10] Gale does not bother to argue for the conclusion that he is able to make philosophically interesting modal judgments about concerns remote from everyday life. Rather, he takes this to be self-evidently true. He is quite sure that I simply refuse to admit that human beings have epistemic powers that they just obviously do have. (He believes that my denial that we have these powers is grounded in a desire to be able to deploy various "for all anyone knows, such-and-such is impossible" judgments in responding to the Argument from Evil, but, for present purposes, that's neither here nor there.) He has said that if my own capacity to make modal judgments is really as limited as I say it is, I must be regarded as modally challenged, as someone who "cannot modalize like normal people do." But I *can* "modalize" like normal people, and so can he. What he *can't* do, apparently, is to discriminate those cases in which his modal judgments are products of his ordinary human powers of "modalization" from those that are based on his immersion in a certain philosophical environment – an environment composed of philosophers who unthinkingly make all sorts of fanciful modal judgments because *they've* always been surrounded by philosophers who unthinkingly make the same sorts of fanciful modal judgments. He is as unaware of his immersion in this environment as a fish is of its immersion in water. He is unaware that the modal beliefs he expresses or presupposes when he says, "We'd have had more room if we'd moved the table up

---

9 What I have called possibility without qualification, some have called "absolute" or "intrinsic" or "ontological" or "metaphysical" possibility. The first two seem good enough names. I don't find "ontological" or "metaphysical" particularly appropriate tags, however. I don't think that unqualified or absolute or intrinsic possibility is in any clear sense an ontological or metaphysical concept. An analogy is perhaps provided by "truth without qualification" (as opposed, for example, to scientific, metaphorical, approximate, or contingent truth). One *might* call "truth without qualification" ontological or metaphysical truth, but these wouldn't be particularly appropriate tags.

10 See Richard Gale, "Some Difficulties in Theistic Treatments of Evil," in *The Evidential Argument from Evil*, ed. Daniel Howard-Snyder (Bloomington and Indianapolis, 1996), pp. 206–18.

against the wall" (e.g., that it was possible for the table to be up against the wall) and the modal beliefs he gives such confident expression to in his writings on philosophical theology have quite different sources. The former have their source in our ordinary human powers of "modalization" (for all that, they are not philosophically uncontroversial: they would be disputed by Spinoza); the latter have their source in his professional socialization, in "what his peers will let him get away with saying." To adapt the analogy I used earlier, he could be compared to a Greek mariner of Homeric times who thinks that his (well-grounded) belief that the mountain that has just appeared on the horizon is about thirty miles away and his belief that the moon is about thirty miles away stem from the same source, to wit, his ability to judge distance by eye.

So much for the modal knowledge I think we do not have. Let me now turn to the modal knowledge I think we do have. Although I do not doubt that we have some modal knowledge, I regard much of this knowledge as mysterious. Some modal statements, I have said, we know by reasoning from what I have called "basic" modal knowledge – simple, obvious modal statements whose truth we are somehow in a position to know – , together with some facts about how the world is constructed. But how do we get started in this reasoning? How do we know the "simple, obvious" modal statements to be true? What is the ground of "basic" modal knowledge? I do not know how to answer these questions.

Let me try to make it clearer what questions it is I do not know how to answer. I do not mean to imply that *all* our modal knowledge is either "basic" modal knowledge or obtained by logical or mathematical deduction from basic modal knowledge and "facts about how the world is put together." We can validly deduce the conclusion "It is possible for there to be orchids" from the non-modal premise "There are orchids." And the proposition "It is a necessary truth that all bachelors are unmarried" can be established by reflection on logic and the meanings of words.[11] Other necessary truths can be established by mathematical reasoning. (And, presumably, some people *know* that it is possible for there to be orchids and that it is necessary that all bachelors are unmarried and that any function continuous on a closed interval must necessarily attain a maximum value in that interval. This knowledge is not based on what I

---

[11] That Hesperus is necessarily identical with Phosphorus can be established by the joint application of the theorem "$x = y \rightarrow \Box\, x = y$" and the semantical thesis that "Hesperus" and "Phosphorus" are "rigid designators" – or at least it can if that semantical thesis has itself been "established."

have called basic modal knowledge and I do not regard it as mysterious.) The questions I do not know how to answer – there are two – pertain to propositions whose truth-values cannot be discovered by reflection on logic and the meanings of words or by mathematical reasoning. First, how can we know that (or find out whether) a proposition is possible when we do not know that it is true – that is when we either know that it is false or do not know whether it is true or false? Secondly, how can we know that (or find out whether) a proposition that we know to be true is also necessary? We should note that it is far from evident whether there is any very close connection between these two questions. We certainly *do* know that it is possible for the chair to have been in some other position at noon; it is less clear whether we know of *any* proposition that it is a necessary truth if it cannot be shown to be true either by reflection on logic and the meanings of words or by mathematical reasoning.

Let us call the area of philosophy that attempts to provide answers to these two questions "modal epistemology." This term (like "possibility argument") should be regarded as merely a convenient label. There are many statements – for example, "If a proposition is known to be an instance of a theorem of first-order logic, then it is known to be a necessary truth" – that it would be natural to call theses of "modal epistemology" but which do not belong to the special domain I am giving this name to.

Modal epistemology is a subject about which little is known. In my view, at least, I know a good deal about the epistemology of non-modal statements. For example, I would say that we know many propositions to be true on the basis of observation. This may not be a very interesting thesis, but it is true and we know it to be true. What *is* interesting is the fact that there is no such truism that one can cite in the case of what I am calling basic modal knowledge. The table could have been two feet to the left. Of course it could have. We *know* that. We know that the table's having been two feet to the left is not among the things that are intrinsically impossible. There is an intrinsic impossibility in the notion of a round square; there is *probably* an intrinsic impossibility in the notion of faster-than-light travel; there *may* be an intrinsic impossibility in the notion of transparent iron. But we *know* – despite the best efforts of Spinoza to prove that falsity is coextensive with impossibility – that there is no intrinsic impossibility in the table's having been two feet to the left. We know – but *how* do we know? Here is one tempting answer to this question: we know this because we have constructed and examined intellectually a counterfactual scenario according to which the table *was* two feet to the left of its actual position (this morning it occurred to my wife that the room would look nicer if the table were two feet to the left, so she moved it) – or, at any rate, because we have constructed and examined such scenarios in many similar cases in the past and know somehow that the present case is like those past cases in all relevant ways. But this tempting answer does not really explain how we know that the table could have been elsewhere. The scenario we construct, after all, will be of no use if it is impossible: even if *p* is a possible proposition, considering an impossible scenario according to which *p* was true would not enable us to know that *p* was possible. It is, moreover, doubtful whether considering a possible scenario according to which *p* was true would enable us to know that *p* was possible unless we *knew* that the scenario itself was possible. It is, finally, doubtful whether constructing a scenario we *knew* to be possible would show us *how* we knew that something involved in the scenario was possible unless we knew *how* we knew that the scenario itself was possible. (And how should we know how we knew that the scenario itself was possible? – by constructing a second, "larger" scenario that included causal antecedents of the events in the original scenario?) But if we know how we know it is possible for my wife to have certain thoughts that she did not in fact have – we no doubt *do* know that this is possible – , we should certainly know how we know that it is possible for the table to have been two feet to the left.

Fortunately, we do not have to have an adequate account of how we know statements of a certain type in order to know some statements of that type or to know that we know some statements of that type or to know that we know a given statement of that type. But I am convinced that, whatever it is that enables us to determine the modal status of ordinary propositions about everyday matters, this method or mechanism or technique or device or system of intuitions or whatever it should be called is of no use at all in determining the modal status of propositions remote from the concerns of everyday life. I am convinced, moreover, that there is no *other* method or mechanism or technique or device or system of intuitions that enables us to do this. (Other than the methods I have already mentioned: "deriving" possibility from actuality, and the use of logical or mathematical reasoning, pure or applied. These methods will sometimes enable us to determine the modal status of propositions remote from the concerns of ordinary life – that there are neutron stars; that there are physical objects whose spacetime trajectories are space-like – , but they will not enable us to determine the modal status of just any proposition remote from the concerns of ordinary life. In particular, they will not enable us to discover whether the crucial modal premises of "possibility arguments" are true or false.) That is, I am what I have called a "modal skeptic."

I will close by briefly considering a recent attempt to explain the basis of our modal knowledge, and will argue that this account supports modal skepticism. Although I am not perfectly satisfied with this account, I believe it has some very attractive features, and is certainly more sophisticated than any other account of modal knowledge. I will neither attack nor defend this account, but will rather try to explain why I believe that anyone who accepts this account should be a modal skeptic.

According to Stephen Yablo,[12] a proposition *p* is conceivable for me just in the case that I can imagine a possible world I take to verify *p*. (A world that I take to verify *p* is simply a world that seems to me to be a world in which *p* is true.) Yablo is well aware that no finite being's powers of imagination are equal to the task of singling out a particular possible world. He reminds us, however, that we can imagine "a" possible world in the same sense as that in which we can imagine "a" representative of any type of thing. If I imagine, say, a tiger, for no number *n* will *n* be the number of stripes of the tiger I imagine – although the tiger I imagine will no doubt have the property "for some *n*, having *n* stripes." The situation is similar when I imagine a possible world (that is, when I imagine a possible world having some specified feature or features).[13] Suppose, for example, that I attempt to imagine a world in which George Bush was re-elected in 1992. It is unlikely that my effort will in any way involve the state of higher education in Pakistan in the year 1957 – although, of course, in every world in which Bush won re-election, something or other was the case as regards higher education in Pakistan in 1957.

Yablo argues that, if I am able to imagine a world I take to verify *p*, I am thereby prima facie justified in believing that *p* is possible. (I will

[12] Stephen Yablo, "Is Conceivability a Guide to Possibility?", *Philosophy and Phenomenological Research* 53 (1993), pp. 1–39.

[13] Yablo rightly distinguishes *objectual* from *propositional* imagining. (Consider, for example, the difference between "imagining a tiger" and "imagining that one encounters a tiger.") The kind of imagining that figures in his epistemological thesis is objectual imagining. Perhaps, therefore, it would be better to state his thesis in terms of "imagining a cosmos" or "imagining a universe," since most philosophers – David Lewis, of course, is the notorious exception – take "possible worlds" to be states of affairs or other such proposition-like entities.

discuss only those parts of Yablo's thesis that pertain to prima facie justi-fication.) This seems to me to be a step in the right direction. To assert that $p$ is possible, after all, is to commit oneself, willy-nilly, to the thesis that there is a whole, coherent reality – a possible *world* – in which $p$ is true, of which the truth of $p$ is an integral part. To assert that it is possible for the moon (or a thing in the moon's actual orbit that looks like the actual moon when observed from the surface of the earth) to be made of green cheese is to commit oneself, willy-nilly, to the thesis that a physical universe in which a moon-like thing made of cheese came into existence and continues to exist is possible, that there are possible laws of nature and possible initial conditions that permit such a thing.[14] (Or, if the object is supposed not to have arisen in the natural course of events, but to be literally miraculous, to the thesis that there could be a supernatural agency that was capable of creating and sustaining it and which either had a good reason to create and sustain a huge ball of cheese in orbit around the earth, or which might create and sustain such a thing without having any good reason to do so.) Although it is in a sense trivial that to assert the possibility of $p$ is to commit oneself to the possibility of a whole, coherent reality of which the truth of $p$ is an integral part, exam-ination of the attempts of philosophers to justify their modal convictions shows that this triviality is rarely if ever an operative factor in these at-tempts.[15] A philosopher will confidently say that a (naturally) purple cow is possible, but he or she will not in fact have devoted any thought to the question whether there is a chemically possible purple pigment such that the coding for the structures that would be responsible for its production and its proper placement in a cow's coat could be coherently inserted into any DNA that was really cow DNA – or even "cow-like-thing-but-for-color" DNA. In a way, of course, it is understandable that this philosopher will not have devoted any thought to this question, for, in the present state of knowledge, it is not possible to devote any thought to it. Either the structural formula for such a pigment is already *there*, lurking Platonically in the space of chemical possibility, or it is not.

---

14 Compare my discussion of the "green cheese" case in the review of Swinburne's *The Coherence of Theism* cited in fn. 7.

15 There is a wonderful article about this that I never miss a chance to commend: George Seddon, "Logical Possibility," *Mind* 81 (1972), pp. 481–494. See also my "Ontological Arguments," *Noûs* 11 (1977), pp. 375–395. (Reprinted in the collection cited in fn. 5.) This essay contains a discussion of the "transparent iron" case. See also Paul Tidman, "Conceivability as a Test for Possibility," *American Philosophical Quarterly* 31 (1994), pp. 297–309.

And – so far as I know – no one has any reason to assign any particular subjective probability, high or low or middling, to the thesis that it *is* lurking there. But if a philosopher has not attempted to do something like this, then that philosopher has not, in any useful sense, attempted to imagine a possible world in which there are naturally purple cows. Therefore, if Yablo's general thesis is right, and if *I* am right in my assertion that in the present state of knowledge no one is able to imagine a possible world in which there are naturally purple cows, it follows that (if there is no other source for prima facie justified modal beliefs than the one Yablo puts forward; he has offered this as a sufficient, not a necessary condition for prima facie justification for modal beliefs), no one is even prima facie justified in believing that naturally purple cows are possible. It must be emphasized that our being unable to imagine such a world in no way lends any support to the thesis that a naturally purple cow is *im*possible. Yablo has an interesting proposal about what imaginings would provide prima facie justification for the thesis that a given state of affairs is impossible: roughly, that for every world I can imagine, I take it to contain the negation of that state of affairs. I will not discuss this proposal. Here I wish only to point out that neither he nor I supposes that if one discovers that one is unable to imagine a world one takes to be a *p*-world, that discovery, by itself, provides one with even prima facie justification for the thesis that *p* is impossible. This is perhaps worth pointing out, since the statement that one is unable to imagine something often carries the "conversational implicature" that one takes that thing to be impossible.

In my view, we cannot imagine worlds in which there are naturally purple cows, time machines, transparent iron, a moon made of green cheese, or pure phenomenal colors in addition to those we know. Anyone who attempts to do so will either fail to imagine a world or else will imagine a world that only seems to have the property of being a world in which the thing in question exists. Can we imagine a world in which there is transparent iron? Not unless our imaginings take place at a level of structural detail comparable to that of the imaginings of condensed-matter physicists who are trying to explain, say, the phenomenon of superconductivity. If we simply imagine a Nobel Prize acceptance speech in which the new Nobel laureate thanks those who supported him in his long and discouraging quest for transparent iron and displays to a cheering crowd something that looks (in our imaginations) like a chunk of glass, we shall indeed have imagined a world, but it will not be a world in which there is transparent iron. (But not because it will be a world in which there *isn't* transparent iron. It will be neither a world in which there is transparent iron nor a world in which there isn't transparent iron.) This sort of effort of imagination will, or so I should suppose, show that a certain proposition has the modal status "possible," but the proposition will be a disjunctive one. Here are some of its disjuncts:

- Transparent iron exists
- The scientific community has somehow been deceived into thinking that transparent iron exists
- A crackpot physicist who thinks he has created transparent iron is the butt of a cruel and very elaborate practical joke
- A group of fun-loving scientists have got together to enact a burlesque of a Nobel Awards Ceremony.

And we *do* know that this disjunctive proposition is possible. We know it because we know of at least one of its disjuncts that *it* is possible and we know that a disjunction is possible if any of its disjuncts is possible. No doubt, by working our imaginations a bit harder, we could imagine a world in which some of the "unwanted" disjuncts failed. We might, for example, add to what we have already imagined a codicil to the effect that all the scientists in the cheering audience are sincere. But this would not rule out the second of the above disjuncts ("mass deception"). To rule *that* out, our imaginations would have to descend to "a level of structural detail comparable to that of the imaginings of condensed-matter physicists who are trying to explain superconductivity." I concede that, although, if we wished to establish the possibility of transparent iron, we should have to operate at the same level of imagined detail as condensed-matter physicists, we might not be subject to the same constraints as they. When we, who are interested in questions of modal epistemology, ask whether transparent iron is possible, we are, of course, interested in "absolute possibility," and not, like the working condensed-matter physicist, only in what is possible given the actual laws of nature. Perhaps, therefore, in attempting to imagine a world containing transparent iron, *we* could properly allow such things as Planck's Constant and the electromagnetic coupling constant to vary in our imaginations. (And perhaps not. It is a profound question whether we should be justified in supposing that it was "absolutely possible" for the fundamental constants of nature to have any values other than their actual values.) In any case, so far as I know no one has imagined, at the necessary level of structural detail, a world – whether its laws are the actual laws or some others – in which there is transparent iron.

I do not know how to argue for this conclusion, but it seems evident to me that if no one has imagined a world in which there are naturally purple cows or transparent iron, then no one has imagined a world in which a perfect being exists (or does not exist), a world in which the imaginer exists but in which nothing material exists (or in which nothing immaterial exists), or a world in which there are vast amounts of suffering for which there is no explanation.[16] I should think that, however hard it

---

[16] As to the last of these: would it not do simply to imagine a world in which vast numbers of innocent sentient creatures fry on red-hot griddles at every moment at which they exist? But this state of affairs is incompatible – this modal term is to be understood in its "absolute" sense – with the existence of an omniscient, omnipotent, morally perfect being. (Or let's assume so. That some state of affairs involving absolutely inexplicable suffering is incompatible with the existence of such a being is the other premise of the possibility argument whose crucial modal premise is the possibility of such a state of affairs.) To imagine a *world* in which this state of affairs obtains, therefore, is to imagine a world in which there is no such being. And what would justify one in believing that one had imagined a world in which there was no such being? To imagine an enormous griddle on which vast numbers of innocent creatures are tortured pointlessly is not to imagine a world, a whole coherent reality. The *absence* of objects "external" to this situation but absolutely incompatible with it must somehow be a part of one's imaginings if one is to have imagined a world in which it obtains. An omnipotent and omniscient being, or so I should imagine, would have to be invisible and omnipresent. How does one go about imagining the absence of an invisible and omnipresent being – as opposed to failing to imagine the presence of such a being? I see no answer to this question. The suggestion that one can imagine an enormous griddle on which vast numbers of innocent creatures are tortured pointlessly is thus very like Hume's contention that one can imagine something's coming into existence without a cause. It is easy enough to imagine something's coming into existence and not to imagine a cause of its coming into existence; it is something else, and rather more difficult, to imagine something's coming into existence and also to imagine the absence of any cause of its coming into existence.

But this is only the first word on this topic, not the last. The issues the example raises are too complex to be resolved in a single footnote. As things stand, it might well be objected that if the argument of the preceding paragraph were correct, a parallel argument would show that one couldn't imagine a chair's having been two feet to the left of where it was at noon today, since one couldn't imagine, say, the absence of an omnipotent being who, for some location, decreed in every possible world in which the chair existed that it be in *that* location at noon today. This is a very good point, but to address it, I should need to leave the topic of modal epistemology and discuss the pragmatics of argument, the purposes for which arguments are offered and the occasions on which various dialectical "moves" are proper. A hint: although I know that the chair could have been two feet to the left of where it was at noon (and therefore know that Spinoza was wrong), it would have been dialectically improper of me to present this piece of modal knowledge to Spinoza – or to someone who really did believe that God assigned to each physical object a spacetime trajectory that was invariant across possible worlds – and to have claimed thereby to have refuted his position.

might be to imagine a purple-cow world or a transparent-iron world, it would be even harder to imagine the worlds that one would have to imagine if (on Yablo's account) one were to be prima facie justified in accepting the crucial modal premise of a possibility argument. If "the Wise Old Beings from the Center of the Galaxy" were to manifest themselves to me in a suitably impressive fashion, I should probably believe them if they told me that they had proved that the existence of transparent iron was, although inconsistent with the actual laws of nature, nevertheless "absolutely" possible. But I should be extremely skeptical if they told me that they had proved that a perfect being or an immaterial intelligence or inexplicable suffering were, although not actual, absolutely possible. It would be hard to convince me that even such beings as they were in a position to know these things – or even to have evidence that was relevant to evaluating their epistemic status.

I have argued that, if Yablo's account of what justifies modal beliefs is correct, we should be modal skeptics.[17] I am inclined to think that if his account is not the whole truth of the matter, it contains a great deal of the truth of the matter, and that the part of it that is right is enough by itself to justify modal skepticism.

[17] Stated with more care, my thesis is as follows. Consider those propositions whose truth-values cannot be determined by logic and reflection on the meanings of words or by the application of mathematical reasoning. Among those, consider those whose truth-values are unknown to us or which are known to be false. If the *only* way to determine whether a proposition in this category is possible is by attempting to imagine a world we take to verify this proposition, then we should be modal skeptics: while we shall certainly know some propositions of this type to be possible, we shall not be able to know whether the premises of our illustrative possibility arguments are true; and neither shall we be able to know whether it is possible for there to be transparent iron or naturally purple cows.

# Index

If an essay is devoted entirely or largely to a topic or a philosopher, and if that fact is evident from the title of the essay, the index-entry for that topic (that philosopher) does not contain references to the pages on which that essay appears. For example, the entries "identity across possible worlds" and "Plantinga, Alvin" contain no references to any of the pages 186–205; that the reader interested in identity across possible worlds (or in Plantinga) should consult these pages is made sufficiently evident by the title "Plantinga on Transworld Identity."

Footnotes in some of the essays contain longish lists of philosophers to whom the author has expressed gratitude. Names that occur only in these lists are not indexed.

# Index

# Index

Printed in the United Kingdom
by Lightning Source UK Ltd.
9725200001B